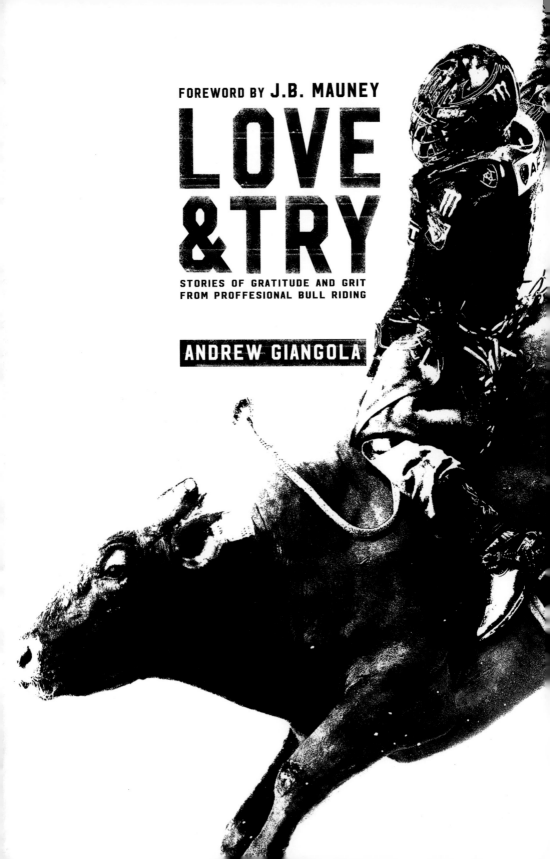

FOREWORD BY **J.B. MAUNEY**

LOVE & TRY

STORIES OF GRATITUDE AND GRIT
FROM PROFFESIONAL BULL RIDING

ANDREW GIANGOLA

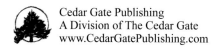

Cedar Gate Publishing
A Division of The Cedar Gate
www.CedarGatePublishing.com

Love & Try
Copyright © 2022 by Andrew Giangola

All rights reserved. No part of this publication may be reproduced, stored in a retrieval system, or transmitted in any form or by any means—electronic, mechanical, photocopy, recording, or any other—except for brief quotations in printed reviews, without the prior permission of the publishers.

For information regarding this title, such as requests on bulk orders, email Cedar Gate Publishing at info@cedargatepublishing.com.

ISBN-13: 979-8-9856255-6-1

Cover photo courtesy of Bull Stock Media

Design by Holden Hill

For everyone, everywhere,
who holds on until their head hits the ground.

FOREWORD
BY J.B. MAUNEY

(Leah Hennel)

If something's not worth dying for, what's the point of even living?

That's how I feel about life and the sport of bull riding, which has been my life for as long as I can remember.

I never wanted anything else but to be a professional bull rider. When I was a kid in North Carolina, I would think about bull riding twenty-four hours a day. My parents used to make me do my schoolwork, and only after I finished would they let me watch my boxes of bull riding tapes. That's all I wanted to do. All I thought about. From the moment I opened my eyes to when I lay down at night.

They'd say if I studied schoolwork as closely as the bull riding tapes, I'd be a straight-A student. I never got those grades. But in bull riding, I paid close attention. I applied myself, as they say, and have done OK. Twice now,

I have won a million dollars that comes with the World Championship. Was I surprised that happened? No. Was that the plan? No. Riding bulls, you don't get too ahead of yourself. I always took it ride by ride, day by day.

You never get to perfection in this sport. Even during my best riding in a championship season, I didn't think I was riding every bull correctly. There's always something you can be doing a little bit better.

And you better always be thinking about improving. The breeding methods in this sport have come a long way, and the bulls get more challenging. Now, there's always been great bulls. There's just a lot more of them today. There's a lot of committed bull breeders trying to make the perfect bucking bull. That makes it a lot harder on my end with nothing but a rope in my hand.

As good as today's full pen has become, I've always believed I could ride every single one of them that unloads. If you don't believe that as a bull rider, there's no point even coming out.

Like most guys, I've had my share of injuries. We know what we signed up for. The next time you nod your head may be the last time you nod your head. My philosophy has been "Don't play the game if you can't take the pain." When you're young, you don't think bad stuff is gonna happen. Deep down, you know it's a matter of time until you get hurt. You just hope it's not too bad.

Still, when you're eighteen, you think you're invincible. In my younger days, I got stepped on bad and lacerated my liver. I didn't know that was the injury at the time. Thought I broke some ribs. They wanted to send me to the hospital. No, thanks. All they do with broken ribs is tape you up and send you home.

I wake up the next day at home, and there's this thing growing out my stomach. Hard as a rock. Finally, I give in and go to the hospital.

The doctor asks me, "When did this happen?"

I say, "Heck, last night."

He says, "That's your liver – you should be dead."

I had eaten breakfast, but they were gonna cut me open immediately, that's how serious it was. I'm in the hospital wondering if I'm gonna keep doing this. And I decide, Heck, I am all in. Always have, always will be.

They said I needed to heal up for eight months. If I rode before then and a horn hit me in the stomach, I'd be dead. I had to take a job in a ball bearing plant, every day head-to-toe covered in grease. If you don't know about ball bearing plants, you're not missing much. But I'll tell you: you don't want to go work in a ball bearing plant. That job sucked. Four months in, I quit. Figured I'd go back to what I do.

I show up at the bull riding, and they ask, "Which doctor released you?"

"Dr. Mauney," I said.

So yeah, even when I was hurt bad, that's what I was thinking about: How soon can I come back? I know it doesn't make sense to most people. In some ways, I think bull riding chose me rather than me choosing bull riding.

I have to ride bulls.

It's who I am.

To be honest, I'd rather watch bull riding than read about it. Most bull riding books are about a certain rider or a straight history of the sport. I'd rather watch the videos. (I'm still watching *8 Seconds* in the middle of the night, but this time with our son Jagger Briggs when little J.B. decides sleep ain't for him.) Still, most bull riding books are a great read. Heck, they're about bull riding. This one's different in bringing you some of the memorable personalities in our sport. When asked to contribute to a book called Love & Try, it made sense, especially with the proceeds going to the Western Sports Foundation to help pay the medical bills of injured bull riders.

You gotta love what you do in life, and you definitely have to love what you do in this sport. If you know me, I don't get mushy. But yeah, there's lots of love shown by the people who bring bull riding to our great fans every week—the bull riders, the stock contractors, and the crew. If you ever have met a stock contractor, you'll see they love their bulls, too.

And the try part? That's in a bull rider's DNA. Anyone holding up that gold buckle proving you're the best in the world that year, or any rider who wins any bull riding event—I don't care if it's in Madison Square Garden, Calgary, or the county fair—they all have something in common. Staying on a bucking bull for eight seconds only comes with try.

Even when it looks easy. Those rides where it goes nice and smooth are like sitting in a rocking chair. It's what you live for. You know that those rides only come by being willing to cowboy up to make it past the bulls who make it feel like you're thrown over a waterfall strapped to a barrel.

From the time I started riding, there were always guys around me with more talent. I have longer arms and legs compared to the stockier guys with a lower center of gravity. I'm always flopping around. They may be built differently or have more natural talent than me. But I always knew I had one thing in my favor: I was gonna try harder, until my head hit the ground.

Try takes you a lot of places in life. It took me to making the whistle on every champion bull I had the chance to pick. And to earning that gold buckle—twice. And I'm not done.

Whatever you do in life, try is the main ingredient for success. I don't care what your job is. Whatever your "rope" is, wrap your hand around it and don't let go.

That's my mentality when asked if I want Jagger Briggs to be a bull rider. If he wants to be a bull rider, absolutely. It's up to him. If he wants to be an architect or a painter or play the flute, I will be fully behind him. So long as he's putting 110 percent into whatever he chooses to do, he's got my blessing and support.

As for me, I'm at the point where my try is focused on achieving goals I had put aside. After winning two PBR World Titles, I decided to go after qualifying for my first National Finals Rodeo and am also raising purebred fighting bulls.

I'm often asked why I still do it. Why do I still try? "At this point, you've accomplished so much, J.B. Ain't riding bulls a big risk?" they ask. "What happens if you fall the wrong way and get crippled?"

"Guess if that happens," I say, "I'll just lie back in bed and think about all the good times I've had."

I hope you have a good time lying back and reading these stories of Love and Try. It's what makes our sport so great. And keeps the world populated.

— **J.B. Mauney**
Cotulla, Texas
October 2021

INTRODUCTION

A ROCK SHOW WITH MEAT

Wearing cowboy boots for the first time since high school (and that was a *long* time ago), I was flying from New York City to Las Vegas for a bull riding event. No laces to fool with at TSA. Pull on the brown Ariats, and you stand straighter and taller. Cowboy boots put a hop in your step and shoot a magical rod up your spine. I felt closer to Superman than a middle-aged cross-country commuter attempting to mine lost confidence even when jamming into the middle seat in the back of the plane across from the stinking lavatory.

A skeptic could point out the new boots were more an accoutrement to a silly, undeserved costume than a revelation of the true me.

You see, that person was no cowboy. He lacked the tin-cup life experiences and calloused qualifications justifying cowboy boots, if such a sartorial code exists for bestowing the "right" to appropriate an accessory central to the identity of generations of men and women, good folks never above their raisin', who, while declining in numbers today, still work this land, keep us fed, and form the backbone of a sport growing in popularity.

It was fall of 2015 as I sauntered to my seat next to the tail-end crapper of the 757 about to leave my city of sophisticates. I was traveling as a guest of the PBR. (That's Professional Bull Riders, not the overpriced hipster beer.) The purpose of the trip was to learn about bull riding in being considered to oversee PR for the sport. Once in Las Vegas, proudly perfecting my new Billy Jack strut, it wasn't more than three minutes into the backstage tour of the Thomas & Mack Center, when, next to the bullpens, I skidded in a creamy pool of pudding. An awkward scissor-leg split nearly ripped me in two. Luckily, I didn't land in the bullshit. My jeans somehow missed the mess, but my self-assurance was in the toilet. The rest of the day, I hobbled feebly, stepping gingerly with equal parts caution and paranoia in my shit-stained boots. Considering my gimpy gait and complete lack of knowledge about Western sports, it must have been Christian-minded charitable pity that led leadership to ask me to take the PBR job.

Really, what the heck was I doing amid clanging steel corrals, horned cattle, and guys named Cody, Colten, and Chase? I live in Manhattan. I ride a subway, not a horse. I'm an *indoor* enthusiast. But success in life is often a matter of stumbling under the cloudburst of dumb luck.

By no means was I a "fan" prior to the Vegas trip, I had only periodically seen pro bull riding while TV-channel flipping. The riders appeared to have lost a few marbles to get on those bulls, and I'd stop in my tracks to watch in the way one gapes at a wreck on the freeway. "Heck yeah, I'm interested," I had responded to the offer to come check it out in person, to see if I wanted to help promote the sport. Work with half-crazy people and you'll never be bored a day in your life, right? (My dad had also taught me that when asked by someone with power over your paycheck if you're interested in a new task, there's only one response, and be sure to make your "yes" seem genuine.)

But I wouldn't need to fake a thing. Everything about the sport was wondrous. I was quickly "roped and tied," as bucking bull owner Bernie Taupin once wrote for an Elton John hit.

For a man who lives in an East Village apartment and makes his living sitting at a desk in an office high above Madison Avenue, every impression of a gathering where the courage in the air could be cut with a karate chop registered as a rousing sensual barrage: the pungent circus-like backstage smell; the blonde shavings you walked through when not skidding on bull dung; the sound of bellowing bulls and crashing metal gates and cowbells at the end of bull ropes dragged across the floor; the roaring crowd abruptly cut silent like a needle pulled off the record when a rider was slammed to the ground and laid motionless; the bobbing sea of cowboy hats on the arena concourse where commemorative rifles, shotguns, and pistols were displayed for sale, all official jackets sold with a "concealed carry" pocket; faces, both sun weathered and peach fresh, respectfully addressing one another as "ma'am" and "sir"; an earnest prayer and then hats over hearts for the national anthem. It felt like America, or at least a throwback of one being canceled.

Loud music boomed over the arena—the power chords of AC/DC, Joan Jett, and The Who, not the twangy country music I'd expected. As one production guy told me, "We're a rock show with meat." The bull rides were by turns beautiful and brutal. (One young Brazilian rider went down with an audible cry, lay still, and was hustled from the hushed arena on a backboard.

Introduction

The arena announcer solemnly asked the Lord Jesus for His healing hand. And then the music cranked up again to restart the show.)

The rodeo clown—who I'd learn is the "official entertainer"—was singing, dancing, and launching hilariously politically incorrect one-liners, contributing to the adrenaline-soaked carnival. Yet, despite my senses working overtime, it was ultimately the cowboys who made me go, "*Whoah!*" The bull riders "too lazy to work and too nervous to steal," as one explained his career motivation, were admirable guys, laughably overmatched by animals more than ten times their size yet projecting the confidence of a four-year-old in a Batman shirt. I wanted to find out what the heck they ate for breakfast, understand their purpose, and help them get noticed. Getting paid to promote rough-and-tumble rebels engaging in blood-and-guts risk-taking, men willingly charging into proverbial brick walls, immune to the hovering fear that paralyzes, completely dismissive to the howling pain that usually follows abject fearlessness? Sign me up! Of course, I jumped at the chance to be part of this magnetic atmosphere and culture.

And if nothing else, I'm a PR man. How does *everybody* not know about these men, these bulls, this outlandish sport? There was a story to be told. And more so, an inner one to be revealed. As I muddled through my fifties in an upside-down world spinning off its axis, intrepid, hard-working cowboys adeptly compartmentalizing fear in reaching for their dream might help me right-size myself. Maybe I could mainline some of the testosterone filling the air, too.

Working for PBR, once in the saddle (geez, there are no bull saddles … sorry), even without official business hosting reporters, I found myself drawn to the locker room, that electric staging area for battle, seeing the cowboys suit up in preparation to go to war. Some could be seen taping up broken forearms and jamming swollen feet into their boots. A few retreated to a corner to read a Bible and pray quietly; the cocky daredevils pulled dinged-up metal folding chairs into the hazy shower area, blaring rock and roll from portable speakers propped against their riding bags as they sucked on cigarettes and razzed one another. Once they prepared their bull ropes by applying a coat of sticky resin, their gear was set, and it was time to start the show. They'd strut purposefully from the locker room to stand waiting in a staging area impatiently rocking back and forth on battered boots until their names were shouted over the arena PA, when each gladiator defiantly marched through the dirt doused with camping fuel and lit ablaze, the giant letters "PBR" in orange flames. And then over the course of the night, they would slap themselves in the face or ram a fist into their chest to climb into the coffin-shaped steel bucking chute, mounting a muscular quivering beast, as if strapping onto an unpredictable carnival ride, part rollercoaster, part roadside bomb. The cowboys approached this mad, primal, insane task with an icy-calm self-assurance that gave me shivers. This was their job. And they could die.

Most were physically small in stature. But, gosh, were they bigger than anyone you can imagine, about to scale the cliff of mortality, voluntarily doing something I knew I could never, ever do, not even during every young man's cavalier period of youthful invincibility. David trying to tame Goliath felt like the grandest, most dangerous, most audacious game of chicken you could imagine. These cowboys weren't crazy. They were *alive*.

Like most others not in the know, I had incorrectly assumed bull riders were merely very brave, half-crazy daredevils. Not much different than the guy shot from a cannon in the circus. Swaggering stunt men in cowboy hats.

Sure, they're bold, courageous, dirt-tough adrenaline junkies. But this sport is no "hold my beer" spectacle of ridiculousness. The riders, beyond the sheer illogical lunacy of their profession, are accomplished athletes— relying on strength, agility, balance, anticipation, and timing. (And not all of them hit the bar; a custom diet and physical conditioning, even yoga, is the latest trend in a sport where real millions can be made).

The underappreciated athleticism required to execute an eight-second bull ride was only part of my intrigue. Danger coats the air in PBR. There's an ever-present possibility of things going seriously wrong in the worst possible way. As one rider told me, "Every time they open that gate, you're knocking on heaven's door." A bull rider must have the fortitude to clear his mind to concentrate on his hazardous task, mentally moving beyond the constant specter of dismemberment and death. With an unencumbered head, muscle memory can take over.

"You think about it all week long. You practice hard. You ride 'em in your head every night. And when you get to the arena, you better forget all that and let your subconscious take over because it's all reaction," said 2001 PBR Rookie of the Year Luke Snyder.

Or as another rider said, "If you're thinkin', you're probably stinkin'."

Introduction

"Physically and mechanically bull riding is difficult, but not any more than any other sport," said nine-time rodeo world champion Ty Murray, a co-founder of PBR. "In any sport there's five basic things you have to do, and if you can do them all well, you're going to be pretty good at that sport. What separates our sport and brings it to another level is you have the same pressures—winning or losing, money and championships—along with the real chance of dying every single time. So, mentally, the pressure is to live in that space and still go for it. What separates the men from the boys is the guys who learn to hit the gas when everyone else is wanting to take their foot off the pedal. It's a very hard thing to do. It's not an accident that I had a family late in life. I couldn't go to the world's most dangerous job every day and put my foot on the gas when every fiber in my soul was saying 'take it off' because I had a wife and baby at home waiting for me. We have the pressure of winning and losing, and also the pressure of living or dying."

As Murray and others describe bull riding, if an athlete is anything less than one hundred percent committed, he certainly won't win. But he can get seriously injured. Because ultimately, the rider isn't the one calling the shots. In the battle between man and beast, the bull always dictates the play, and is never the one to back down.

"Take car racing for example," Murray said. "You're still the one with the foot on the gas or the brake. You're the one in control. Riding bulls, they've got the throttle, deciding what level it's going to go to. It's up to you to have the mental toughness to say, 'OK, how far are we going to take this.' Champions in this sport say [to the bull], 'You take it to the level, and I'm going to go with you. Right now.' When that gate opens, you gotta be able to turn it on to the max. You have to be one hundred percent committed."

Each bull rider prepares differently for that task of staying on for eight seconds. Listening to Murray and other riders explain their calling, they all share one thing in common. It was how they used the word "try." And how often they used it to describe their job.

"*He rode that bull because he had a lot of try,*" they'd say.

"*That guy's got a great future. He's got talent and try.*"

Or "*I can pick up some points and ride into World Finals. I just need more try.*"

Usually, riders talk about try without saying the word. In the first rider interview I sat in on, two-time World Champion J.B. Mauney told the reporter, "To be successful in this sport, you don't quit until your head hits the ground."

I may have put on my cowboy hat *backwards* the first time I tried to wear one (an experiment on tour that lasted one night, for any day AG puts on a cowboy hat becomes Halloween), but even I got it. J.B. was talking about try. Through his own try, Mauney became the richest athlete in Western sports history (more than $7.4 million in career earnings) and created a legendary persona that ESPN's Marty Smith said makes the North Carolina cowboy "the next last American hero."

From Mauney on down the line, cowboys are more about actions than words, whether it's watching Chase Outlaw come back from a devastating facial injury or fourteen-year-old Najiah Knight taking her lumps in her unflinching dream to become the first girl to make it to the top. Meet a bull rider of any age, background, and gender, and you'll hear a story of incredible try. You'll get to meet a few of those incredible cowboys and cowgirls in these pages.

PBR is a sport where nothing is given to anyone. Riders in the premier series have no contracts or guaranteed salary. They get paid only when they're ,successful in staying on their bulls. "It's money or mud out there," retired bull rider Bobby DelVecchio, from the Bronx of all places, told me in explaining the rider's motivation. But even if a competition were unpaid, for bragging rights only, these cowboys would still be giving it their all.

I'd spend a weekend at a bull riding and then feel a dull, aimless letdown, like withdrawing from popping potent "thrill pills." Who would want to hang out with regular people when you can be with cowboys?

Along with "try," something else was ever present in the sport. It was a feeling floating in the background, an acceptance in the air, a big wash of *love*, first shown to any outsider discovering the sport by the way insiders speak about and treat the bulls, whom they call "animal athletes."

At first, I wondered if this so-called love for the four-legged athletes was to keep at bay the whacky all-animals-should-be-set-free crowd. The most vocal practitioners of *kumbaya* can turn out to be some of the cruelest individuals to walk God's green earth, eh? In this sport, every ride is scored 50 percent for the rider, 50 percent for the bull. Of course, the bull is important. Without animal athletes performing well, there's no sport; certainly not one on network television and selling out major arenas coast-to-coast. I wondered

Introduction

if the bull is essential to PBR like a racecar is in NASCAR. You invest in the car, give it a lot of attention, put in the best parts … then run the darn thing into the ground, sometimes a wall. The car is used up to the max. You may appreciate it, but you don't love it.

Calling the bulls "athletes" in trying to humanize them sounded like clever spin. But like other things in life, when immersed in something new and easy to prejudge, the scales quickly fall from our eyes. The relationship between the men and women who own, raise, train, and haul the bulls turns out to be deep, meaningful, and inspired by love. Because these animals provide their handlers a living, the constant care and feeding of the bulls creates an emotional bond like a member of the family. Similar to a devoted parent constantly checking on a child, bull stock contractors are obsessed with the health and happiness of their bulls. It's the first thing on their minds when waking up and the last thought before going to bed at night.

As bull raiser Tiffany Davis told me, "When our bulls pass, they get a grave." I would witness a bull stock contractor crying when one of his prized bulls died due to old age. This was no relationship of transactional practicality. Working in NASCAR, I'd never witnessed a race car owner bawl his eyes out when a car flipped and disintegrated.

I learned the bulls have it pretty good. Think of it this way: nearly every bovine born on this earth goes into the food supply at three years old. A fortunate few get to compete "as athletes," then retire to stud. Instead of a baked potato on your dinner plate, they get a tombstone on a ranch after passing from natural causes at about fifteen years old. That's some good love there. The sacrifices made for the bull athletes are plentiful, to be covered in these pages.

PBR is situated within a Western lifestyle that's simultaneously in vogue with the masses (the cowboy drama *Yellowstone*—really, a Shakespearian tale about powerful fathers and family succession, think *The Godfather* on horses—is at press time the top-rated show on cable television) while treated with clumsy stereotypes and clueless suspicion. This book isn't a sociological analysis (though take what you want) or an orderly chronological history of the sport. We jump years and miss important events and personalities, not intentionally. Write about what you see and feel, my favorite teacher had advised. This is what I saw and felt and the people I have met within a simple, rugged sport I fell in love with. The lens is the curiosity of a gung-ho newcomer, an outsider still unsure of where to step, who is flattered to be welcomed in. Because everyone is welcome.

PART I

LOVE

PBR bucking bulls are powerful, graceful, and valuable athletes. They're lucky, too, considering the dire fate of any bull not fortunate enough to make it to the PBR.

The men and women who raise these animals are confident the bulls would tell you that, if the lucky animals could only speak. A talking bull might point out that competing on a nationally televised bull riding tour is like a five-to-midnight stay from the governor because any bull *not* in the PBR is Dead Animal Walking.

You see, the unlucky ones—those cattle not blessed with the bloodlines or inclination to kick, spin, jump, and thrash, who therefore *don't* get into the PBR—face a death sentence by the time they're three years old. That's about one fifth of the way through the full life of a top bull athlete. In human terms, it's as if everyone were bid *adieu* from God's green earth at fifteen years old, except a few lucky pampered athletes blessed with great genes, who work for eight or sixteen seconds a weekend for a few years, then get to bask in the sun, sleep when they want, and procreate during a long, leisurely retirement.

The depressing specter of the inescapable early demise of those heading for your dinner plate is a grisly way to introduce you to the bull stock contractors who lovingly raise the magnificent animals escaping this fate. It will get fun, I promise, as we head to North Carolina to go behind the scenes with two Mount Rushmore types, who raise the star bulls of the sport. Next stop: The friendly home of "the first couple of the PBR"—Jerome and Tiffany Davis.

1

THE FIRST COUPLE OF BULL RIDING

(Bull Stock Media)

When PBR swings through Greensboro, North Carolina, fans have the opportunity to get a down-home insiders' look at big-time bull stock contracting by visiting the Davis Rodeo Ranch in Archdale. Bull riding enthusiasts are welcomed with open arms by two beloved figures in the sport, who, when Jerome Davis's career was cut short by injury, turned to raising bucking bulls to compete in the PBR, hosting smaller events in their own arena, and housing and training bulls for outside partners.

At the Davis Ranch, fans are made to feel right at home, getting an easy-to-follow, soup-to-nuts education on these animals—along with a scrumptious home-cooked Carolina meal and plenty of laughs as they tour the couple's sun-drenched one hundred acres in golf carts driven by Jerome and Tiffany. On one tour in September 2018, fans boarded those carts for a bumpy ride along a bucolic path cutting through the ranch's rolling pastures. The carts would periodically stop, and then Tiffany—driving the one out front—would bound out, step onto the grass ridge, and loudly introduce each bull, finding a way to veer off onto hilarious riffs, like getting engaged to a young, rising bull rider.

As told by Tiffany: "I started off as a buckle bunny," she joked. "No, to be serious, I was raisin' bulls early. I have known Jerome since high school. I worked at Pizza Hut; instead of a car payment, I had a cow payment. Girls, the way to get a cowboy is not through cookin'. It's through cows. One Christmas, I gave Jerome twenty-four head—twelve heifers and twelve bulls. Well, Jerome and I were together for a while, and one day, Jerome says, 'We need to get one of those engagement rings. You better go get one.'"

That was nearly a quarter century ago. The couple have a number of "children" who fans met on the tour—in fact, about seventy of them, weighing up to two thousand pounds each, casually roaming the lush hills of the ranch. The bulls are fed early, every morning, hot or cold, rain or shine.

"You don't have snow days. You don't have off days. You don't have holidays. Bull raisin's a 365-day-a-year job," Tiffany said. "And these bulls eat a whole lot better and healthier than us. On the road, we eat at truck stops. They have this expensive organic feed we take. We even take our own hay. We pack the bulls' food, and meanwhile we grab what we can find."

The Davises are part of a growing bull industry that has become big business as PBR has become more popular. Some top bulls are worth hundreds of thousands of dollars. When they retire, their semen can be worth up to $10,000 a straw.

The down-home folksiness of this ranch tour is a microcosm of a sport that feels like a large family traveling around the country to provide wholesome family entertainment. Yet for all the warm informality, the animals in the sport are produced by sophisticated, high-tech breeding techniques yielding predictable bloodlines. For the past twenty years, bucking bulls have been carefully bred like racehorses to make them more "rank." Breeders like the Davises have at their disposal a computerized registry of about a quarter-million cows and bulls from American Bucking Bull Inc., which is jointly owned by PBR and the independent breeders. It's the world's second-largest animal DNA registry.

The bulls breed with cows known to have a history of producing the most powerful and fleet-of-hoof bovine athletes. Both male and female parts of the equation are critical. (It takes two to tango, right?) But over the years, it has been discovered that, in this most masculine of sports, the cow is the predominant factor in producing bucking greatness. As bull breeding advances, the entire industry trains its eyes on the resulting bloodlines.

Unlike many stock contractors who buy into a promising or already proven bovine athlete, the Davises raise their own bulls on their ranch. When their bulls are ready for competition, they haul them to nearly two dozen events in PBR's top two U.S. tours each year, including the richest and most prestigious one, World Finals in Las Vegas. There, the couple also gives sold-out tours at bull housing behind South Point Hotel & Casino. Sometimes they join other stock contractors and important figures in the sport like PBR cofounder and Director of Livestock Cody Lambert to showcase more than 750 bulls making their homes at bull housing during championship week.

At any of these tours led by the stock contractors, speaking to the fans is a chance to set the record straight on some of the most misunderstood and unfairly maligned athletes in sports. "These bulls don't work for us; we work for them, and they let you know it pretty quick," Tiffany said. "I got seventy bosses to report to every morning. Except it's a boss that you truly love and care for."

On the tours, fans learn about that love and care, manifested in the time and energy devoted to keeping the bulls healthy on the ranch, on the road, and in the arena. For example, fans will notice that the bulls have flattened horns, which Tiffany explained is a result of getting their horns tipped. "We want to keep the bulls safe from each other and, as much as we can, the cowboys safe from the bulls," she said. "The rules say you have to be able to lay a fifty-cent piece on the horn. Tipping's like getting your fingernails cut. Takes those sharp edges off and doesn't hurt the bull in the least."

Like people and their hairstyles, each bull has a unique appearance and personality and horns to match.

"You see that bull over there, that bull with the downward-pointing horns?" Tiffany asked. "That's Heartbreaker, and those are banana horns. We call him Heartbreaker because you can see a heart on his face. He's probably broken the hearts of a few cows, too. Next to him is a muley, which is what we call bulls with no horns. Some of them are mean. Maybe there's some resentment. Do we have any animal psychologists here? One of the worst hookings Jerome got was from a muley."

Tiffany, who turned a story about her husband into a PBR lesson that at times feels like unintentional stand-up comedy, does the lion's share of the talking. That's just fine with her affable, laid-back husband, who was known as "The Carolina Cowboy" back in 1995 when he was the PRCA World Bull Riding Champion.

"I can't hardly hear, so I'm loud; he's the opposite," Tiffany explained, though most on the tour had already arrived at this conclusion. She believes part of her appeal to Jerome was her fireball loquaciousness and openness to accepting any new task or adventure. Once, when they began dating, they were driving to Georgia for a bull riding. Around 3 a.m., Jerome was getting tired. "I said to Tiff, you take some of them No Doze, so you can stay up and drive," he remembered. "So, we bought some at the truck stop. She takes them with Mountain Dew. We get to Atlanta, and I wake up in the back seat and look up, and she's driving and scratching her hair. Just scratching and scratching. I say, 'Are you alright?!' She says, 'I don't know, Jerome. It's like I got ants in my hair. I'm all jittery. My nerves are shot!' I think she took too many."

Tiffany required no assisted caffeination or amplification when showing fans her bulls at the Davis Ranch. But later that year she did have to borrow a portable speaker from her good friend and fellow stock contractor LeAnn Hart in Las Vegas, where the tour swelled to eighty people, which included Chad Berger—the most successful bull raiser in PBR history—and fellow stock contractor Kenny McElroy of K Bar C Bucking Bulls.

"Every one of these bulls is like one of my kids," Berger, wearing his trademark jacket bearing the logo of his bull raising operation, told fans in Las Vegas. "These animals mean so much to me, my family, and everyone who works for us and they treat them accordingly."

Berger is an eleven-time PBR Stock Contractor of the Year, an honor he's received more than anyone else. He has been feeding bulls every morning since he was six years old. He now raises more than 225 bulls on his ranch outside of Bismarck, North Dakota, some of them fifteen and sixteen years old. Like other top bull stock contractors, he spares no expense in giving them the best.

The First Couple of Bull Riding

Chad Berger loving on his bull Beaver Creek Beaux (Chad Berger)

"These bulls get to do what they love," he said. "They have the best food and medical care. Instead of going to a slaughterhouse, they retire to hang out on a beautiful ranch with their girlfriends. They live a great life. If there's such a thing as reincarnation, I want to come back as a bucking bull in the PBR."

Bull stock contractors will bring in chiropractors and acupuncturists, Tiffany explained. They invest in expensive cold-laser therapy devices and electro-pulse therapy to increase blood flow and loosen sore bull muscles. Bulls swim in giant pools that stock contractors install on their ranches, enjoying their own spa treatment.

"These bulls got it better than me," Tiffany said. "I don't get no acupuncture or lasers; I can tell you that. These bulls have had a pedicure three times since the last time I had one."

J.B. Mauney said it another way in telling me, "This sport ain't animal cruelty; it's human cruelty." While Mauney's comment was in jest, in his inimitable way, he was making a valid point about who gets injured (him) and when (often), and how well the pampered animals who make the sport go and have helped make him the richest athlete in Western sports are treated.

While some bulls are ornery, others are sweethearts outside the bucking chute. Tiffany tells the story of surprising the crew when helping in the production of the film, *The Longest Ride*. "I was giving the bulls a bath and wiping their butts with Baby Wipes. They had the perception we keep them all mad for going into the chutes. You don't want them wastin' their energy and goin' crazy! After the film shoot, the crew was hugging us, sayin', 'You do love these bulls! You're makin' it so we can enjoy this sport!'"

Some bulls are outgoing, attention-loving hams. Other bulls are shy and could do without people around. Many are more finicky than humans when it comes to their food and drink, giving stock contractors another way to please them. For example, at World Finals the Davises' bulls are reluctant to drink Las Vegas water, which, beginning as snow melts in the Rocky Mountains then flows into the Colorado River, tastes different than the water drawn from the groundwater tables of North Carolina.

"You want your bulls to be well hydrated. We'll put in a little Gatorade to encourage them to drink it," Tiffany said. Other stock contractors like McElroy bring their own water supply. The Davises take their own special hay on the road as well.

"They show on Instagram and what-not the wives of the PBR packing before they leave home. I wish they showed how we pack for our bulls," Tiffany said. "Oh, we spoil them. By the time I've packed for the animals, I don't care what's in my own suitcase.

"The bulls are well aware of the schedule when the season is in swing. They can tell when it's time to travel," she said. "They see the trailer loading up, and they're prancing around like boxers getting their game on. We call it being 'on the muscle.'"

The animals' journey to bull housing, which is usually located twenty to thirty minutes from the arena, is a smooth and comfortable one. Trailers are specially equipped with "Air Ride" suspensions. Stock contractors will put twelve to fourteen inches of shavings over a spongy trailer bed floor to remove shocks from the road. "The bulls basically glide down the highway so they're ready to go when we get there, not worn out or shook up by the ride," McElroy said.

Members of the tours are shown how to "hang the flank" in the chutes to encourage the animal to buck when the gate flies open. At the Davis Ranch, fans come right up next to the bucking bulls and learn to tie the bull's flank, or rope, as instructed by Tiffany. Some fans assume they need to tie the soft cotton rope around the animal's haunches. That's not how it's done. "It's not a Christmas present!" Tiffany warned. "Put it loose, to encourage him to kick up, like a kitten tries to get rid of a ribbon light around her paw."

The biggest misconception and the most misunderstood part of the sport, the disinformation repeated ad infinitum to take on the surging life of a debilitating lie, is the placement of that flank strap. Some people who say they love animals also love deceiving others. They've conjured up a painful mistruth, claiming the flank strap is used by the bull handlers to tie up the bulls' testicles to abuse and torture them. Whether or not the so-called "animal activists" did the research, checked the facts, and then still consciously choose to lie is immaterial. They choose to spew a world-class whopper of a graphic lie that travels faster and farther than the truth. And nobody knows the difference. But here's the thing: *the flank strap never goes near a bucking bull's genitals, and it never hurts the animal.*

Those who take the time and effort to do the research and speak with bull stock contractors will find out there is one thing tortured in professional bull riding: the truth.

Cody Lambert is a third-generation cowboy from Texas who rode broncs and bulls for a living as a younger man and retired from competition after the 1996 PBR World Finals. He's now known to be the world's greatest "bull picker," scouting the four-legged talent on one end of the bull rope that helps make PBR so successful. Along with Jerome Davis, Lambert was a cofounder of PBR, which makes him—and the nineteen other cofounder cowboys—among the world's most savvy businessmen for parlaying a $1,000 investment into a $4.2 million payout fifteen years later. As head of livestock, Lambert is the only cofounder who's still working full time for the organization. To pick the bulls that get to compete at the big show, he peruses a black book with information on thousands of bulls to choose. Each of those bulls is equipped with a flank strap, which he described as a soft cotton rope, neither abrasive nor tightly bound to the bull, that serves as an object the bulls simply try to kick off. "The repeated accusations of allegedly irritating the animal's genitalia with this strap to encourage its performance are ludicrous," Lambert said.

"If a bull's testicles were tied or touched, he wouldn't move as well; he certainly wouldn't buck. Touching a bull's genitals is cruel and is banned in the PBR. Of course, it's not allowed. But beyond that, why would anyone do that? It would defeat the whole purpose of the sport, which is to have the bull buck hard to the best of his ability."

(Mauney, who for most of his PBR career lived about thirty-five minutes up the road from the Davis Ranch, put it this way: "Let me kick you in the nuts and see if you want to jump around, or just lay there on the ground wishing you were dead.")

While the flank strap encourages the bulls to kick without hurting the bull, these special animals buck first and foremost because of genetic breeding, Jerome Davis explained on his ranch tour. "Where we are today with these bulls is the result of a hundred years of breeding," he said. "You can't force a bull to do anything he doesn't want to do. It's the bred bloodlines that make them want to buck. We put a dummy on a calf and get a good idea of what he can do. That's the beginning of a bull's development. You see which bulls then have a natural bucking inclination, and the potential to go further."

The Davises raise their bulls from birth. Any bull making it to the elite level of the sport generally begins their PBR career at two to four years old. They compete for four to six years on average, then retire to stud to make more bucking bulls, enjoying a very restful, comfortable lifestyle, and generally passing of natural causes around fifteen years old.

Jerome's ever-gregarious wife greatly enjoys hosting people and making them feel at home. Tiffany's *casa es su casa*. But her biggest motivation for doing the tours is educating anyone who'll listen about how the bulls are treated.

"If you really love animals, you should be a PBR fan, not standing outside arenas in leather shoes holding your leather bag and shouting about animal abuse," she said. "These bulls live out their lives with us. They get a grave site. They don't have to worry about getting eaten. I'd be a member of PETA if I could get a chance to sit down and explain how we treat these bulls, and people would listen. These bulls are happy here. You can see it. And they love what they do. You can't make a bull buck if he doesn't want to."

But, as we've established, bulls don't speak. Tiffany and Jerome Davis and Chad Berger are by all counts honest, straight talkers, and in their many quiet acts of kindness extremely caring and charitable. Berger is often seen on tour in hotel lobbies late at night quietly chatting with fans facing disability or other hardship. He once privately and without fanfare drove three hours each way across North Dakota to drop off a Chad Berger Bucking Bulls jacket to a sick fan who he heard loved his bulls. These don't appear to be folks who make things up to purposely deceive anyone. They believe what they're telling us. But how can anyone be certain the bulls love what they do?

Berger points to Little Yellow Jacket, a legendary competitor who, along with Bushwacker and Sweet Pro's Bruiser, is the only bull in PBR history to win three World Championships.

When Joe Berger, Chad's father, had once brought his bovine lineup to Austin, the famous 1,750 pound bull with one horn pointed upward and the other going down was not scheduled to compete on the first night of the event. As Berger's other bulls were leaving for the arena, Little Yellow Jacket tried to get on the trailer. He then impatiently paced the fence line all night long, digging a ten-inch trail deep into the dirt.

After Little Yellow Jacket retired, when bulls going to the next event were being loaded onto the trailer, he would bellow and cry. He'd run beside the trailer as it was pulling out. A few times he tried to take a short-cut route to sneak in with the other bulls.

"Little Yellow Jacket would sleep in the horse stables. He was the most human-like bull I'd ever seen," Berger said. "I can tell you with one hundred percent surety that this bull loved to buck."

On a rare occasion when a bull may be injured in the arena, stock contractors will spend thousands of dollars on the best medical care. When Mississippi Hippy, one of the largest bovines ever to compete in the PBR at 2,460 pounds, hurt his hip muscle, Kenny McElroy brought the popular bull to Texas A&M University for evaluation.

The prognosis was not good. Surgery wasn't an option. McElroy invested $30,000 in a MagnaWave machine for the giant brown and white bull whom he took home to his ranch in Southwest Ohio. Following successful electro-pulse therapy to heal his stressed muscle, Mississippi Hippy enjoyed five more peaceful years under a big oak tree on a ranch in Ohio.

These fan tours of bull housing and the stock contractors' ranches give fans a chance to hear stories like that from legends of the sport and allow the men and women behind the star animals to spread their passion.

"If it weren't for y'all, we wouldn't be able to feed our bulls," Tiffany told the group which had registered for the special premium experience before PBR bucked off in Greensboro, one of many up-close experiences PBR offers such as Cowboy Brunch, bull housing tours, and seats in the Can-Am cage in the middle of the arena, akin to watching a baseball game from the pitcher's mound or finding out your ticket to an NFL contest is on the fifty-yard line where they do the coin toss.

When he got his start in the sport, Jerome had been a fresh-faced, easy-going and likable nineteen-year-old kid, leaving home to rodeo with his heroes Ty Murray, Ted Nuce, Jim Sharp, and Clint Branger. In the early 1990s, he turned pro by entering the Professional Rodeo Cowboys Association (PRCA). He traveled with Cody Custer, a talented bull rider from Arizona, watching him win a world title. The two cowboys would drive to rodeos in the Dodge pickup that Custer had won in winning the Dodge RAM Circuit Finals sponsored by the automaker.

"He was a backwoods kid who'd never been away from home—seeing the world for the first time," Custer said.

Custer, eight years older, first saw Davis get on a practice bull in West Texas when he was going to college in Odessa. "Right away, he was special," Custer remembered. "I said, '*Who is this kid? He's gonna be somebody*!'"

The two hit it off immediately. When Davis turned twenty years old, influenced by Custer and riders including Murray, Cody Lambert, and Tuff Hedeman, he made what would turn out to be the smartest and most financially lucrative decision of his life. At the outset, however, when Davis barely had two nickels to rub together, there was hardly any indication of a monetary upside to helping found the new sports organization. As a kid doing what he loved then invited to join the colorful band of rodeo cowboys who were forming a new standalone bull riding league, the invitation in itself was worth all the money in the world.

The riders, seeking a better pay day for their efforts, had all gotten together in a Scottsdale, Arizona hotel room—about fifteen guys cramming in, as Custer remembers. Neither rodeo partner knew if the concept of "Professional Bull Riders" would succeed. For his part, Davis was just thrilled to be along for the adventure with heroes he idolized. A thousand dollars seemed like a worthwhile investment, since many individual rodeos were paying out maybe only three or four times that much, nothing was guaranteed, entry fees were required, and each rodeo was drawing the top bull riders, making a good payday even more challenging.

For a more established rider like Custer, forking over $1,000 to be part of the new bull riding league, even if his check was hot (meaning there were insufficient funds; he'd need to cover it by winning money at the very next bull riding), was a no-brainer.

"I could spend that kind of money to travel to and enter a rodeo, fall off, and get nothing," he said. "The story today is how smart we were. We really were a group of determined guys in the right place at the right time who believed in what we were doing. We were committed to being bull riders for a living. We weren't looking so much into the future as immediately taking care of ourselves and our families after riding for minimal money."

It was a big honor for Davis to be invited into an exclusive bull riding league with men he considered to be "a group of Elvises." But he only had $500 to his name. Still, the happy-go-lucky Carolina Cowboy was all in to be part of the new league.

"I was the youngest guy there," Davis said. "If they told me, 'We're gonna go rob banks!' I'd have said, 'Okay, let's do it!' I'm a kid from North Carolina, who had only seen these guys on TV, and now I'm rodeoing with them!"

Davis gave $500 to PBR's business manager, a small, potty-mouthed man named Sam Applebaum, who had big ambitions for the cowboys he represented and a caustically effective confidence that got deals done. Jerome promised Sam he was good for the balance the next weekend. He went out to California, made the whistle on a few bulls, sent in the prize money, and became the youngest owner of the new league founded at the end of 1992.

In terms of exposure, sponsorship, and rider pay, the new sport was of course nothing like it is today. Initially, the living wasn't easy. Jerome and Tiffany made their home in the old homestead house on the dairy barn, leaky roof and all.

He was happy.

"There was no guy that loved the sport more than me; I was my own boss and made a living. I would get on up to 175 bulls a year. To be able to win a world title, you have to live it, drink it, walk it, talk it. It takes up every minute of your day. I was good with that."

He almost died in 1992 when stomped by a bull, breaking his collarbone and ribs and puncturing his lung. "I could tell I was suffocating; they ran a tube up into me," he said.

The Carolina cowboy healed up, came back and finished in the Top Five. And in 1995, at twenty-two years old he secured his name among rodeo's elite by winning the bull riding title in the PRCA. He was the first rider from east of the Mississippi to claim that world title. Jerome finished third in the world in both 1994 and 1996, when he won the most money to date in the PBR, allowing him to purchase the ranch from his family.

Two years later, early in the season in March, Davis was number one in the world, leading the PBR standings. He'd only been thrown off three bulls all season. In Fort Worth, he was set to face a bull called Knock 'em Out John. They already had shared a violent history. "He had hit me in the face once before. He'd rock you back and pull you in and hit you in the face," Jerome said.

Tiffany was sitting in the bleachers in Fort Worth next to a girl who didn't like that bull; he'd knocked her husband out a few weeks earlier. Knock 'em Out John stayed true to habit and name. He jumped forward, rocking Jerome backwards. Then the bull's momentum pulled Jerome into him. The young rider turned his head and was knocked out before he hit the ground.

"It was like diving headfirst into a swimmin' pool without enough water," Tiffany said.

The First Couple of Bull Riding

At the Hollywood premiere of The Longest Ride (Bull Stock Media)

When he came to, he knew it was bad. "I asked the doctor to take my glove off," Jerome said. "He looked at me and said, 'Man, I already took your glove off.'"

Tiffany met Jerome by the ambulance as he was about to be rushed to the hospital. For the first time since they'd met, she saw fear in his eyes. At the hospital, the doctor broke the news he'd never walk again. "First thing Jerome said is, 'You mean I won't ride bulls anymore?' He thought about that more than the walking part," Tiffany said.

Jerome couldn't accept the finality of the doctor's words. Surely his legs could heal. "I asked for the percentage. *Give me a percentage.* The doctor said 'I can't. There's nothing there. You won't be walking.' I kept persisting. 'Come on Doc, give me a percent!' He finally said, 'Jerome, I will give you 1 percent.' I said, 'That's good enough.' You know, I'm on twenty years now and still working on it."

"I always say we are still in denial," Tiffany said. "We are not accepting it to this day. One way to look at it is that Lane Frost's parents were there with us. Of course, they'd never get to see Lane again after he had passed. And Jerome is still here. We have him."

After the wreck that left the rider also known as "Jerome Danger" paralyzed, his life would of course forever change, and Tiffany's was thrown into turmoil. As if the stress level wasn't high enough, the couple's love, and her commitment, would be questioned.

Tiffany was standing in the hospital with her future mother-in-law and Jerome's attending physician, who was outlining next steps in caring for a twenty-five-year-old man who'd been paralyzed. The fall had crushed two vertebrae in Davis's neck, and to repair the damage, surgeons had grafted a bone from Davis's hip onto the damaged vertebrae. The doctor was addressing Jerome's mother, without even acknowledging Tiffany. As if she wasn't even in the room. He finally snidely offered, "Oh, she'll be one of the 90 percent." Meaning, those who following a traumatic injury of a partner leave the relationship.

The crude, insensitive, off-hand insult just made Tiffany, who was then twenty-three, more determined and resolute. She was in love. She was loyal. She was better than that. *They* were better than that. God would look over and care for them, as He always had. And she knew she would continue to love Jerome with all her heart no matter the shape of his legs. There was a wedding date set, two months away.

Jerome encouraged his fiancé to leave him, so she wouldn't have to be a caregiver to him the rest of his life. He knew he needed Tiffany more than ever, but felt it was the right thing to do. And so he extended to her an out, a way to go on with her life without feeling guilty.

"I tried to run her off," he told Flint Rasmussen on his "According to Flint" podcast. "I didn't want her to go down that road. I loved her of course.

But I felt she didn't need five years down the road to be hanging out with a crippled guy."

Tiffany would have none of it. "We were best friends before we ever started dating, and you wouldn't leave your best friend in a situation like that," Tiffany told the *High Point Enterprise* in a 2014 piece about their long and happy marriage. "So, I told him to hush up and that was the end of that."

There would be no May wedding. It was moved to October. She became Mrs. Davis seven months following Jerome's accident.

Tiffany had always been there for Jerome, like driving all night to help get him to rodeos far from the Carolinas. Now she was doubling down. "We had a few cows to go on but not much," Tiffany said. "People sent in money. It was like a gift from God. Our hospital bills got paid by donations from all these good, generous people, most who were strangers. Our living bills got paid. Jerome said to Randy Bernard (who ran PBR at the time), 'My bills are paid. I feel bad taking more money.' That's how the Rider Relief Fund got started by Randy, and it's helped so many riders over the years." (This fund, which paid severely injured riders' medical and living bills, was relaunched as the Western Sports Foundation in 2018, adding a range of new services including access to medical specialists, counseling, and wellness services. Proceeds from this book will support this fund.)

Doctors told Jerome he'd only have 15 to 20 percent of his body functioning. While still in the hospital, he began dialing up riders and sponsors to plan the first Jerome Davis PBR Invitational bull riding event. It's now PBR's longest-running outdoor event, well into its second decade.

For a time, Tiffany sold bull whips and trick ropes to continue to keep the lights on, as the couple transitioned to finding a sustainable way to earn a living on their own without relying on the help of others. They invested in bulls, haulers, bucking chutes, and other equipment to host their own events. Tiffany became the first woman to flank bulls in the chutes. At first it was intimidating, especially under the no-nonsense eye of Cody Lambert. But Tiffany knew what she was doing. She was serious and disciplined at her new job while exuding love, warmth, and positivity. And everyone of course loved Jerome and wanted the Davises to succeed. Tiffany was fully accepted as a stock contractor, paving the way for many others now seen preparing bulls for competition at PBR events today.

"I'm not the smartest person, but I know I'm smart enough to do something I'm passionate about," she said. "This is a lot of hard work for what you're making. But the friendships and lessons in life you get, I wouldn't trade for anything. I've always thought the most important thing in life is how you treat those people around you. The PBR is such a good group. We have a deep love. It sounds corny, but it really is like a family."

One member of that family who has always supported and inspired Tiffany is LeAnn Hart, who would also become a stock contractor with her husband, J.W. Hart—the 1994 PBR Rookie of the Year—after he retired from riding in 2008. Even with all Tiffany was dealing with, she would encourage LeAnn in her struggles, especially the devastation of thirteen miscarriages.

"Tiffany stood on her faith when she and Jerome went through what they went through," LeAnn said. "We know we were created to be tougher than to feel sorry for ourselves. At some point in life, you're going to have to nod your head. Nobody's going to do it for you. You need those people in your life. Tiffany is one of a handful of people in my life to help get me out of myself and my bad moods, my hurt and anger and brokenness. That's what she does, and what I hope to be."

As the PBR family welcomed the new stock contractors, led by a hard-working brassy blonde who loved what she did, the couple's financial lot would eventually improve markedly as a result of Jerome's decision a little more than a decade prior to kick in every dollar to his name to join his fellow riders in forming a new bull riding sport. In 2005, a company called Spire Capital would acquire the PBR, producing a windfall for the founders. Lambert, one of the heroes Jerome looked up to when he first joined the nineteen other cowboys forming a new sport, got to make the best phone call of his life to inform Jerome that he was about to become a millionaire. Jerome and Tiffany used part of the windfall to build on the ranch an impressive Western-themed, three-story log cabin, complete with an elevator. Its roof would never leak.

"For a while, every time it rained, I'd still want to look for a bucket to catch them drops, even when we had the new house," she said.

"Best thousand bucks I'd ever spent," Jerome added, referring to the money he scraped up to invest in the audacious new bull riding league.

At first, after Jerome was hurt, Tiffany's faith had been rocked to the core. She'd question why it was Jerome who was hurt. He was one of the good guys! Then she began to understand the mysterious and challenging workings of God's divine will. Jerome's accident did have a purpose. He has helped and inspired many more people in a wheelchair than he would have if the accident hadn't happened, she believes.

Today, the five thousand-seat Davis Ranch Arena on their property hosts a handful of rodeo and bull riding events each year. Fans enjoy concessions and shop at a souvenir shed filled with branded Davis Rodeo Ranch merchandise. The week before the 2019 Greensboro Invitational, the ranch had welcomed the Christian Junior Rodeo, Tiffany's favorite event of the year because the Davises give back to the community just as the community helped when they most needed it. Fans who had attended the church service in the bleachers and brought two cans of soup for a local community charity were admitted for free. The event drew two thousand fans and five hundred entries.

A week later, on the premium experience tour, Jerome and Tiffany fed their guests a stomach-pleasing fare of homemade North Carolina barbecue with chicken dumplings, potato salad, and mac 'n' cheese. The dessert table was laid out with trays of banana pudding, white chocolate cheesecake, and persimmon pudding—"something old Southern ladies make, which is why Cracker Barrel doesn't have it," Tiffany said.

The food was as good and satisfying as the homespun wisdom and laughs served up on a memorable afternoon starring two of the genuine characters making the PBR family so special, a couple bound by a special love and enduring faith that spills over to their community, their sport, its fans, and, of course, the animals.

Love & Try

2

BEVERLY HILLS COWBOY

(Tiffany Davis)

Growing up in rural North Carolina, little Jerome Davis never doubted his intended professional path.

When Jerome was a baby, his dad would lull him to sleep on horseback. He told his first-grade teacher he was going to be a bull rider one day, and she laughed at him. He didn't get sour or put up an argument—you didn't speak to your elders like a smart aleck. The polite kid with self-assurance beyond his years knew deep down he'd have the last laugh.

"All I ever wanted was to put my hand in a bull rope," he said. "It was almost like I had a disease. I was infested with it."

Jerome was lucky to have a partner in crime of sorts—his own dad, who let his son miss fifty-two days of high school to go to rodeos. One time a teacher was giving him problems. "She was getting into me for missing school," Davis remembered. "I told her I can't afford going to school." He would show her his pay stub—proving he was earning more than she was.

After high school, father and son plotted to find a place where Jerome could continue his education, if that's what you called it, while rodeoing. Odessa Junior College in Odessa, Texas, would allow rodeo to come first, and Davis's school schedule could be set up around attending competitions. He tore up his knee early on and did not make the eight second whistle on one bull the first half of his first season. Then Davis went on a tear. He didn't get thrown off a single bull in the second half, winning the National Intercollegiate Rodeo Association's Bull Riding Championship as a freshman.

Even while attending college, his mind and focus was on bull riding. There was no backup plan. "As soon as you have a backup plan, you're not committed to bull riding," Davis said. "You're either a bull rider, or you're not a bull rider."

When Davis helped establish PBR, TNN was televising events and Bud Light was the main sponsor. Rider payouts were growing, but the big paydays were still a few years away. Going into the 1993 Del Rio bull riding event, Davis found a way to make a few guaranteed greenbacks. The film company on-site in Texas shooting a Lane Frost bio-picture was paying bull riders $50 to dress up like Luke Perry, the *Beverly Hills 90120* heartthrob, who was impressing everyone by flexing serious cowboy chops in playing the rodeo star. A quintessential no brainer, Davis donned the requisite plaid shirt and found a black cowboy hat along with a handful of toilet paper.

"I had a straw hat because it was starting to be warm. Luke was wearing a big, black felt hat, so I needed something to keep it on my small head," Davis recalled.

Minus the cranial TP, three or four other bull riders also turned up looking like Lane Frost, whose life, five years earlier, had been cut short at twenty-five years old by a misplaced bull horn at the Cheyenne Frontier Days Rodeo.

"There were only a few guys dressed like Luke. Not everyone was as broke as I was," Davis said. The pot for doing so, though, was even sweeter.

If the ride footage of any Luke Perry lookalike made it into the movie, *8 Seconds*, he'd earn an additional $500.

Davis produced what he called one of the top five rides of his career, riding a bull named Playboy for ninety-two points to take the George Paul Memorial Bull Riding XVI in Del Rio, his first PBR win. "The arena announcer said it was ninety-seven points, but we're pretty sure he was drunk," joked Jerome's wife, Tiffany, chuckling about the good old days of the PBR.

Hollywood heartthrob Luke Perry flexed serious cowboy chops in playing legendary bull rider Lane Frost. (Tiffany Davis)

"Wasn't a bad weekend for me," Davis said. "I got on a few bulls and won $18,000 wearing those clothes. The movie shows Lane winning Del Rio, and I actually won that bull riding, so that was kind of cool."

Fans of *8 Seconds* will remember the scene where Davis rides Playboy as Stephen Baldwin playing gruff, tough bull rider Tuff Hedeman, whose anger in being bucked off once became so intense he gritted his teeth so hard he broke a tooth and who told Lane Frost to "cowboy up." Unfortunately, Davis hurt his knee and was unable to perform additional stunt work for filming the rest of a movie that earned Luke Perry critical praise, gave rodeo pop culture validation, and attracted new fans.

Bull riders can be skeptical of outsiders daring to put on a pair of chaps. But Jerome would forge a lifetime friendship with the actor who didn't even know how to ride a horse in pre-production yet would study and train so he could mount rank bulls. Beneath Perry's radiating Hollywood fame, Davis couldn't help but observe a hard-working cowboy. When Luke arrived in the bull ring, he was completely committed to his first leading role in a motion picture. He put in the work, learned to ride bulls, and he convincingly captured the realism of the sport and Lane Frost's spirit in a film beloved by PBR fans to this day. Perry, who passed away in March 2019 at fifty-two after suffering a stroke, is at the center of *8 Seconds'* success and iconic place in Western sports history.

Ask any bull rider, and chances are, he's been influenced by the film. PBR Ring of Honor member Luke Snyder watched *8 Seconds* as a ten-year-old and knew he'd be a bull rider, learning from Lane Frost that even more than your riding record, what people will remember is the way you treated them outside the arena. Future Ring of Honor inductee J.B. Mauney still watches the film in the middle of the night when his son, Jagger, is having trouble sleeping.

To help Perry portray Frost, the writers drew on the counsel of his other traveling partners like PBR cofounder and nine-time World Champion Ty Murray. When Murray walked into the first script meeting in a hotel in San Antonio, he saw Perry dressed like Frost and already acting like his buddy.

"It was freakish how much Luke looked like Lane and took on his mannerisms," Murray said. "For a split second, it was like you had seen a ghost. I knew right then they picked the right guy to play Lane. He loved the cowboy lifestyle and respected bull riders. It was important for him to do justice to the cowboys in *8 Seconds*."

Perry worked hard to portray an athlete who was such a nice guy that his physical and mental toughness as well as his intense competitiveness could be overlooked. Lane Frost did *not* like to get bucked off, even if he had scored on a dozen bulls before that. He did a good job publicly masking his frustrations, but his riding buddies knew that deep down he was *mad*.

"It didn't matter if it was a thousand miles to the next rodeo; none of us had to drive after Lane got bucked off," Cody Lambert said. "Lane was gonna punish himself and drive. You just hoped it wasn't in your car. I had a Chevy Caprice Classic, and he had that whole thing shaking so hard, going at least 130, as fast as he could go, as long as he could go. Now we all hated driving; it was like a contest to see who could get out of it, so we wouldn't complain. Lane drove as far and fast as he could. One time, he'd driven all night and was ready to turn it over. Finally, one of us would have to say, 'Lane, we thought you had him.' And he'd get mad and grit his teeth and be good for another two hundred miles."

Perry would later say that while he played many athletes, he was most connected to the bull riders of the PBR.

"He was initially known as a very famous actor on a very popular show about Beverly Hills, but you could see Luke was a cowboy," Davis said. "It felt like he was one of us, and he was. He just fit in when he was around. I didn't look at him as the *90210* star. He was just humble ol' Luke."

Perry exuded easy generosity in a quiet, unassuming way. Five years after filming at Del Rio, he would turn up in the Davises' life and exhibit extraordinary kindness after Jerome's bull riding accident left him paralyzed.

Perry had found out the local North Carolina community supporting Davis was pulling together a fundraiser for the injured rider. He got ahold of Jerome's number and called the Davis ranch, intending to support the event. Tiffany answered the phone. Assuming it was a prank, she disconnected. Perry called back and had to convince Tiffany it was for real.

He'd do whatever was needed to help. Just one thing: he needed a ride from the airport to the charity bull riding and auction. Tiffany called her sister who often drove bull riders from their flights to the Davises' rodeo arena.

"She said, 'Yeah, sure,' and asked, 'What time is the flight, who is it, and what does he look like?'"

"I just said, 'It's Luke Perry,' and she hung up."

Tiffany immediately called back.

"Quit bein' stupid on me," her sister replied and hung up again.

Tiffany had to call her mother to persuade everyone this was no joke.

Perry laughed when a full entourage of Tiffany's family picked him up. He was gracious in meeting fans and signing autographs. He even brought a personal painting to auction off to help make the event a success.

"After that, we got to become buddies," Jerome said. "Luke would call out of the blue to see how I was. He felt like an old friend every time we talked. I can't say enough good things about him; he was just a super nice guy."

The last time Perry rang up Jerome, he was south of Nashville, just checking in to see how his friend was doing.

"It showed what kind of guy Luke was, and it made me feel good," Davis said. "He was good, grounded, and humble, and I'm so sad he's gone."

3

HEART OF HARTS

(Bull Stock Media)

LeAnn Hart always wanted to be a mama. As a little girl, she'd stand outside her family's dairy farm in Louisiana in the afternoon sunshine with a pillow stuffed under her shirt. She'd put one side of her body in the sun. The shadow of her distended belly, spread onto the ground, looked funny when cast from her small body. And it was comforting, too. She loved her baby bump. She smiled imagining the pillow one day replaced by a growing boy or girl.

LeAnn would never have a problem getting pregnant. But thirteen straight times, her baby was lost.

"You start asking the Lord, 'What's your plan? Because mine ain't working out'," she said.

LeAnn and her husband, bull rider J.W. Hart—a.k.a. "The Iron Man," who retired from PBR competition in 2008 to become one of the sport's top bull stock contractors with LeAnn, as well as a guest analyst for PBR on CBS—leaned into their faith. They prayed hard about the situation.

The Lord revealed a plan for the Harts to become parents. The couple would adopt. And adopt again. And again. They now have six children ranging from four to thirteen years old.

For those not familiar with today's adoption process, it's not like ordering shoes from Amazon. Adopting a child in the United States can take up to three years after navigating a labyrinth of rules ostensibly written to assist neither a child in need nor would-be parents ready to provide a loving, stable home. Through their faith, the Harts kept a patient mindset, understanding that delays don't mean a denial from God. They endured the long and time-consuming steps six times over, while managing their 240-acre Southern Oklahoma ranch where they raise more than one hundred bulls.

The first child the couple had adopted, Wacey Dalton Hart, was born in March 2009. LeAnn, pregnant while the blizzard of papers was going through, had another miscarriage. Doctors were perplexed; nobody could tell her what was wrong.

"Who knows if I'll be like Sarah in the Bible, ninety years old and pregnant," LeAnn said. She laughs about it and can sometimes get upset. On those occasions, she disarms her old self, brings her emotions into check, and accepts her role in God's grand plan by turning over the joystick to Him. "I've always tried to allow the Lord to have control," she said. "Not everything's about me or us, even when it sure seems to be about us. Sometimes things happen *to* us. And it's always for a reason."

The Lord's plan the couple patiently accepted didn't end with adopting six children, as gigantic and impactful a responsibility as that has been. Over the past dozen years, LeAnn and J.W. have also served as foster parents to more than fifty children. Many of the kids were removed from heartbreakingly unhealthy situations—violent homes, abusive situations, exposure to drugs. It wasn't always a workable fit. Several kids had to be sent back due to safety concerns for the Hart's own children. One foster baby kept getting sick; LeAnn found out there had been methamphetamine in her baby bottle.

While some placements didn't work out, many more did. The couple's open hearts and home provided a fighting chance to dozens of children who couldn't fight for themselves.

"You get a chance, whether it's two days, two months, two weeks, or two years, to give those kids some stability," J.W. said about being a foster parent.

The bureaucratic dance for foster parents who just want to provide a stable, loving home is exhausting. Government processes don't encourage input from foster parents, who have virtually no rights, no matter how well-meaning they are.

J.W. Hart with his children Makayla Raine (L) and Wacey Dalton (Bull Stock Media)

"The system is broken," LeAnn said. "Everyone thinks everyone else is out to do someone wrong. You have to have a hard nose to keep looking out for what's best for the kids. It will wear you out physically, mentally, and spiritually."

Along with her no-nonsense cowboy husband, LeAnn never shied away from the daunting challenges, daily frustrations, and depressing setbacks of navigating the foster and adoption systems. "I grew up working hard," she said. "You appreciate things more that way."

She was raised in a musical family, mostly by grandparents who sang with the popular gospel group, the Happy Goodmans, known by millions as one of the flagship groups in "the Gospel Singing Jubilee" and then their own TV show, *The Happy Goodman Family Hour*. Her grandparents toured with the Grammy Award-winning Goodmans at churches throughout Louisiana.

When LeAnn was three, she sang "Jesus Loves Me" in church. She may have cried all the way through, but it was clear the young girl was blessed with a tremendous gift. As her dad competed in local rodeos, she would sing the national anthem more times than she could count.

At seventeen, she graduated high school early and wanted to go to Nashville, where an aunt lived, to pursue a music career. It was recommended that she avoid performing in bars; instead, she was referred to an audition at Dollywood located in the foothills of Tennessee's Great Smoky Mountains. She'd never lived outside of Albany, Louisiana, but wound up performing in "Paradise Roads—the Life & Songs of Dolly Parton," a Broadway-style show celebrating Parton's career, and she sang in the classic country theater show for two years.

LeAnn had always been drawn to cowboys for their grit and resilience. She'd dated a bull rider before meeting J.W. in 2003 at a bull riding event in Tampa when, during a break in the Dollywood show, she was on her way to Louisiana. Tiffany Davis was there, too. As good a tour guide and bull raiser as Tiffany is, she's a better matchmaker. Sensing LeAnn was the one girl who could handle the cocksure J.W. Hart, she whispered to J.W. that that pretty girl, LeAnn, over on the other side of the bar, was going to be his future wife.

J.W. recognized the stunning blonde with the disarming movie-star smile. A few years earlier, at a bull riding event in Fort Worth, his dad had pointed out LeAnn, saying to his son, *"Why can't you find one like that?"*

Hart walked up to LeAnn and declared, "You're my date for the night."

She knew a bit about the former Rookie of the Year who'd won the PBR World Finals event the previous fall. He'd come from a poor family, in a home often without electricity and heat even in cold Oklahoma winters. How cold? Well, one morning J.W. had woken up, and the toilet was split in two. The toilet water had turned into a chunk of ice. J.W. was gruff and hard-nosed, a fighter who had earned everything in life through hard work and an uncompromising will. "I never was the best bull rider in the world. Never was—any era, any year, very seldom any weekend," J.W. later told Matt Merritt on his *ROADCAST* podcast. "I was as good as I was because I tried very hard, as hard as I could, because at a very early age I learned it was easier to ride bulls than to work in the oil field, where my dad came from." As a bull rider, J.W. was known to be cocky and could back it up. He had set the PBR record for competing in 197 straight events (later broken by Luke Snyder). J.W. was a straight shooter, hardheaded and stubborn, not known to mince many words. LeAnn even thought he could be full of himself. "J.W. was a butt," she recalled, laughing.

And something clicked.

She was twenty-three and, while she was from a family of huggers who said "I love you" whenever bidding goodbye to one another, she'd never told a boyfriend she loved him. Within a short time, she would say that to J.W.

"We just hit it off," she said. "The cowboy mentality of 'never give up' is pretty contagious to a lot of women. There's a bad boy exterior but a big heart underneath, and I got to see J-Dub's heart."

An enduring love affair began that night in Tampa. The couple dated for nearly two years and were married in 2005.

"She's the most loving, charitable person I know," J.W. would tell Keith Ryan Cartwright for a PBR story when LeAnn was given the Sharon Shoulders Award at the end of the 2016 season for her contributions to the sport. "At the same time, she'll stand up and go toe-to-toe with anybody."

LeAnn feels it's her responsibility to work just as hard as her husband in tending to their cattle, mending fences, and hauling bulls to Velocity Tour events when J.W. is headed to the Unleash The Beast.

"LeAnne Lambert told me to stop showing J-Dub what I can do so I won't have so much on my plate," she laughed. "But I wanted to be a cowgirl. This is what I do. We have ranch horses. We gather and work our cattle on horseback, work the bulls and give them shots. We do what cowboys do daily; it's our livelihood. Whatever J.W. does, I do. It may take me a little longer, and he may sometimes disagree with how I do it, but I get it done!"

"I have a grown man who works for me, and he can't do as good a job as she does when I'm gone," J.W. told Cartwright. "When he can't pull the slack, she goes and takes care of it. Cattle, horses, and kids. She feeds a crew of guys on branding day, takes the kids to school, saddles horses, helps to gather cattle, brand cattle, and then she does all the charity work for the kids."

When she had first met and married J.W., full of newfound confidence from singing in the Dolly Parton show, LeAnn was considering her own musical brand at the Grand Ole Opry rather than branding cattle on a ranch. She was in Nashville, writing and releasing songs, including one called "Where Jesus Is."

One of hundreds of renditions of "The Star-Spangled Banner" (Bull Stock Media)

Launching a successful solo music career, however, was challenging for a young, impressionable girl in the cutthroat music industry viewed by controlling executives as fresh clay to mold into the vessel they wanted her to be. She recalled her grandfather's advice: *Do not conform to the patterns of this world.* She was also planning to start a family with J.W. LeAnn would withdraw from her country music career but never give up singing.

The song of choice was the one she publicly sang the most—"The Star-Spangled Banner."

First at a bull riding event promoted by Jerome and Tiffany Davis (who are now godparents to all six of her children) and then just about everywhere PBR went, she performed the song that means so much to her. During hundreds of renditions, it never lost its impact, and it still brings butterflies. "I'm nervous every time I sing it," she said. "And every time I tear up staring at that flag and what it represents—those who did for us what we can't do for ourselves. Freedom is never free. There's always a cost of blood spilled, and incredible sacrifices made."

Even when singing the national anthem more than anyone else in the life of the sport, LeAnn is more likely to be known as "the crazy girl who talks about Jesus," she observes. "Some women at PBR have said, 'It's a little weird how much you're into your faith.' I say, 'It's weird you're not!' I was a partier and a girl who knew how to have a good time. I was also raised in faith and had grandparents who walked in relationship with Jesus. They treated others the way they wanted others to treat them. You grow into that as you mature and work into the legacy others have left to you. I love people. I love to talk to them and hear their stories. I always wanted to talk about the goodness of God. I'm good with all J.W. and I have walked through because there's a purpose to it."

Since the couple began adopting children and sharing their story, LeAnn has been asked to speak about her experiences grounded in her special faith. She was raised Baptist, but now attends a non-denominational church and has even spoken at Catholic churches. Her ministry often happens on social media—sending devotionals, often on the fly, from the pasture, a stop along the road, or bull housing at an event. Bull riders have approached her in the back pens of PBR events, asking her to pray with them.

She's not out to prove a point, just to "be the evidence of what you believe" and share what's in her heart. Her daddy once told her to stop trying to convince people all the time. It was hard at first. She eased into it. She wants to show the goodness of God by the purpose of her walk. She's working toward walking consistently rather than running toward perfection.

It's been observed of this couple in the Western sports limelight that J.W. Hart toughened LeAnn up, and she in turn softened him. As much as there's truth to that, each has admitted that all those kids in their home have had a larger effect on their relationship as a couple and who they are as individuals—especially with the six that are now their own.

"Every one of them, they each take a piece of your heart," J.W. said.

What the former bull rider didn't add is this: nobody can take anything from your heart. It's all given freely.

PART II

TRY

Their whole life, they're told not to do it. It's dumb. It's insanely dangerous. It's no way to support a family. It will get you crippled.

They do it anyway.

And is it ever difficult. And does it ever hurt.

There are no instant stars. To do it well means first enduring failure—miserable, frustrating, and painful. Nobody walks away unscathed. No matter the size of their talent or the strength of their will, they will eat dirt and break bones.

Maybe it is ill-advised insanity. Until the day the level of their brimming confidence surpasses the crest of their fear. And then they know the quest is unstoppable.

They are different than you and me. They are a breed apart. They are bull riders.

4

HEART OF A WARRIOR

(Bull Stock Media)

Now that PBR is part of a thriving global public company with tentacles flung into sports, fashion, art, media, events, and entertainment, lots of ideas are kicked around for accelerating the sport's charge into the mainstream as random producers ring up the league seeking to partner on the next *Yellowstone*. One such idea is a sports comedy feature film. Think *Talladega Nights* meets *Blazing Saddles* with a splash of *Slapshot* … set in the world of bull riding.

If it happens, when casting begins, the part of bull rider Chase Outlaw *has to be played* by Chase Outlaw.

Chase Outlaw—like Endeavor, this unique multinational company that owns the sport he competes in—defies easy description. I'm flattered that you're reading his story. But the tale of Chase Outlaw would resonate a whole lot better in the ear, in an audiobook, for there is no more glorious, greasy, Southern-fried, gravy-smothered, vowel-extending, and syllable-stretching accent than the one from the man from Arkansas known as "The CEO of Outlaw Nation."

To beat the Hollywood analogy to a pulp, if they were making an animated movie, for Outlaw's character think The Tasmanian Devil crossed with a bull riding Yosemite Sam. At 5'6" 140 pounds, the high-spirited bull rider is a fireball-hurricane commandeering every room he blows into.

Take, for example, Chase meeting Bozoma Saint John when the ultra-connected chief marketing officer of Endeavor was coming to her first event "to discover my inner cowgirl," she said. Boz (pronounced "Boze")—a brand unto herself (her Instagram moniker is *@badassboz*) and formerly a top marketer at Apple, Beats, Pepsi, and Uber—chose the 2018 World Finals for her PBR indoctrination. (She would move to oversee marketing for Netflix). Like Outlaw, Saint John is larger-than-life, and not only figuratively. Off the jet at McCarran International, out of the black Cadillac SUV, and stepping into T-Mobile Arena, she had to be 6' 3" in cowboy boots, pushing 6" more with the hair and cowboy hat. She was decked in enough head-to-toe denim to draw the envy of J.B. Mauney, who, as the joke goes, was born in Wranglers.

Queuing up for the metal detector outside the arena, Boz was a formidable force field of jangly jewelry, multicolored nail bling, and eruptions of deep laughter. And who whirled in like the perfect storm landing ashore next to the towering figure? It was the spry Arkansas cowboy, with a ping-pong-ball-sized chunk of chaw in his cheek.

This is going to go extremely well, or very badly, I was nervously realizing, as the PR guy responsible for escorting the senior executive into her first bull riding event and down to the exclusive "dirt suites" set up on floor level. That said, "caution" and "deliberation" are terms that have never appeared on one of my performance reviews. Learn to swim in the deep pool. If Boz was going to meet any bull rider on the day's outing, it might as well be Chase Outlaw. I introduced the two.

Off came Chase's cowboy hat. He craned his neck to look up to her. Big smiles from both. Boz's bright white teeth looked like they were plugged into a nearby solar panel. Chase's? What with the tobacco habit, not so much.

"Pleasure meeting you, ma'am. Chase Outlaw!"

"That's one heck of a clever (and should I say, appropriate?) stage name. Chase Outlaw!" Saint John said.

"Oh, no ma'am! Came out of the hospital, that name right on that birth certificate. *Chase Ethan Outlaw!* And did you know there was a woman who just had a baby and they wanted to name her child *Ee-than Al-len*, and she looks over patting her big stomach still sore and goes, '*EE-THAN AL-LEN, THAT'S A F--KING FERN-IT-TURE!*'"

Whoosh, the hat was back on, and Tropical Storm Chase had blown out to sea. Outlaw was gone, and Bozoma Saint John was in stitches, the way Chase Outlaw often leaves them. "Now, *that* is a personality America needs to know!" she was left saying.

Go big or go home. I get to stay.

In a good-time, scary-dangerous sport full of cowboys who appreciate every fragile moment and lack the disingenuity to sugarcoat things, Chase Outlaw is as real and entertaining as they come. What you see is what you get. When Chase is pissed, you know it. When he's happy, which is a lot more often, you know it, too.

He is in a happy element when bounding into the arena. There's a spunky hop to his step, except for the times he enters more slowly, quiet, and serene, because he's holding the hand of a sick child. (Chase has never declined a Make-A-Wish request, including Kye Davis, pictured above, who only wanted to be a cowboy, and Chase ushered him across the blue carpet outside T-Mobile Arena leading into World Finals in 2017. Kye passed away in 2018.)

Chase Outlaw doesn't need much to get his motor running. Arriving at the arena, particularly the locker room, is a reliable kick start. He is jacked to be *a professional bull rider, yessir!* It is his life's dream, what he always wanted to do, what he's hoped to be since he was a little boy asked by his second-grade teacher to write a letter to himself. Little Chase Outlaw took that assignment to heart. He thought about it, but there was only one answer. He sat in his bedroom, took out a No. 2 pencil, and wrote out "I *am going to be a professional bull rider.*"

That was it. Just like the mythical heroes in natty chaps and dusty hats he worshiped on the TV.

"There's no way I wasn't gonna be a bull rider," Outlaw said to a reporter I had brought into the locker room at EagleBank Arena in Fairfax, Virginia, in late September 2019, as he was getting his gear ready for the Unleash The Beast event during an epic run to the PBR World Finals. "No, ma'am, no way I wasn't gonna be a professional cowboy in that way. There's just something about having that cowboy hat on."

For most of his career, Outlaw rode in a cowboy hat. In 2012, PBR instituted a rule that every participant born after October 15, 1994, would be required to wear a helmet. Veteran athletes like Chase were grandfathered in and exempt from the helmet mandate. Some said a helmet threw their balance off. Others comfortable in their ways just didn't appreciate mandated change. It was their choice.

In pitching the sport, the cowboy hat is very good for business. Many a morning show has committed to segments when figuring out the talent could goof around in cowboy hats. That hat is an entrée to Western intrigue. One time, a radio host who'd done his research was recounting how riders may place a lucky talisman in their hat, like a photo of a sage grandfather.

"Do you have something lucky you put in your hat?" he asked J.B. Mauney.

"Yeah," Mauney said. "My head."

A handful of other riders, including João Ricardo Vieira, Fabiano Vieira, Guilherme Marchi, and Outlaw, continued to shun the helmet and go with the cowboy hat. But after Cheyenne, when getting on a bull, Chase would have no choice but to trade the felt- or straw-brimmed hat for a protective helmet.

Cheyenne. It's a tour stop every rider looks forward to, tops for some. To many fans, the word "Cheyenne" conjures images of Lane Frost, one of the biggest stars of rodeo who lost his life after taking a horn to the back in the iconic outdoor ring at the age of twenty-five. And now they'd also think of Chase Outlaw, after another wreck in Cheyenne that would enter bull riding lore. Heck, it would even make its way onto the pages of outlets like *USA Today*, which usually doesn't give a lick about America's Original Extreme Sport. Outlaw refers to what the newspapers were covering as "The Accident." Sometimes it's "That Damn Accident." Many assumed that after the damn accident, his dream had completed its run, no matter how tough anyone had said Chase Outlaw was.

This chapter of Chase's life, the open-ended one on extended-play repeat because it's become the part of his story everyone insists on dwelling on, started in the summer of 2018. July is when cowboys traditionally head to Cheyenne Frontier Days, the world's largest outdoor rodeo, held in the place once called "The Magic City of the Plains," where the Union Pacific Railroad laid its tracks and spawned a bustling boomtown teeming with dance halls and saloons, an edgy destination for the hard living who'd take what they believed was theirs for the taking, a city where men and women alike slept with more than one pistol under the pillow. That group who enjoys Cheyenne's atmosphere includes Chase's friend, Bonner Bolton, recently retired from bull riding, after an accident broke his neck and temporarily paralyzed him. Bonner hadn't been to a PBR event for a while, and he was looking forward to spending time with Chase. "When given the chance to hang out with Chase Outlaw, hang out with Chase Outlaw," Bolton explained.

In the chutes, Bolton helped tie Chase's rope onto a bull named War Cloud. The bull wasn't cooperating. War Cloud was quivering in a forbidding way; it took two tries to get the rope wrapped around Chase's left hand. Old school in his cowboy hat, Outlaw nodded. The gate flew open. War Cloud detonated from the chute, kicking his front legs to the right. The forceful move threw Outlaw's timing off. He was moving forward, out of sync with his dance partner, jerked down toward the animal just as the bull rose, spinning to the left. Chase was unable to counter the forceful pull. He was head butted with a ferocious shot to the face just 1.51 seconds into the out.

It happened so fast, and the blow was so furious, fans didn't realize the gravity of what had just happened. But when they saw the ride slowed down in slow-motion replay, it showed the tremendous force of the collision, like being whacked in the face with a heavy pipe. Outlaw sprawled backwards onto the dirt. Bolton knew it was bad.

"The way I saw it from the chutes, the bull came across one side of his face so hard, it busted up the whole other side," said Bolton, who would stay overnight in the hospital. It turned out the bull broke both sides—Outlaw's entire face. He staggered to his feet and was able to walk out of the arena, blood splattered across his cheeks and nose.

Dr. William Wyatt, the on-call physician, didn't initially believe the injury was as bad as it turned out to be.

"I felt his nose and could see that his cheeks were pushed in, but I still did not realize the extent of his injuries," Dr. Wyatt told Marty Klinkenberg, an award-winning reporter with *The Globe and Mail,* who would write a stirring feature story about Chase's comeback. "He was alert and said it felt like his nose was swelling. Then he blew it, and blood filled his sinus cavities and ran into his eyes."

Seeing Chase's bloody eyes, Dr. Wyatt put Chase in an ambulance and separately rushed to Cheyenne Regional Medical Center to further attend to him. Soon Dr. Wyatt would be reviewing the x-rays and scans of Chase's face. He was looking at the worst facial damage he'd ever seen.

Chase's wife, Nicole, was there, too, along with his sister, Brittany. "In the hospital, the doctor comes back and says 'Every bone in Chase's face is broken. This is a lot more serious than we thought when he walked in the doors,'" Nicole said. "He said, 'We need to do something immediately.'"

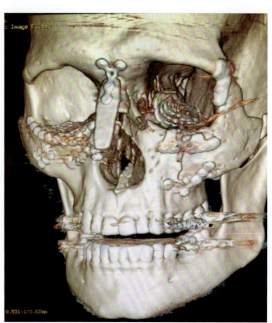

Chase the Cyborg—with 68 screws, 11 titanium plates, and 4 pieces of mesh in his face. (Chase Outlaw)

War Cloud had destroyed Chase's face. The injury was what doctors call a near panfacial fracture—meaning just about every facial bone (thirty for Chase) was broken, even his eye sockets. "We get him into the O.R. and after you find good exposure, you start assessing all the pieces," said Dr. Wyatt. "And you juggle them around until you get them to fit, and then you start fixing him."

"It was important to operate fast and accurately to stop the bleeding," Dr. Wyatt said. If Chase had continued to bleed, his condition would turn significantly more serious.

"I remember everything that night up to the hit. I remember putting my rope on, I remember nodding my head," Outlaw said. "And then I remember being in the hospital, and Dr. Wyatt came in and said, 'Hey we have to have you in surgery within the hour. Pretty much every bone in your face is broken.'"

In twelve hours of delicate and complicated surgery, Dr. Wyatt essentially rebuilt Outlaw's entire face with twelve plates, sixty-eight screws, and four pieces of surgical mesh. A piece of his skull was used to fix the top of his nose.

Outlaw woke up from surgery with a swollen pumpkin face. "I was thinking, 'What the heck. *Maaaan?* You let one done git ya!" he recalled.

And then Chase said something that surprised even Nicole. He asked the doctor when he could get back on a bull.

"I was shaking my head when I heard that," she said. "It was the first question he wanted to know the answer to."

Nicole had told Klinkenberg, "I would have been okay if Chase had decided not to get back into it. I told him, 'If you don't want to do it anymore, don't worry about how you are going to provide for your family. We will all work together and take care of that.' When I said it, he looked at me like I was crazy."

Chase decided he'd be riding at World Finals.

Not *next year*. The 2018 World Finals in Las Vegas—less than four months out.

"This was the same arena that Lane Frost lost his life in," he said. "It very well easily could have been the same situation with me. But heck, you could get T-boned on the way to the Walmart. That doesn't mean you're never gonna get in your truck and go back to the store."

The mere possibility of quitting never crossed Outlaw's mind. The good Lord had a plan for him, and He'd created face masks for a reason, right? In this sport, ride your bulls and pick up points. If he got back as soon as he could, and rode his butt off, a top thirty-five finish or winning the Velocity

Finals, the sport's No. 2 tour—both scenarios qualifying a rider into World Finals—was not impossible. He would use the accident to fuel his drive.

"I was wondering, 'How quick can I get back?'" Outlaw recalled. "They told me four months, and I said, 'The hell with that.' I cut it to two. I know my body. I'm not gonna jeopardize myself. Being able to come back and face that giant is what separates the men from the boys."

It wouldn't be the first major challenge God had put in his path. Outlaw had been through mourning the deaths of his grandmother and mother, as well as, more recently, his best friend, Mason Lowe. He reminded himself that the loved ones he has lost are watching him ride.

Yet, coming from a serious injury to play at a professional level is a lot more complicated than just waiting for bones to heal. Even more so in bull riding.

"Your bone or ligament heals way before your mind understands or trusts it," nine-time World Champion Ty Murray explained. "When you've babied something for six months, even though it feels great, your brain still wants your body to protect that injury."

During his career, Murray would run through a series of physical and mental exercises to get his body back into shape and coax his mind to forget that his body had been brutalized in the first place.

"I knew what the consequences of bull riding could be every time I got in there," he said. "You have to recognize you're taking something that is dangerous to a plateau few people know. The guys who nod and just want to feel how far this is going, well, those guys won't win a championship and can get seriously hurt. All of our brains work differently, but champions know they have to take it all the way to the level the bull wants to go to."

Outlaw may not have articulated it the way Murray did. He said it in the way only Chase Outlaw can.

"It's like a fist fight out there. You can't have no remorse in the bucking chute. Without fear, there's no courage. You overcome fear, or fear overcomes you. Champions don't talk about it. They're silent warriors. The fear? It's an everyday walk of life. The top thirty-five in the world, we just go out and do it."

Outlaw returned to competition just seventy-five days after the Cheyenne wreck and proceeded to mount one of the most impressive injury-comeback runs in Western sports history. He was ranked No. 76 in the world when he returned at the elite tour event in Milwaukee. He would shoot past sixty cowboys to finish the year ranked No. 16. He would qualify for the 2018 PBR World Finals by earning 865 world points at five events—including a runner-up finish in Nampa, Idaho, at the final elite tour event of the season, and the week before World Finals adding a huge win at the Velocity Tour Finals

With Molly Steffl to visit, Outlaw shaved his head. (Bull Stock Media)

at South Point Arena in Las Vegas, the second of his career.

The hospital bed proclamation came to be. Outlaw had punched a ticket to the World Finals.

At one point during his surge up the standings, Outlaw rode eight consecutive bulls, a streak that was snapped in the championship round of the Velocity Tour Finals.

Several weeks before that, going into Minneapolis, Chase shaved his head to prepare to meet a very special girl coming to tour the locker room. Nine-year-old Molly Steffl had been born with a cleft lip and palate. She had been bullied brutally. The ensuing stress had caused all of her hair to fall out. Chase heard Molly would be visiting and promptly found a razor. He turned his head into a cue ball.

"She ain't gonna be the only bald one in the locker room," he proclaimed.

When Chase removed his cowboy hat in meeting the courageous girl to reveal a shiny white pate, his gesture of love and solidarity brought her parents to tears.

Fast forward to World Finals: the big boys were riding lights out and registering high scores every night inside T-Mobile Arena. But even with Marco Eguchi, José Vitor Leme, J.B. Mauney, Derek Kolbaba, Cooper Davis, and Cody Teel hanging on for gigantic ninety-point rides, the loudest roars were for the gritty cowboy riding the year's most improbable and stirring comeback story. Inspired by another Make-A-Wish kid, Chase Outlaw was one of two riders to go an impressive five for 6, nearly catching Eguchi, who was knocked out cold after a ninety-point ride but passed the next day's concussion test, kept riding, and won the event and a cool $300,000. Boy, did ESPN miss out in passing up this one.

Outside T-Mobile Arena on Toshiba Plaza, next to the faux skyline of New York, New York, for the streaming press Q&A with the night's top riders, moderated by PBR arena announcer Matt West, Outlaw was sitting in a director's chair, again living up to his name. After the requisite "How were you able to ride that bull?" questions were asked, Chase grabbed the mic and said, "Hell, this is World Finals! Y'all are in Las Vegas, I don't know why y'all are sittin' here listening to us!"

To end a presser, that sure beats, "If there are no more questions, we'll wrap up, thank you, and have a good night."

It was good for the sport to have Outlaw back, foot on the gas. He returned to competition five days after Eguchi edged him to take the World Finals event title, tying for the win at one of the first events awarding points towards the 2019 standings, a lower-level Touring Pro Division stop in New Town, North Dakota.

Asked about Chase Outlaw's decision to keep riding, Dr. Wyatt said, "People with goals are successful because they always know where they are going, and that's Chase. He knows where he wants to go."

Nobody needs new reasons to root for Chase Outlaw. Yet, hearing his story and listening to his nearly obsessive drive—to not just show up, but to prove to everyone he's the best—and seeing him give every ounce of *try* to go for that World Championship, even after his face exploded, well, a person must lack humanity to not pull for that breed of human.

"When you leave the house for a PBR event, your goal is to win. If you don't plan on winning, you might as well stay at home," Outlaw said matter-of-factly, one eye still slightly bigger than the other following his Cheyenne wreck, as he came back from shoulder surgery early in the 2021 season. "This is what we do to put shoes on the baby's feet. It fuels my passion and is something I love to do. If you love what you do, you don't work a day in your life. Man, to have fans in the seats spending their hard-earned money to come watch what my passion is, and what I love to do, it's very humbling. It's something I've loved to do since I was a little kid. When you get to do your job for eight seconds and people stand up screaming for you, it sends chills down your back. It can't be better than that."

The sparkplug who never stops firing is dead tired of talking about busting his entire face. He wants to move on from Cheyenne, keep it from defining him, bury it in the story instead of letting it be the blaring headline. But he realizes the gravity of the accident and has never avoided the hard introspection of coming to peace with its meaning.

"Maybe I needed that injury to push me over the ledge, see how strong you are, what your full potential is," Chase said. "Having that accident made me evaluate a lot of things. Made me realize how lucky I was to have this talent that I got and not take it for granted. The good Lord tested me to see, '*Is this what you really want?*' Yeah, this is what I want. To be a world champion."

Getting on the world's most dangerous bulls with a face-full of hardware—even with a helmet on—isn't about trying to write some dime-store comeback story. It's not about cruising for accolades or seeking more attention. For Chase Outlaw, there's nobody left to impress. He does it because when you set out to be something in life, and then attain it, you don't go and run away from the chosen path. PBR is what separates the men from the boys. Once a man, you don't go back to being a boy.

Chase Outlaw is a professional bull rider. And, man, does it feel nice.

"When you're riding good, you can see a speck of sand fly off that bull's back," he said. "Ain't nothing like it."

Love & Try

5

SAY HER NAME: JONNIE JONCKOWSKI

(Dan Hubbel Rodeo Photography)

Jonnie Jonckowski. It's a name every sports fan should know. Yet, when asked today, most would respond, "Who's he?"

First, *he* is a *she*. Those on the road with Jonnie hitting jackpots and rodeo invitationals and anywhere else offering a chance to earn a few bucks hanging onto bucking animals who don't recognize personal pronouns will surely attest to that.

Jonnie Jonckowski. The name is bigger than rodeo. Or at least it should be.

In a proper world, the name *Jonnie Jonckowski* would evoke the same starry ring of familiarity as "Mickey Mantle." If the universe were a fair and logical place, that name would be on the tip of the tongue of any sports fan who reacts to myth-busting achievements with ga-ga appreciation and a wallet open to purchasing the related merchandise. It would be a name known by all those who appreciate a fierce story of blood-and-guts triumph, who enjoy a steely tale of indomitable human will trouncing man-made barriers.

Jonckowski is a champion trailblazer in the same rarified sense as Althea Gibson (the first Black athlete to win Wimbledon, the French Open, and the U.S. Open); Janet Guthrie (the first woman to qualify and compete in the Daytona 500 and Indianapolis 500); and Babe Didrikson Zaharias (who won gold medals in track and field at the 1932 Olympics before switching to golf and winning ten LPGA major tournaments).

Jonnie Jonckowski was the first woman to compete against men at a championship level in professional bull riding.

Like Guthrie, Jonckowski's gigantic first came on a grand stage, riding in the men's bull riding World Championship at the Justin World Bull Riding Championship in Scottsdale, Arizona, in 1992. She was invited among an international contingent, considered one of the world's top thirty bull riders.

Like Didrickson, Jonckowski was an incredibly gifted athlete across several sports. She wasn't born in Fargo, North Dakota, in July 1954, as much as she burst into the world revving to make a mark. Early on she was an incorrigible tomboy withering to no challenge. She wanted to be first, the best, the highest, the strongest. Had to outrun everybody. And when that person turned out to be a boy, so be it. The rougher the horseplay, the better. Jonnie's mom made her wear jeans because she kept tearing up her dresses. ("Mom wound up wishing she hadn't done that," she said.)

Rambunctious little Jonnie didn't stay small. In high school, she shot up nine inches to 5'8", growing into a lanky, rangy girl who loved winning track and field events. With "the Olympics on my brain," she was second in the country running collegiate track at Flathead Valley Community College (a small school in Kalispell, Montana, that held its own against NCAA powerhouse universities) and appeared headed for the 1976 summer games in Montreal. In the final qualifying event for the Pentathlon, however, at full speed, she clipped a hurdle and went sprawling. Jonnie badly injured her back, crushing her dream.

She left college. For two years, she could barely walk. She was lost and despondent. One afternoon with her mom at a restaurant outside Billings, she saw a sign advertising an all-girls rodeo. She was no longer able to run like the wind but figured she could sit on an animal doing the work. She was twenty-two.

In ten years, Jonnie Jonckowski would be a world champion bull rider.

Yet it is perhaps Billie Jean King, a household name for integrating professional tennis and pushing for equal rights for female athletes, who Jonckowski most deserves to stand beside, as she would succeed in securing women riders a place for their league to compete at men's bull riding events, including sanctioned events at shows for the PRCA—the leading rodeo association—at Cheyenne Frontier Days, the rodeo considered "The Daddy of Them All." Jonnie often competed against men, but the women's circuit she helped lead remained separate. She was okay with that. The girls were riding. The crowds were cheering. Progress was being made.

Unlike King, who in her tennis whites played a fierce game but never risked catastrophic injury on a tennis lawn, Jonckowski's sport was a vicious one. She won her first World Championship in the now-defunct PWRA (Professional Women's Rodeo Association) by taking her last ride with a crushed leg after being stepped on in the final round leading into the championship. Her damaged leg had blown up like Popeye's arm. Doctors warned that a blood clot from the injury could kill her. She didn't need a high score, just one successful ride to win the championship. Jonnie made it to the bucking chutes on crutches and had to be hoisted onto the final bull. She rode him.

She had her gold medal.

Jonckowski would fly to New York to sit with David Letterman, who commented, "You thought track was too dangerous, so you tried something safer ... like bull riding."

Earning that buckle the hard way, fair and square, allowed for good-natured joking. She didn't want to be a martyr, or recklessly stupid, just recognized as the world's best. Jonnie wore the buckle upside down. Whenever she looked down, she wanted to see "W O R L D   C H A M P I O N." Before then, though, those believing they were protecting a misguided girl way out of her lane had come swooping in without the cheeky humor of Letterman. Everyone seemed to have a righteous opinion, so self-assuredly opposed to a naïve girl exhibiting her free will while planning her own funeral.

Others got a charge from helping the curly-haired young lady with the big smile, easy laugh, and outlandish plans. After seeing that rodeo poster, Jonnie went to a local bar and found an experienced cowboy to teach her riding basics. "I was so naïve, I didn't even know to be afraid," she said. "If others could do it and survive, how bad could it be?"

She started getting on bulls—with only one hand in the bull rope, not the two hands other women were told to use. She lost count of the times she heard that girls shouldn't be riding bulls because *strong, able men have been killed doing so.*

The loudest voice, the one that rang through her head the most, came from her own father.

"My journey as a bull rider was so painful, physically and mentally, especially in a family who didn't understand it at all," she remembered four decades later.

The Jonckowski family lived in Montana, but Jonnie, who had two older brothers, was more of a city girl. Billings may not have been New York or Chicago with rows of office towers scraping the sky, but Jonnie wasn't on a farm getting on sheep or going to rodeos like other kids who'd go on to ride bulls.

Her dad, who managed a local Toyota dealership, kept repeating his version of reality: *It's just a phase. A stupid, reckless one. She'll grow out of it, find something more ladylike to do. Something safe. And proper. And sane. It's only a matter of time. Yeah, she'll get this out of her system.*

Only, Jonnie didn't. The more she tasted the rush of the rides, the hotter the fire burned.

"You don't do it to get hurt," she said. "You do it because it feels great when it goes right."

Her dad would never understand her unquenchable drive or the absolute elation of doing something deemed off limits for half the people walking planet earth by virtue of rigid expectations attached to birth chromosomes they didn't choose. He certainly couldn't fathom toying with the lopsided risk-reward ratio of a sport like bull riding.

Jonnie's mom became her quiet supporter, finding marital middle ground to navigate her husband's immovable displeasure by quietly acknowledging and encouraging her daughter's beautifully fierce fighting spirit. Even when a show of support went against every protective bone in her body.

"Mom was always there when I flew out for a rodeo, but never when I came back," Jonckowski said. "She always thought that when I left, it would be the last time she'd see me alive."

Leather-tough as Jonckowski is, her voice cracked in sharing a revelation she only found out about years after she hung up her bull rope. "My mom had that fear, but she stayed supportive," she said.

It was a learning experience for both mother and daughter. Jonckowski had heard bull riding was dangerous, but knew little else about the sport.

"At first, when I started, I had no equipment and had to borrow a rope and spurs. I knew nothing about bull riding. I didn't know I had to say 'go' and nod my head to get out of the chutes! I'm in there on my bull, and the gate guys were all looking around asking, 'Is she ready? Is she ready?'"

Once Jonnie understood the "go" decision was up to the rider, her first out lasted a very respectable four seconds.

"That really turned my crank," she said. "I'd gotten on broncs and rode bareback. This was a whole different thing. Yeah, it was a case of hook, line, and sinker."

In practical terms, a mother's fears and a father's recalcitrance were justified. In Jonnie Jonckowski's ongoing project of cooking up a mean dish of crow to jam into the gaping mouths of each and every singer in the Choir of Negativity, she would nearly lose her life on more than one occasion. The injuries came quickly. When she first began, she just about lost her nose.

Jonnie wouldn't have been in the position of facial disfiguration if it weren't for her plucky stubbornness. She had been rejected for admission to dozens of bull riding schools and camps. None would take a girl. Finally, she called one to enter a "Johnny." They had no idea Johnny was not a boy. She showed up in Fountain, Colorado, and would train in a school run by Chris LeDoux, a stunning multi-talent who won a bareback World Championship and sold more than six million records singing country music, former saddle bronc World Champion Bobby Berger, and rodeo World Champion Bruce Ford.

The quality of the school's motley assortment of bulls was all over the map. There were some jumpers and a few tough spinners. There were bulls who lunged wildly without rhyme or reason. And so, the student body was dwindling. Guys were dropping out by the day, some out of quaking fear in being fated to an unpredictable bull, others frustrated when quickly eating dirt every time out. The one girl standing tall was a strong-minded athlete with something to prove.

But girl, boy, it didn't matter. Nobody was going to outmuscle these bulls. The game was one of anticipation, balance, and finesse. Staying on for Jonnie actually came pretty easy. Attendance in the school, which began with more than one hundred would-be rodeo stars, was shrinking fast. She kept riding. One day she got on nine bulls.

On the final day, down to ten riders, a school champion would be determined. She drew a bull named Spotted Dog. "I didn't like that bull from the get-go," she said. "He didn't have a rhythm or any pattern. He had big horns and was built like a big ol' yak in pioneer days pulling a cart. There was nothing about him I liked."

Jonnie made the ride, and when she pulled the tail of her rope to dismount, the bull tripped. She was ready to throw a leg over him, but Spotted Dog hooked a horn and flipped. She was half sitting on the ground and saw a hoof coming at her.

"I thought, 'Oh God, he's going to kick me in the face!' My head snapped back. I didn't feel a thing. I thought he missed me. I jumped to the side but couldn't see well. Bobby Berger and Bruce Ford ran out and said, 'Jeez, your nose is torn off!'"

Then LeDoux ran out and said, "That you did. But you stayed on. You won!"

Her face looked like it had come out of a blender. Medics applied compresses and loaded her into the ambulance. The motor turned and turned, producing a depressing sound of scraping metal— a dead battery. They climbed into the second ambulance, sinking to one side. Flat tire. Finally, Jonnie was rushed to the nearest hospital—forty minutes away. Her rotten luck since being matched with Spotted Dog took a turn. A humongous, beautiful, life-altering, face-saving turn. A national plastic surgeon's convention was in town.

The out-of-town specialists who were summoned were excited to see her, as Jonckowski remembered. "A bull had exploded my face apart. I was ripped from my hairline down through my eyebrows across the bridge of my nose. It was a good project for them."

Jonnie's rearranged face was fixed by the very best in the business. At no charge.

"They put me together for nothing. I was like a Humpty Dumpty test dummy. They were thrilled to have me," she said with a laugh.

Jonnie had mastered track and now had tried her hand at bull riding. Because she stayed on Spotted Dog until the whistle and got a good score, she was school champion, even though nobody would officially admit that. She had nearly lost her face, but they couldn't lose face by giving the buckle to a girl.

She wondered what was next. The injury, she realized, was actually freeing. She'd get back to riding bulls as soon as she could. "My rationalization was 'I'm too ugly to do anything else, I gotta go back!'" she said. "Besides, God wouldn't have healed me up so fast if he didn't want me to go out and do it again."

Sure, that dumb bull Spotted Dog went and tripped before kicking her in the face. But even with a better bull, there was no guarantee she wouldn't be badly hurt again. She couldn't control a one-ton animal, but she could build her body to increase the odds for being in a better position next time.

"I was a gangly, skinny kid for a long time—big knees, all elbows. I looked awfully skinny," she said.

After feeling the power of riding on top of a freight train, realizing the gravity of continuing to compete, and being wired to do whatever it took to not fail, Jonckowski didn't stay skinny for long.

"I was beat up where you literally throw up all night," she told CBS newsman Ed Bradley in the early 1990s. "If I can feel physically strong enough, I can convince my mind I can do this. If my mind believes it, it tells my body it can do it."

Once Jonckowski began riding full time, she claims she "lived in a gym seriously building my body." Soon, she was ripped, boasting 7 percent body fat. She got that way from running through high-intensity cardio routines, lifting weights, and creating her own exercises like putting a basketball between her knees, turning her toes out, and jumping around. (Do not try that at home.)

"You gotta be strong through the middle to ride bulls, and my abs were ridiculous. I was a tough son of a gun. A big part of bull riding is reflexes to counteract the bull. As an athlete, I knew that reflex doesn't go through fat well. Other girls riding were flopping all over the place. I was in control, so I'd get the points."

Jonckowski also knew when and how to play off being a woman and utilize her body. She'd show up at the cowboy's locker room—and there was only one—in a dress and heels wearing red nail polish.

"I didn't want them to think I was macho. I was all woman and didn't want any mistakes to be made by anyone."

And then she made sure no errors would be made. As the other riders were getting ready, Jonnie would morph into cowboy-athlete stud mode unlike anything they'd seen.

"The other guys were stripping down to the buff, so I'd strip down to my panties and a sports bra to scare the sh-t out of them! And then I put on my riding gear," she said.

The transformation jacked her confidence in a sport said to be at least 90 percent mental. "I may have shown up in a dress and everyone's thinking, 'She's a joke, she's gonna get killed.' But when I put my boots on and pulled my hat down, it was like, *'Yeah, I'm a bad ass. I can do this.'*"

And how she did. There was a bull called Mr. T who had not been ridden in forty-two outs by the best riders in the world in the top rodeo association, PRCA. (This was a few years before twenty PRCA rodeo cowboys broke away to form PBR.) Jonnie rode Mr. T in South Dakota.

Conquering a rank, nearly impossible bull like that was a very big deal, she said, and it helped win the respect of the other riders seeing her earning her stripes, sometimes literally ... like breaking twelve bones in her arm or getting hit so hard in the back of her head it broke bones in her face, giving her kaleidoscopic vision for two months.

"At first it was like a high school dance. I was on one side of the arena, and they were on the other side. They wouldn't touch me with a stick".

Jonckowski as Chance on the CBS show "Wild West Showdown" (Courtesy J. Jonckowski)

That changed fast. Once the riders got to know Jonnie, she received nearly universal acceptance. At one rodeo event, Bradley and Dan Rather from CBS were researching a piece on her. They pulled various riders aside for their opinion about this new gal. What did they think? Did she belong? The veteran newsmen were anticipating juicy conflict—hostile cowboys eager to show her the door. They couldn't find anyone playing to the expected narrative.

"I'd been up and down the road living in a pickup, sleeping in a room with twenty other people. The guys knew I'd paid my dues and earned my stripes," she said.

Jonckowski deftly courted attention without throwing shade on genuine stars with years of accomplishments like Ty Murray and Tuff Hedeman. Yet she also knew she could cut her own path as a serious draw. She could do the interviews and be gracious to everyone. YouTube clips of her appearances on Letterman's NBC show and CBS's *48 Hours* show a happy, humble cowgirl just thrilled to be part of the big show. She knew if she looked good on the bulls—just don't get dumped right out of the chutes, or worse, be thrown before the gate opened—she'd avoid being treated like the tossed, tumbling clown in a sideshow spectacle.

"At first, I was living out a small bit of fantasy in my life. But I got serious early on and put in the work, and knew I could compete," Jonnie said. "I thought as long as I don't look foolish out there, with my sex appeal, everyone's gonna know who the hell I am."

The best of intentions. Jonnie had no idea how quickly she'd get that attention. Riding in Wyoming alongside the men in 1988, she received an urgent call from the press trailer. "Get down here *now*" was the order. The packed, buzzing media center looked like when the Beatles had first landed at JFK. Rows of reporters a hundred feet deep were snapping photos and screaming questions at her. Jonnie-mania had arrived at Cheyenne Frontier Days. While the lads from Liverpool could play off one another like the Marx Brothers, faced with similar questions that had an undertone of doubtful skepticism, Jonnie only had herself.

Dozens of cameras were trained on her, in the press room and in and around the bucking chutes. The pressure became nearly overwhelming. "I was sick to my stomach, throwing up," she remembered.

An important figure on the American sports scene helped her through. Prior to *SportsCenter* on ESPN and ubiquitous game highlights a click away on the internet, sports reporter George Michael had a popular national TV show serving up those clips. Michael was a longtime fan and supporter of rodeo. No one in mainstream media did more to legitimize rodeo than Michael, who appreciated good rides, but more than anything, loved to tell a good story. And in the mid '80s, one of the best sports stories was a vibrant, joyful blonde from Montana taking on the big boys in a sport that could kill. *The George Michael Sports Machine* began covering Jonnie, and Michael proved to be a savior amid the Cheyenne media crush. "George was making jokes and giving the levity I needed so much with all these cameras four feet from my face," Jonckowski recalled.

Later, athletes and celebrities were available for fan autographs. Country music legend George Strait drew a long line. Hundreds of fans were also patiently waiting to say hello to a hot, young Oklahoman strongly influenced by Strait by the name of Garth Brooks. But one line snaked ever farther around the iconic fairground's pebble shrimp po boy and smoked turkey leg stands. Everyone wanted to see the famous female bull rider, the one and only Jonnie Jonckowski.

Jonckowski, a two-time world champion and 1991 inductee into the Cowgirl Museum and Hall of Fame, retired from riding in 2000 at forty-six years old.

"I didn't quit it, it quit me," she said. "My body couldn't take it, or I'd still flippin' be out there. To this day I'll see four or five of those bulls in a performance, and I say, 'I wish I had a rope. I could ride that one!' Probably a bad thought, but I still have it. You can't do something for twenty-five years, get on fifteen hundred bulls when you count 'em up, feeling and feeding off the crowd, the lights, the mud, the blood, the whole thing, limpin' out of the arena draggin' the rope, you can't have that adrenaline poppin' out and flushing through your body all that time and still not crave it."

Toward the end of her career and in early retirement, Jonckowski would appear on television shows like *What's My Line*, *To Tell the Truth*, *American Gladiator*, and, its wild Western-themed precursor, *Wild West Showdown*, where she played a character called "Chance," who she remembers as a "back stabbin', horse stealin', bank robbin' son of a gun." Jonckowski was the only character cast for the show who had no real acting experience. *Wild West Showdown* gained a solid, loyal audience in 1995, but was ahead of its time and would be canceled by CBS. Slowly, little by little, the limelight dimmed.

At sixty-seven years old, she has a slightly crooked smile and a scar running down her forehead that would have been a lot worse if it weren't for a plastic surgeon confab in town on exactly the right day. For a long time after hanging up her rope, she wondered, "What was I thinking? I'd look in the mirror and say to myself, 'What have you done?'"

What she did inspired so many. And scars are nothing but tattoos with better stories. They help her story, which will live on, because the limelight was never fully extinguished: a biopic film called *Baby, Hold On*, written by Gigi Levangie, a *New York Times* bestselling author (and wife of sports photographer Chris Elise featured in this book), is in development. When Jonckowski's incredible life is brought to the big silver screen, a new generation of young girls and boys alike will have fresh permission to do anything.

She blazed paths and sold countless rodeo tickets and charmed millions on the shows of Letterman, Johnny Carson, Maury Povich, and Charlie Rose. Today, Jonckowski wouldn't be considered wealthy. But she is undoubtedly rich, compensated by a heart as big as her try. Jonnie pours her time, energy, and every extra dollar into a charity she founded, Angel Horses. The human service organization uses rescued horses and donkeys to give veterans, cancer patients, senior shut-ins, and their caregivers comfortable, compassionate therapy all at no cost to them.

"We had two old cowboys I'll never forget, eighty-eight and ninety-one years old, driven in from assisted living in a big, black Ford pickup," she said. "The two of them looked like an eggbeater walking toward their horses, they were so bowlegged. Silver scarves around their necks. We saddled them up, and they'd ride maybe a hundred yards, park under a tree, and for two and half hours just talk. Their hands wouldn't stop. They'd toddle back to their truck and go back to assisted living. That's what we do. We provided an environment where they could be cowboys again."

Bull riding is a constant itch Jonckowski won't ever scratch again. But she's now as passionate about Angel Horses—giving animals a second chance, who then improve the lives of those in need—as she was about staying on any bull, even the ones the cockiest guys couldn't ride.

You don't meet many one-of-a-kind legendary American originals. Jonnie Jonckowski is one. Her name will be known.

"I didn't plan on being different," Jonckowski said. "All I knew my whole life is to be all out. It takes guts to go out there to do what your heart tells you to do at full bore. I was a bull rider, and if you're not all or nothing, you probably won't be a very good one."

Love & Try

6

NETHER REGIONS: AN IMPROBABLE STORY OF CELEBRITY STARDOM

(ABC Publicity Photo)

"The first piece of very good news was that I wasn't going to die," said the bull rider from the hospital bed, on his back immobilized in the way they keep you still to prevent making a move that will kill you. "Then I found out that one day, I'd be back on my feet. The minute the doctor said I'd walk again, I wanted to jump right out of this bed and dance."

Fourteen months after a nearly fatal bull riding wreck, he was dancing all right—on ABC's hit series *Dancing with the Stars* ... where he made it to the semifinals.

PBR fans, along with those who devour the cheesy celebrity suck-up and put-down magazines, know the star of this story.

Bonner Bolton was reaching the height of his career with a great future ahead. He had won a title in CBR (Championship Bull Riding) in 2007 at the age of twenty then moved to where the big boys get on the rankest bulls—PBR. Bonner began to realize his potential by finishing fourth at the PBR World Finals in 2015. He came into the 2016 season on fire, leading the season opener in Chicago. On Championship Sunday, at twenty-eight years old, he had never felt better, physically, and mentally. He always had the swagger. Now he was earning the right to be cocksure. He would be first to ride in the second round at Allstate Arena, the position bull riders call "The Gunner."

"There's extra pressure being 'The Gunner.' The moment is a little bit more intense to start the show with a bang. But you love it. Everyone wants to be that guy," Bolton said.

He had last seen the bull, Cowboy Up, in 2015. Most riders don't get analytical about their bull matchups. These are, at their core, wild beasts. But any creature, even one whipping with such ferocity to sling a rope of snot twenty yards, has tendencies. Bonner knew enough about Cowboy Up to believe the bull fit his style. It was a great matchup for a dance that he hoped would lead to his first elite series event win.

His plan was simple. *Make the eight and get this crowd rocking for the national TV audience of more than a million fans tuning to CBS. That puts me in the championship round, where the top fifteen riders in score get to pick their bull. Choose one who can generate a good score. Get on him and hang on for another eight seconds (maybe fling out the boots and flash the chaps for extra style points) and win Chicago. Then go with my buddies and celebrate in epic fashion. At least there will be photos to remember what's gonna happen over this weekend. With a fresh $40,000 check in my pocket, I'm buying.*

Bull riding is a sport of vast extremes—a deceptive calm bursting into an all-out storm. Bonner lowered himself onto the staid bull, knowing that when he was ready and nodded his head, Cowboy Up would detonate from the opened chute, discharging from statue-like stillness to rapid chaos in a fraction of a second. The rider had spent years training himself to muster up every bit of courage to try to come out on the other side of the hard, violent storm unscathed.

Bonner wrapped his hand and nodded his head. The gate swung open, and the duo blasted from the chutes. He held his rope tight. Above his sticky, gloved hand, the bulging bicep that had been surgically reattached after being torn clear from the bone on a rank ride was doing its job.

By the time the gate slammed shut, Bonner was up on the bull, centered, a split-second ahead of each of Cowboy Up's violent moves. Bull riders don't think it through. There's no advance planning. Not a lot of game film or X's and O's. Spend any time on a bull anticipating his next turn to strategize your counter move, and you're launched. It's all muscle memory; any reaction is instinctive. Riders who think too much are on the ground before they even can process what they're trying to figure out. Use your head, and you're on your head.

Bolton's body was matching the bull's twists and kicks. The eight-second horn sounded, signaling a successful qualified ride. A great start to the weekend—and the season—was going to get better. In that instant, it appeared the night's drinks would indeed be on his tab.

"Move for move, the ride was perfect," he remembered. "Then the ride ended, and it came time for me to eject and dismount and come off. I wanted to get away from him. But the way he was bucking rolled me off his back, and the momentum shot me straight up instead of away from him."

Bolton was launched like a midlife-crisis billionaire's rocket.

Bull riding is the one sport where an athlete can hit a grand slam home run and wind up in a wheelchair. He can score the game-winning touchdown and never walk again. A bad dismount after doing your eight-second job on the bull can be disastrous. Spiraling up and out of control, Bonner landed on his head, pile driving perpendicular into the dirt.

"It's like someone grabbed a baseball bat, took a swing, and lit me up," he said. "I heard a sickening crunch. I can see bull's feet stomping around. I'm thinking, 'He's gonna get me and I'm gonna die.' Guys do die in the arena, and their faces all start flooding into my head. My life is going to end right here in this arena. I'm never going to see my family and friends again."

In the ensuing years, he has had a lot of time to think about the next few seconds and what could have been ... but, fortunately, didn't come to pass.

"The real miracle is the bull goes over me and all four feet lightly graze around me. He even puts his head on me, like he's going to mash me into the ground. He has me dead to rights. But he holds back. I think he sensed I was hurt; he didn't want to kill me. My life was in his hands, and he decides to spare me—a magical, unexplainable thing, right? The bullfighters are jumping in, and the bull miraculously steps around me. I believe there was an angel over us right there."

Bolton looked out at his arm stretched across the dirt. It was like observing someone else's limb. It wouldn't move.

"My mouth is full of dirt. I can't feel anything in my body. I can see my hands out in front of me, but I can't feel them. I lift my head a bit and think, 'Maybe I'm just knocked out, and shit's not functioning.' I finally put my head back in the dirt. The medical staff rolls me over. The looks on their faces are devastating. I know it's bad.

"I'm being strapped to the back board. They're trying to get the dirt out of my mouth. Then I'm going into the dark ambulance, and they're closing the doors on me. It's Chicago in January and it's cold and it's getting harder to breathe. All my friends, the other bull riders, still have to ride. It's not like they can jump down and skip out on the competition. They need to finish their spot. We're all riding to split fifty grand that day.

"There's one guy who knows me, Todd, the team chaplain. I'm thankful he's there to ride in the back of the ambulance, hauling me off to the hospital to save my life. Todd keeps telling me: '*breathe, breathe, breathe.*' I'm remembering my yoga classes, trying to breathe. I'm trapped in a body that's now just a shell, telling, pleading to God, 'If you're not taking me home today, I really would like to use my arms again to wrap them around the people I love and let them know how much they mean to me.' Stuff in your life really becomes clear then. It's the people you love and that love you that matter most. That's all I can think about: wrapping my arms around my loved ones, and just hoping I can have that chance.

"I am fading in the ambulance, and they give me an adrenaline shot. At the hospital, they do the MRI and CAT scans. Todd was good to stay with me. Then my buddy, Douglas Duncan, comes. Stetson Lawrence and Tanner Byrne from the tour stop in and give me some humor to keep my spirits up and stay with me through the night. All of us were crying. None of us know if I'll be able to walk. Everyone's thankful I'm not dead or paralyzed from the neck down. I'm concentrating and trying to get feeling in my hands. Finally, it feels like a wave in my stomach turning over. It kind of scares me. Am I bleeding? Then I realized, *I just felt my stomach*. Then my fingers. Then my toes, and I can feel up through my legs and back. I am so stoked. I want to jump out of bed and celebrate. Every doctor who comes in, I'm telling them, 'You're gonna walk me out of that hospital.'"

Bolton had shattered his C2 vertebra. He would have spinal fusion surgery performed by four talented doctors working six hours to fuse his C1 to C3 vertebrae. Four days after the surgery, he was able to slowly get on his feet.

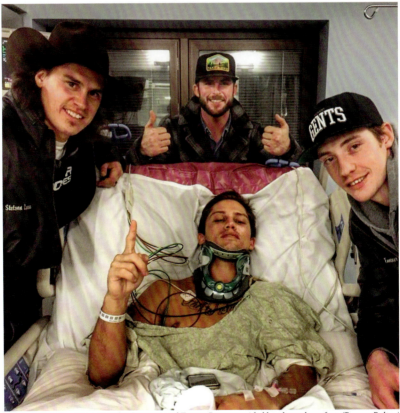

Stetson Lawrence, Douglas Duncan, and Tanner Byrne provided laughs and comfort. (Bonner Bolton)

"They have to hold me, so I don't fall to the side, but I am pretty much walking on my own," he said. "They say I am maybe 2 percent of people who walked away from that kind of spinal injury. To regain feeling before surgery was miraculous and then to not have damage after surgery, and you gained mobility, they had their mouths open. It was a lot for me to take in under heavy medicine. It still dumbfounds me today. I don't really have an explanation other than I'm thankful for the angels looking over me, and obviously, I have some good ones."

Bonner's injury was the same one suffered by Christopher Reeves. However, the famous actor had transected his spinal cord when thrown from a horse. Superman would never walk again. Bonner was luckier. His nerves weren't cut. He had only badly bruised his spinal cord. It could heal.

He was flown on a private jet to his parent's ranch in Texas for a long convalescence, during which he hit rock bottom. The next three months, immobile in bed, tethered to a constricting neck brace, popping painkillers like Tic Tacs, were the nadir of his life.

"There were hard, dark times when it was hard to hold onto any positive thoughts," he said. "I was immobile on pain medicine. My thoughts were so bad. I wondered if it was worth going on. But in the end, I refused to believe I was going to be lame. I finally flushed the pills away after two months. I wasn't going to accept that. I wanted to get my body working right and prove to the doctors I could do it."

Lying in his bed, Bonner promised himself that no matter what he did in life, whether back on a bull or not, that he'd be successful. Or die trying.

"It was like part of me died on the dirt with the injury," he said. "It was hard, and still is, difficult to come to terms with that. You don't know if you'll ever fully recuperate to live a normal life. On one hand, I had to accept that 'death' and what happened, but at the same time also fuel my fire to recover as hard as I could and give myself every fighting chance to make the decision on my own whether to ride. I didn't want to leave it in the doctor's hands. I just wanted to give myself the best chance I could to get to good health and make the choice mine."

Seven months after the Chicago wreck, he was back to running, swimming, steam room sessions, and hot yoga. To get back in shape and regain flexibility and agility, he did water therapy in a hot tub, tai chi, and core kinetic workouts.

Not long after flushing the pain medicine down the toilet, another break went Bonner's way.

A few months before the Chicago accident, at the PBR World Finals in Vegas, he'd been photographed by Cass Bird, a photographer represented by IMG, a sister company of PBR under the bull riding organization's new owner, Endeavor, a global leader in sports and entertainment. Executives at IMG Models, the parent company's modeling division, liked how the photos showed cowboy confidence bursting off the images. Beyond that, there were new political and cultural shifts under way. With Donald Trump newly elected as president, the entertainment gatekeepers and cultural tastemakers in New York and Hollywood were jolted into rediscovering middle America. In November 2016, the taste-making gatekeeper overlords of media, fashion, and mass entertainment were essentially doused with a bucket of ice water. Trump's shocking ascendancy stoked new demand for men who were raw, authentic, masculine, and untamed. It was a good position for a great-looking guy with or without a cowboy hat who'd been pursuing a risky, dangerous living just as dirt under the fingernails was becoming the new clean fingernails.

Bolton was signed by Ivan Bart, head of IMG Models, to global representation at the world's largest modeling agency that's also one of the world's savviest star-making factories for personalities like Gigi Hadid, Gisele Bunchen, Kate Moss, Christie Brinkley, Alessandra Ambrosio, Karlie Kloss, and Ashley Graham.

Backed by a team of agents, Bonner would be named one of *Us Weekly*'s Hot Bodies. He'd sit in the front row at a Victoria's Secret show. He'd pose for the world's most famous fashion photographers and land on the front page of the *Wall Street Journal*. He would meet interesting people living in a rarefied sphere at exclusive parties and soirees and receptions he'd never imagine being invited to. The best part was he got to be himself, wearing his big buckle, boots, and cowboy hat—for everyone who wanted to meet the new midnight cowboy.

"The most common comment overheard and relayed to me was how women were whispering they'd leave their husbands for me," he remembered, laughing. "I'm always trying to see the bright side of things. But, man, there must be a lot of unhappy ladies out there!"

Bonner wasn't even out of his neck brace when Ivan Bart had entered the picture and offered the modeling gig that could be credited with saving his life; it certainly thrust him into a new one.

"The second chapter for me all started there with IMG," he remembered. "It was still hard for me to hold a fork, but I started working with the company to get introduced to the modeling world. What's amazing is Ivan and his team had followed my story and had faith in me while I was still on my back to believe I'd come back to full health and gain my mobility. But I don't even think they expected me to do what I'm doing now."

Some were skeptical about the kid from Texas's foray into taking pictures for premium fashion magazines fans had never heard of and attempting to work with mainstream consumer brands. His wild ride as a top model wound up lasting a heck of a lot longer than eight seconds.

The Texas cowboy's first major campaign broke with American Eagle as a face for *The New American Jean* collection. Then, as further evidence of America's rekindled fascination with cowboys, he was *The Cosmo Guy* in the August 2017 issue of the iconic magazine seminal to female empowerment, *Cosmopolitan*. The American Eagle campaign was shot by Bird, who had trained her lens on a dozen bull riders at the 2015 PBR World Finals in Las Vegas. Photos of the then twenty-eight-year-old Western athlete caught the eye of Bart, the star-making head of IMG Models.

When Bonner was still immobile and recovering, I had set him up with a print reporter to discuss the accident. We began the interview, and, forty-five minutes in, I suspected this may be a story unlike any sports coverage I'd worked on. Bonner was vulnerable and introspective, vivid and harrowing. He told the story of laying on the arena floor, looking at his motionless arms, mouth full of dirt, his dreams and his life fading away. It was riveting. And he plumbed the ultimate human darkness, which is when we contemplate in plain sober rational terms taking our own lives.

When it was over, I wondered if it was too much. Should we be putting one of our athletes out there like that—naked on a cliff about to throw himself off? Bonner said it was therapeutic, and I could certainly sense that. We continued.

Bart, reading the subsequent press clippings, was intrigued by the Texas cowboy's openness and vulnerability. Being a successful male model today is as much about a story and platform as the strength of a sculpted jaw. Bart also recognized that all Bolton knew was bull riding. If that were to end, he needed a new profession. Bonner was signed to the world's leading modeling agency while still in that neck brace after the wreck, just two months after Cass Bird photographed him.

"In this business, careers are made based on who you sit next to at the right party," said Bart, who, even in his role of running the agency, played point on a team creating the champagne-and-hors d'oeuvres connections for the cowboy *du jour* that put him in the right parties, helping spawn a campaign for Saks Fifth Avenue and photo shoots with world-famous photographers Mario Testino, Terry Richardson, Bruce Weber, and Steven Klein.

Bolton's first big fashion spread hitting the glossies would be with one of the most famous faces in the world, fellow IMG model Joan Smalls, who has a social media following as big as a small European nation. The two shot a steamy session on a horse in inner city Philadelphia. In one photo with Smalls, Bolton is naked, shot from the side with a leg being toweled off while strategically raised on an old washtub.

"This stuff is all art … and I've intended to push the boundaries," he said after the shoot. "Some of it might get a bit edgy at times and push the limits. But that's also how our sport is. It's all extreme."

And then, amid the rising demand for raw authenticity and the shifting cultural winds blowing real America into our living rooms, came Tom Ford. Bolton was chosen as the face of a new cologne, "Ombre Leather." The stark black-and-white ads shot by Steven Klein are seen everywhere from Sephora stores to glass-enclosed Tom Ford airport displays to a giant billboard on Rodeo Drive.

Since pile driving into the dirt in Chicago, Bolton's life took turns onto paths typically not tread by ranch-raised cowboys making a living barnstorming the country to ride bucking bulls. Fourteen months after nearly buying the farm, he fully embraced his cosmic reprieve.

While artistic in nature—dabbling in songwriting, playing guitar, and taking acting and art classes, influenced by his mother, an art teacher, and having lived in France as a child— professionally, all Bolton had ever known was the Western lifestyle and bull riding. His family had moved from Central Texas in 1903 in covered wagons to the west quarter of Texas and staked out a four thousand-acre ranch that's still there.

Toya, Bonner's dad, retired from his rodeo career in 1991. Soon after, he was recruited by Euro Disney to star in the Buffalo Bill's Wild West attraction. Five-year-old Bonner and his family wound up in France. Looking up to his dad—a real cowboy who rode bulls and one who played an adventurous cowboy shooting fake bullets in the Disney show—young Bonner, like so many other bull riders, knew what he wanted to do. The sport is so challenging and dangerous, it takes that kind of passion to stick with it, especially after the first major inevitable injury. Little Bonner liked the real bulls best.

He had developed the mindset to endure the no-payout weekends (subsidized by the winning ones), the torn muscles and broken bones, and he had finally made it to the top. And then it all came crashing down in Chicago.

For months after the wreck, Bolton debated whether he would attempt to get back to the PBR. He'd have to get into peak physical condition, and then receive a doctor's clearance.

"I wanted to say, 'I'll know if I'm strong enough to do it myself.' I can tell you I became strong enough to try to ride a bull again," he said.

Dancing with the Stars was a large part of an unconventional, painful physical rehab. The money and fame the ABC show would provide were nice, but the reason he entered the competition was to not let the injury intimidate or define him. Learning to dance competitively on national TV wasn't exactly mounting War Cloud in Chicago. But it still presented a very big challenge.

Nine-time World Champion Ty Murray had blazed trails for bull riders on the show a decade earlier and made it to the fourth round of competition. Murray told Bolton that even without his neck injury limiting his mobility, this would probably be the hardest thing he'd ever done.

Murray remembers an important prep call with the network before the tapings would start. Toward the end, the talent booker asked for questions. Murray had none. "She burst out laughing," he recalled. "She said, 'You have absolutely *no idea* what you are getting yourself into!'"

She was right. Each day after grueling dance training sessions, Murray would wake up feeling like an eighty-year-old man. "Muscles I didn't know I had hurt," he said. "You're dancing for six hours in these weird little shoes. It felt like every bone in my foot was broken."

While cowboys can be cocky, Murray readily admitted he wasn't much of a dancer. But cowboys can be proud and stubborn, too. He trained so hard,

Nether Regions: An Improbable Story of Celebrity Stardom

he wound up eating a bucket of ice cream every day just to keep his weight. Despite the relentless physical grind, the hardest part was remembering the choreography—"what to move on your body and where to go," as the nine-time world champion put it.

"There is no faking your way through that show," he said. "Dancing is an art form that takes a whole life to learn. The pros have spent years of disciplined practice to get where they are. And now you're attempting what they're doing."

Ultimately, the advice the legendary Western athlete known as "King of the Cowboys" gave to Bonner was to work hard and have fun, despite the physical pain to come. He was right. Bolton had to bear down hard for six to eight hours a day seven days a week for ten weeks (two weeks prep and eight weeks of competition). When he finally reached the semi-finals, he felt strong enough to ride a bull again. While he'd need to go to the PBR doctor to get officially cleared for competition, in his mind, that was enough. Physically, he'd made it back.

The bull rider's physical challenges remained formidable. Although he was pulling his full body weight in chin ups prior to the dance competition, that metal clamp fusing his C2 and C3 vertebrae would for the rest of his life be stationed precariously close to a vital artery along with eight inches of metal in his shoulder holding together a collarbone shattered in four places by a bull's horn.

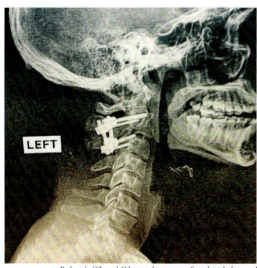

Bolton's C2 and C3 vertebrae were fused and clamped (Bonner Bolton)

"I knew I'd have to baby my neck and avoid certain dance moves," Bonner said. "I was putting my faith in my dance partner, Sharna Burgess."

Burgess's first task was to give Bonner the confidence to move freely and avoid the instinct to protect his neck.

"He had a massive injury, and dancing puts a lot of strain on the body," Burgess said. "But I love a challenge. With Noah (Galloway, her previous partner who, in the Iraq War, had lost his left arm below the elbow and left leg above the knee), we worked our way around it, and I expected to do the same with Bonner."

Burgess drew on lifelong experience, starting to dance ballet as a five-year-old and leaving Australia for England thirteen years later "to chase my dancing dream." She was known to work very well with athletes, making it to the semifinals with Olympic ice dancer Charlie White and race car driver James Hinchcliffe. She had also partnered with NFL stars Antonio Brown and Keyshawn Johnson.

"I love people with depth and truth and stories, who are willing to bare their soul," she said.

As the red-haired Aussie charted the choreography to reveal Bolton's story, the Texas cowboy was memorizing intricate new steps, working his body toward its best shape since smashing his C2, and studying film. His IMG agents sent a list of movies to study, including *Magic Mike, Dirty Dancing, Singing in the Rain,* and *An American in Paris.*

"Had *Magic Mike* been cast today, I believe Bonner would have a role," Bart said with a laugh. The head of IMG Models wanted Bolton on the dance show drawing up to fifteen million weekly viewers to not only continue to inspire those with physical challenges; the exposure would also help catapult him into a new modeling and entertainment career.

"We live in confusing times; men aren't quite sure what true masculinity means anymore," Bart said. "We need role models representing the new modern man. Bonner is a genuine, down-to-earth cowboy. America fell in love with Bonner in large part due to *Dancing with the Stars.*"

Outside of personal brand-building, the therapy was world class. Yet the by-products of his elevation in fame were unexpected, leading to awkward, potentially career-busting situations.

"Surreal is an overused word. But what I've experienced is truly otherworldly bizarre," Bolton said from the ABC set in April of 2017. "My childhood idol, Mr. T, (a fellow competitor) thinks I'm a tough guy! I'm hanging out with Dennis Quaid on the Hollywood press gauntlet after every show,

The dancing couple, meeting for the first time on set in Texas (Author photo)

shooting network promos seen by tens of millions of people each week and training for hours on end with a beautiful flaming redhead live wire from Australia to learn how to tango on the number-one show on broadcast television Monday nights."

Even if Bolton didn't win (a colossal longshot since he'd never be loose of limb again), appearing on the show would be a major victory. Hopefully, he'd last long enough to be an inspiration to anyone dealing with an accident, injury, or illness, helping motivate others who have challenges.

Bull riding had taught him what it's like to be in front of cameras and a crowd. Still, he was more nervous doing the tango than getting on Rango, an ornery bull he rode as Scott Eastwood's stunt double during a pressure-packed midnight shoot for a key scene in the film, *The Longest Ride*, based on the Nicholas Sparks best-seller.

"That first dance on network television was as big a rush as getting on a rank bull that could kill you in a heartbeat," Bolton said. "My heart was like a freight train running through my chest. It was insane. Would I remember my steps? Would I be able to move the way I wanted with a clamp holding the top of my spine together? I'm used to channeling my adrenaline in the bucking chute getting ready to hold onto the bull for eight seconds. Bull riding and dancing are similar in that both require timing and rhythm and balance. In bull riding, the bull leads, and you follow. Sharna would lead, too. The big difference is Sharna isn't as mean or unpredictable as a PBR bull. And she's a lot smaller."

The duo stepped out to Luke Bryan for their first dance and, while not exactly fluid as Fred Astaire, Bolton looked good considering his nearly catastrophic injury. The audience, particularly the ladies in the house, hooted and hollered like it was after midnight at a bachelorette party.

"I felt good," Bolton said. "I could barely hold a fork a year ago and had to relearn a lot of basic motor motions, so my timing was slightly off. Sharna had cracked the whip and drilled me up all week. But it was worth it. The place was going bonkers, and I think we did OK."

ABC knows how to prime its audience, and, with these two, juiced a potential romance. Before Bonner and Sharna danced, the taped set up was like a promo for a Harlequin novel—all golden sunlight, neighing horses, and shots of the bare-chested cowboy.

"It was high-quality Harlequin, and I was proud to be in it, and I do not regret the decision to remove my shirt, which you should know had been pre-debated at the highest levels of my management representation," he said. (He's not joking; a conference call was held debating pros and cons of baring skin.)

Following that first dance, while analyzing the replay of the previous couple, Bonner would be fully baptized in the world of celebrity. A "caught-on-camera" incident would light up the celebrity tabloid press.

"I knew from being out there how tough that is to do, and I was watching their dance. I wanted to share the moment with my partner. My arm went out to bring Sharna in, and I hooked her. My hand accidentally moved a bit south and glanced across her nether region."

Video replays on *Extra* and *ET*, among other places, where "The Grab" was the top story, showed Sharna, for a microsecond, startled, then promptly moving Bolton's hand away, with efficient professionalism.

A mischievous UK headline read "Groping with the Stars." For twenty-four hours, the tape was slowed and reversed and blown up under forensic analysis like the Zapruder film. In the US, entertainment media was calling it "Handgate." Nixon lives on.

The fabricated scandal clashed with Bonner's press team's strategy to win Middle America and capture the Walmart and Cracker Barrel vote. Yet, had the whole unfortunate incident been helpful? It could be argued the news story was a gift horse helping the dance duo get higher scores, because the producers knew millions were tuning in out of curiosity to see what the rascally cowboy would do next.

Bonner was fortunate to have soundbite-savvy Sharna, highly skilled with media, leading the response. Without hesitation, she confirmed to everyone who asked, and everybody was asking, that this was purely an accident, because her partner is nothing but a Southern Gentleman.

"And even, hypothetically, if I weren't, I'm not gonna cop a feel on national TV with my mother and sister in the audience a few feet away!" Bolton explained when I was asking for the off-the-record God's honest truth, because that's always where to start in crisis management.

Sharna told everyone as much, in an incredulous tone that didn't sound bossy or haughty. Try that at home.

Her quick-thinking responses in a delightful Australian accent helped quickly snuff out Handgate. The following night Bonner and Sharna went to a cowboy bar near Hollywood to practice a few dances. They wrote "Date Night" on the call sheet, knowing the tabloids would see it, and again, it became the top story on outlets like *Extra*, *ET*, and People.com, which each season had already been dabbling in speculation on Sharna's love life and were desperately seeking evidence of knowing looks and visible chemistry among the dance partners with the investigative zeal of a young Bob Woodward.

"Throughout the show, I learned a lot from Sharna—of course, tons about dance but also how to both provoke and be disarming with the media," Bolton said.

It would be a useful skill in navigating a show that sends a weekly email to each star's agents and managers stipulating in bold letters highlighted in

(Author photo)

yellow, just to be sure the message fully resonated, "**Please make sure your clients have a bag packed in case they are eliminated. Dancing shoes included! AND a government issued ID approved for travel.**"

Dancing shoes are a must-pack travel bag item because eliminated contestants are whisked to LAX for the red eye to JFK airport in New York to dance on *Good Morning America*, the place where cast members were initially introduced.

Bonner often wondered what that final dance would be like. A slow dance at a funeral? Or a sprightlier victory lap of sorts?

Neither he nor Mr. T, Charo, Nancy Kerrigan, Chris Kattan from Saturday Night Live, nor NFL star Rashad Jennings, who wound up winning his season, were professional dancers. Just making it to the show and finishing that first jig to get your score, no matter how high, is victory.

A year earlier, Bonner had been on his back in bed in a neck brace numb on painkillers debating the point of continuing. He knows he was invited onto the show because of the notoriety of his bull riding accident.

"I was still, first and foremost, a bull rider," Bolton said. "Bull riders are famous in Western circles, but we are still niche in pop culture."

Nether Regions: An Improbable Story of Celebrity Stardom

(Author photo)

But even so, cowboys as pop culture icons have had ebbs and flows in popularity that surges and dips. Their popularity was starting to crest again in PBR. In 2018, Jess Lockwood was the first bull rider to be photographed by *Interview* magazine, in a package making PBR's youngest world champion at twenty resemble a reincarnated James Dean. (Lockwood would hate the look and made it clear that in future photo shoots he'd be portrayed as nothing but a working cowboy.) Brazilian Guilherme Marchi, the sport's Babe Ruth with the most qualified rides ever (635), made the cover of *Men's Fitness,* pictured on a bull to boot. J.B. Mauney was a late-night guest with Stephen Colbert after winning his second championship. Ezekiel Mitchell has been a guest on

Good Morning America. Who knows how far away the day is when a Chase Outlaw will host *Saturday Night Live?*

For three decades, PBR had always been a scrappy fighter, week in and out clawing for attention and continuing to grow. The sport was selling out arenas like Madison Square Garden in New York, STAPLES Center in Los Angeles, and T-Mobile Arena in Las Vegas. On certain Sundays, head-to-head against the traditional stick-and-ball sports, professional bull riding had drawn more television viewers.

"If bull riding keeps growing, it's not inconceivable to be up there in the same breath as baseball and football," Bolton said. "I can see it."

(To make itself more relatable to sports fans who are used to watching games, in July 2022 PBR will launch a new league, The PBR Team Series. Riders will join eight teams based in Arizona, Texas, Missouri, Oklahoma, Tennessee, and North Carolina, playing five-on-five bull riding games in a ten-event regular season leading to a championship in Las Vegas. The biggest development in the sport since those twenty cowboys broke away from the rodeo is expected to create new fan rooting interests, sell some very cool merchandise, and double the bull riders' annual compensation.)

Bonnor is doing his part to continue to help grow the sport while also making an entrepreneurial play to reap rewards in its expansion by bringing together technology experts and financial backing, along with his own funding, to create the PBR fantasy game *Rank Ride*, which launched in spring 2021.

"I do realize everything that's happened to me is a big deal for a kid who lived on a ranch in West Texas," Bolton said. "It's a different path than most taken by cowboys raised on ranches."

For a time, he lived his dream, grabbing his gear bag and heading to a new city to do what most people understand to be an act of certifiable lunacy: getting on the back of a powerful two thousand pound animal bred to whip you off his back.

Stay on for eight seconds a few times each weekend and be successful a third of the time, and you make a very nice living. Do it at an even better percentage and you can wind up winning a million bucks in Las Vegas, along with the belt buckle that allows you to say, *I am the best and baddest mother in the world, doing something mere mortals will wet their pants even thinking about trying to do.*

Most cowboys don't talk like that. Some might. My hyperbolic purple prose aims to convey the bull riding cowboy's indescribable outlier mentality: the outsized risks they take, the triumph in conquering the beast, the inevitable punishment endured, the rare guts to do it again.

Bonner Bolton would take the risks and accept the pain. He'd enter the brotherhood of cowboys who share the unspoken, uncommon freedom granted to those who court grave danger and cackle in its face.

Then he was planted face down and rendered powerless, letting go to prepare to meet his maker. It just wasn't his time. Breaking his neck was a terrible turn of events, but it would turn out to be the opening scene of a second act.

Bull riding is the domain of the relentlessly optimistic. For anyone to harbor the notion he will be able to consistently tame a beast more than ten times his size then walk away, unharmed, is an exercise in sunny delusion. There are no unscathed bull riders.

Some pay the rest of their lives. Some pay with their lives. And then sometimes, after a scary bad wreck, a bull rider will get lucky. His reprieve defies explanation. It's God's dirt they play in. Maybe He decides.

For the fortunate bull riders given a second chance, getting knocked down doesn't define us. What counts is what we do when finally getting up.

Love & Try

7

A LIGHT SHINES ON EZEKIEL MITCHELL

(Snap Inc.)

A blazing young sports talent brimming with big dreams, vast potential, and rocket-ship fuel for crossover fame carries on his strong shoulders a weight heavier than even his own looming expectations: the fate of his large family. He's at the top level of a high-stakes profession where he's been given the opportunity to charm the cameras now trained on him, soak in the fan adoration, privately enjoy the personal satisfaction of elevating his siblings ... and possibly put himself in a wheelchair for life.

For his isn't a contact sport. It's *a collision sport.*

He's a professional bull rider—the equivalent of being involved in a few high-speed car crashes each weekend ... sans seat belt. It's a job full of pride and pain, one he admits he can't quit. Bull riding is in his blood. It's what he's meant to do. *More importantly, it's his way out.*

Yeah, there's the lure of the bright lights and the big cities. But get sucked into the distractions easily found on the road, lose your focus, and when those bulls quickly fling you like a rag doll, you get paid nothing. Your mother and dad and ten siblings will still love you. Start to question yourself, hit a dry spell, get dropped from the top tour, and what have you really done for them?

And those who said you had no business being up there in the first place? Well, they get to preen like roosters in mating season doing the see-me strut.

Those are the dramatic parameters of the life story of Ezekiel Mitchell, which played out on social media in early 2021 in a Snapchat docuseries, *Life By The Horns*. The high-octane series followed "Zeke," aka "Blue," on a life-or-death journey to stay on bulls, become recognized as one of the sport's best riders, and carry his family to the promised land.

Oh, and Zeke would scoff at one qualification some people will add, because his career isn't any kind of political or sociological statement—*he's just a cowboy.* But, if his dream comes true, for the record books, he'd be the first Black cowboy ever to win PBR's gold buckle.

The fast-paced, ten-part Snapchat series captured the matrix of a young man of many talents, boundless energy, and abundant paradoxes. Zeke's raw talent, beaming smile, dance moves, spectacular rides, frustrating buck offs, and occasional swig from a whiskey bottle are contrasted with the plight of two other young riders pursuing their dream: the harder-working, more reserved Andrew Alvidrez and Zeke's less-heralded cousin Ouncie, who after breaking his femur is questioning his commitment to the sport.

Zeke has no such questions, just hard-earned realism about the nature of his calling.

"Bull riding is like being in a toxic relationship," he said. "But you still love that person."

His business manager, mentor, and "brother from another," Max Maxwell, said, "For all these guys, there's no Plan B. They're fighting for the love of the sport. For the culture of being a cowboy. For the financial freedom of their families."

Maxwell's full-on immersion in bull riding was serendipitous. It began when he spotted Zeke on a *Vice* documentary about Black rodeo athletes. He would tell *GQ* magazine he was intrigued by "a young hustler who doesn't

(Author photo)

have the right opportunities." Maxwell saw opportunity far beyond the arena dirt. Shows like *Deadwood* and *Yellowstone* were massively popular. Lil Nas' "Old Town Road" was breaking multiple *Billboard* chart records. Cowboys and cowboy culture in general were hot, while mainstream cultural tastemakers were craving to acknowledge African American trailblazers. Here was a confident and charismatic Black cowboy with model looks doing something special in a tough, exciting, growing sport.

Maxwell contacted Mitchell. At first, Zeke didn't know what to make of the self-proclaimed real estate mogul projecting an impressive aura. Max was willing to fly in to meet him, and Zeke was always open to advice, especially someone who appeared genuinely interested in his career. It felt too good to be true, but he drove ninety miles to take the meeting. When he shook the warm hand of the bearded, well-dressed Maxwell, it felt like being introduced to a new big brother.

PBR is a unique blend of sports entertainment, and Max saw the bigger picture of an athlete like Zeke becoming established in the broader world of entertainment. He had great ideas about what Zeke needed to do to succeed. He felt bull riders, putting their bodies on the line, deserved more in sponsorship money. And instead of filling a rider's vest with competing logos like a NASCAR driver, he advocated a "less-is-more" approach: fewer, higher-paying sponsors who'd get more exposure to pop on a cleaner, less cluttered rider uniform. (Ariat would buy into the concept, and Zeke's gleaming new look would set a new standard for PBR riders.) He even offered to help Zeke with new equipment.

Maxwell would eventually move Zeke from Houston, where too many so-called friends were glomming onto his increasing fame, to a fresh start in North Carolina. Max owned the land, and, away from negative distractions, they could focus on building his body, his will, and his brand. They even had a name for the project: Operation Superstardom.

Maxwell is so confident of Zeke's projected career arc, he says he still hasn't taken a penny from the rider. It's a passion-project investment in a man he loves like a younger brother, poised to be a superstar transcending rodeo. Maxwell appreciates the platform of bull riding; Mitchell is a cowboy lifer who has bought into the vision. Both believe bull riding can be a launch pad to stratospheric stardom. What Dwayne Johnson accomplished in pro wrestling, Mitchell seeks to replicate in bull riding. "Yeah, I want to be just like the Rock," Zeke says.

Historically, the story of Black cowboys was largely neglected by Hollywood and Madison Avenue. "Culturally, it was more appealing for Caucasian men to be seen and portrayed as strong, bold, independent, rough and tough cowboys," Mitchell said. "It was easier to leave us out of the picture."

In order to "launch" Mitchell, and write new history, changes had to be made. Many athletes take basic home stability and infrastructure for granted. Maxwell has given that to Zeke. For now, the twenty-three-year-old is building a media and social media presence (Maxwell constructed a studio for interviews during COVID-19 and hired a talented social media storyteller, the videographer Dave Harding to chronicle Zeke's life.) More importantly, Maxwell knows Zeke must advance his bull riding craft. He recognizes that the Rock also grew up in a poor family, unable to afford Thanksgiving dinner one year. He became a giant in wrestling before building an entertainment empire that has made him for a few years running the world's highest-paid actor with more than three hundred million social media followers and head of a successful production company, among other businesses. Johnson's most recent big splash was purchasing the XFL professional football league.

Nobody handed anything to Dwayne Johnson on a shiny platter. He was hungry and was always the hardest worker wherever he went. For Zeke, step one is to do the work to make it in bull riding, win events, build his name, and maximize his earnings. Sure, the money at PBR's elite level is great. "But you can't take it into the ground," he says. The purpose of money is what it can do for others, mainly his family—the ten brothers and sisters he can put on his back.

Zeke had spent his childhood back and forth between Baytown, Texas, not far from Houston where his mom resided and Rockdale, a small town in remote Texas where his dad lived. He remembers being a child captivated by the energy of cowboys getting on bulls at a local rodeo. "I was just a kid in awe hanging on the rail, watching. One guy was riding his bull looking out at the crowd, kinda cocky. It was like he was looking right at me, waving to me. I loved the way cowboys conducted themselves. They were mysterious and cool. I don't think there was ever a time in my life when I didn't want to be a cowboy."

When Mitchell's family could finally afford cable, he'd watch PBR from his bunk bed. Most riders have fathers or brothers who could give advice on riding. Zeke's dad was a horse dentist, providing him some familiarity with horses and exposing him to the cowboy culture, but he didn't have mentoring or a chance to get on a bucking animal. He turned to YouTube. Zeke would study bull rides for hours on end to learn about form and technique. Then he'd string a barrel between two trees outside his mother's house and mimic those moves he'd memorized.

"Bull riding was my way out of poverty," he said. "I told my mama from the beginning, 'If this goes the way I want to, you'll never have to struggle, you'll never have to worry again.' My whole life, I watched my mom, my stepdad, and my dad struggle. I never wanted to be there again. This seems the best way to make it out."

This being a beautiful, brutal, unforgiving sport where anyone, no matter their level of talent or preparation, can be taken. When Mason Lowe took his last ride in Denver in January 2019, Ouncie was in the chutes scheduled to ride immediately before Mason's out. Zeke was up next, scheduled to go out right after Lowe, a friend with an easy, sly smile who shared his mischievous sense of humor. Zeke watched his cowboy brother get rammed in the chest, take two steps, and then succumb right in front of his eyes. That night, Zeke hit the bars, went home, and cried himself to sleep. A rider can think hard about things like this, and he did. But then it's time to move on, or it messes with

your head, and you'll get hurt. You cowboy up. Zeke got back in the practice pen two days later.

The danger of it all never goes away. Off the dirt, Zeke may be dancing around in black crocodile boots with a cognac sole, sometimes shirtless, or proudly sashaying in his latest neon blazer—an influence of his dad who loved to get into his Sunday best. During competition, when at his own best, he's in a clean, uncluttered, star-studded blue and white custom vest backing

(Bull Stock Media)

up the bravado with flashy ninety-point rides on the toughest bulls. But behind the smiles and quips, the TikTok videos and post-ride two-step celebrations, the specter of serious injury is always looming.

"A lot more people die in car wrecks than bull riding," Mitchell reasons. "Not another day is promised to any of us. I respect the bull. We're partners dancing together. He's doing all he can do to get me on the ground. I'm doing what I can to stay on. He leads. I follow. Eventually, when it works out, it's party time. When you dwell on the ifs, bad things can happen."

A mother's protective instincts dwell on the ifs leading to those bad things. "What if he gets hurt? What if I lose him? He lost a little sister in 2000," Ezekiel's mother, Janie, said.

She doesn't want to come near that feeling again. At first, Janie had forbidden Zeke to ride bulls. Her son didn't have a car, and he would secretly jog ten miles from his home in Baytown outside Houston to the practice pen. He'd be first to get there and last to leave—getting on as many as twenty-four bulls in a night. At home, the strong difference in opinion over Zeke's desired profession became a source of consternation. He would move out of the house, creating physical and emotional distance from his mother. Zeke says it didn't take long for him to appreciate that his mom's concerns were coming from a place of great love. His maturity as a man has helped mend the broken fences.

"Every time I talk to Ezekiel I tell him, 'I'm proud of you, and you didn't let anyone stop you, not even your mama,'" Janie said in an episode of *Life By The Horns*.

The blunt series didn't shy away from the injuries that happen in bull riding. Over the course of the 2020 season, Alvidrez, finally riding more consistently and making a run for the World Finals, was pile driven to the ground, breaking his neck.

"You are the underdog, two thousand to one," he said. "This bull is faster than you, he's stronger than you. They don't care if you're world champion. They'll throw you off their back, and if you land in front of them, they will hurt you."

Alvidrez was proud and defiant, even while speaking stiffly in a neck brace recovering from injury.

"I was sitting on top of the world and those bulls just humble you," he said. "Just like that they remind you, you're human. I'm used to failing. I'm used to eating the dirt, man. But guess what. I'm a stubborn SOB, and I know how to get back up. A lot of people assume (breaking your neck) would just crush you. Honestly, the first thing that came to mind is: *Can you imagine the comeback story?*"

Mitchell, like other riders, on occasion refers to bull riding as a dance. Viewed through the quick-cutting in-your-face presentation in *Life By The Horns*, it's more like dancing with a semi-truck driven by someone who's impaired. The series was available to more than a hundred million Snapchat users in the U.S.—a giant coup for PBR to reach new, younger audiences, the elusive Holy Grail when viewership of other major sports is off. The series quickly gained 300,000 subscribers, introducing Mitchell, Alvidrez, and their sport to a new audience.

"Bull riding is jam-packed, fast, and doesn't take a huge attention span," said Trevor Paperny, the show's creator and director. "It really worked out for Snap's platform."

Paperny, a self-described adrenaline junkie who off-roads, surfs, and climbs rocks, initially was introduced to bull riding when filming a commercial that happened to include Ezekiel Mitchell. He and his partners, Benjamin Scott and Alastair Ramsden, knew right away they needed to make a show about bull riding. They started watching PBR and were well-enough versed in the sport to sound convincing and they got a commitment from Snapchat. Soon, they were ready to hit the tour, COVID-19 compliance officers in tow. One story angle grabbed their attention: Ezekiel Mitchell's humble background, how he started, and the giant expectations on his shoulders.

"Overall, it's a beautiful story, and then you have the backdrop of the full, explosive nature of bull riding," Paperny said.

None of the producers expected to see the crucial role the bulls play in the sport, inextricably tied to the riders. The bone-crunching bulls are feared and respected; they're both opponent and teammate. "The whole sport is an amazing dance with the beast; the cowboy and bull become one, riding together, scored as one," Scott said. "That's one thing I loved about Zeke. He says, 'I pray for myself, and I pray for the animal.' I'm from New York City and had no idea that bulls had personalities or were treated in such a caring, loving way."

The producers learned that bulls have their own chiropractors, and they were surprised to see the animals treated like royalty—eating the best food and getting massages and electro-pulse treatments.

"We found out they are bred to buck and love it," Scott said. "Some of the bulls will come up to you and want to be petted. There's mutual love and respect for the animals that I honestly didn't expect."

During the filming for the series, produced by 21st Street Creative & Beneficial Entertainment, the creatives accompanied Mitchell to remote Oklahoma to attend a fundraiser for a bull rider who'd been seriously injured.

"Zeke was the only Black guy there," Paperny said. "I'm a white, long-haired dude from California, and I have to admit I was nervous. But there was nothing but love. Everybody wanted a picture and autograph from Zeke."

The crew traveled to sixteen states, observing cowboy values at every event and in the ranches they were invited into. They too, feel as if they were accepted into an extended family that starts with the riders.

"It doesn't matter where you come from, what you look like," Paperny said. "If you have the balls and heart to get on that animal, you're accepted as a bull riding cowboy. Period."

The star of their acclaimed series is a work in progress, learning about himself, still trying to calibrate the balance that includes enough preparation and try necessary to be a world champion.

As two-time PBR World Champion, Justin McBride said, "Zeke has got so much natural ability, it's both a blessing and a curse all at the same time. He can get by with things most guys cannot. As a bull rider I think Zeke sometimes lives in the future instead of in the moment. This guy wants to be a world champion. He says all the right things. He knows what to do. He just has to go do it day in and out."

Just getting by won't win a World Championship, and, deep down, Mitchell knows that. He says he wants more—to be one of the all-time greats even as he settles in as another fun-loving friend in the locker room, one more ballsy cowboy who, during a cocky, in control ride, will lock in on a young kid and make him believe. He's now got that power. He's also one of PBR's most-covered stars by virtue of something he didn't choose—his color. The questions of race bubble up when he only wants to talk about his match up in the draw. How the heck did every bull ride become the freaking March on Washington?

"True fans of bull riding just want to see guys ride bulls," he told ESPN in an interview before he competed in the Bill Pickett Invitational Rodeo, broadcast on CBS to become the first all-Black rodeo on network TV. "It doesn't matter what you look like. I'm an African American in a sport that doesn't see a lot of African Americans at a high level. It's about believing in yourself and shutting down any ignorance. You're the only person who matters."

He's in the limelight like few other bull riders have ever been. He's been anointed to bear a cross he never sought. It's a heavy weight for a twenty-three-year-old just starting to make his mark.

The saving grace in the predicament of Ezekiel Mitchell is that if he does his job, and the results catch up to his talent, the buckles and bucks won will speak the loudest.

"At the end of my career, I hope to influence people that anything is possible," he said. "This is the prime time of our lives to push the envelope. I don't want to prove anybody wrong; I want to prove myself right. Cowboy doesn't have a set color. Nothing in life has a color. If you work hard in this life, you can be anything you want to be."

He says he wants to be world champion. We are all watching.

Love & Try

8

OPENING THE TENT IN MUSIC CITY

(Dean Allen)

The 2019 PBR season had gotten off to a blistering start. Jess Lockwood—his swagger back after failing to repeat as world champion in 2018—won the season opener at Madison Square Garden. The 2017 World Champion—the sport's youngest ever at nineteen—was one of the guys with the sport in their blood since they began walking. It was even before that for Jess. When he was a week old, his mother wrapped him in a blanket and took him to a rodeo in their home state of Montana.

Love & Try

It's what parents do in a rodeo family. Little Jess got on his first sheep and calves before he was three years old.

Lockwood showed true superstar potential in winning the title in 2017, but then slacked off the following season. He had said so himself. Going into the Garden event to start a new year afresh, we get to introduce cowboys to reporters wearing skinny jeans instead of the usual boot cut. I took Jess to an interview with a high-end men's fashion magazine. He was brutally self-introspective, saying "there were times in 2018 when I didn't want to ride bulls. I was pretty weakhearted … and pretty disappointed in myself. I've definitely kicked myself in the ass after last year. If I'm gonna do this, I'm gonna do it right."

The self-administered butt-kick lit a fire. Jess won at the Garden then grabbed the event buckle the next weekend in Chicago, taking a firm hold of the top spot in the standings. Lockwood was so confident, commanding, and athletically sound—he's a former high school wrestling champ— he appeared on track to run the proverbial table for another championship. At the time, only one rider in PBR history, Brazilian Silvano Alves, had won back-to-back world titles, accomplishing the very difficult feat in 2011-12. However, about a month after winning in New York and Chicago, Lockwood went down hard in AT&T Stadium in Texas, breaking his collarbone. He'd be out for three months. Surging Chase Outlaw took over the No. 1 spot in late March.

Lockwood returned to competition in mid-May in Albuquerque, and he began to mount one of the most dominant summer campaigns in league history, winning five lower-level Touring Pro Division events in both the United States and Canada to enter the first event of the second half in Tulsa No. 3 in the world. In the BOK Center, Jess put up ninety-two points on a bull named Bezerk to tie for the win in the 15/15 Bucking Battle, then went three-for-three in the regular event, winning it with a ninety-point ride on Biker Bob in the championship round.

Heading into Nashville, Lockwood, the reigning world champion, was back at world No. 1 confident as ever.

Meantime, another athlete from another sport, the reserved, intensely focused Brazilian phenom José Vitor Leme, working nearly as hard to learn English as keeping his compact body fit, was showing his own impeccable technical form, centered on just about every bull—yet pulling moves making the ride look a little harder than it actually was, thereby increasing his scores. Leme had played professional soccer in Brazil. The previous season, he got on an airplane for the first time and showed up in Las Vegas to win the World Finals. Clearly, the sport had a new star on the horizon.

College boys Dalton Kasel and Daylon Swearingen had also burst onto the scene with veteran-like poise and huge rides. Swearingen, a mild-mannered cowboy from upstate New York, was making a run to be called the hardest-working cowboy in Western sports. During the spring and summer of 2019, he logged more than thirty thousand miles on his truck, crisscrossing North America to enter bull riding events. One weekend in late May, Swearingen competed on PBR's elite series in the U.S. and Canada, going from a WCRA rodeo competition in Green Bay, Wisconsin, to traveling abroad and riding in Halifax, Nova Scotia.

Months ahead of World Finals, the sport's very best were hanging onto every bull as if the gold buckle were on the line then and there.

In Nashville, the highly anticipated Music City Knockout was twenty-four hours away from bucking off with a ton of points on the line.

Inside Bridgestone Arena, located adjacent to the strip known for twanging country music streaming from the open windows of honky-tonk saloons lining an avenue serving as the main thoroughfare for processions of squealing bachelorettes pedaling away inhibitions and alcohol calories on ubiquitous mobile bars, final preparations were being made for the year's final PBR Major.

The road crew was assembling bucking chutes and spreading truckloads of dirt above the ice surface where the Nashville Predators play. As always, the crew would be responsible for removing every morsel of dirt from the arena after the event, even though the onset of preseason hockey was still weeks away. For now, another sport would thrill the Wranglers-and-Ariat faithful traveling in to see their favorite Western athletes along with the prowling party groups up for any sort of action, adventure, and revelry. On a steamy Saturday night in late August, it would be professional bull riding filling the arena and drawing the largest crowd the sport had seen in twenty-one years in this booming place, fast claiming the title of Funtown, USA—a suitable location for hosting America's original extreme sport.

That PBR road crew had been working double time. They'd been enlisted to build two dirt rings inside the arena. A full day ahead of one of the season's most meaningful events, they put down the first dirt field in an unusual place—the arena's back loading dock, where a contained commotion was breaking out. In a city that bashes with the best of them, the undisputed top party that Friday night was in full force, complete with cheering fans, blaring live rock music, and gung-ho cowboys climbing aboard furiously bucking bulls.

It was a made-for-TV event, invitation only, unspoken, and unknown to the fan base outside of those with solid connections or a keen ear to the ground leading them to an old-school hootenanny in the bowels of Bridgestone, where a cold nondescript concrete space had been transformed into a smoky, good-time barn reeking of Tennessee red cedar.

The CBS broadcasts of PBR open each week with an upbeat musical introduction, and this was the scene for filming a new broadcast lead in. The loading dock had been turned into a movie set with authentic touches like a hayloft overlooking the dirt, antique lanterns, steer horns, and vintage gas station signs surrounding a real rodeo arena. The bands that were playing while the bulls bucked for the cameras performed in front of a large, illuminated BE COWBOY sign.

It may have looked like a Hollywood production, but in the bucking chutes, the cowboys were no stunt men. This was real as can be. Grave business was at hand.

Patrolling the dirt were the U.S. Border Patrol bullfighters Jesse Byrne, Shorty Gorham, and Frank Newsom. At the front of the house, Dr. Tandy Freeman stood on call in the event of a bad fall or vicious stomping.

As the party raged, the crowd scenes were great. The music performance footage from Eddie Montgomery, Chevel Shepherd, and Black Stone Cherry, each belting out the new song, "Be Cowboy," written by country music legend Wynn Varble and David Frasier on commission from PBR, looked spectacular.

"I can definitely say I've never had a bull stare me in the face at any other shows," said Black Stone Cherry vocalist and lead guitarist Chris Robertson. "Something primal kicked in when the bulls and riders were that close that made us go that much harder."

Yet, the key ingredient—the bull riding—was thoroughly lacking.

As the chutes opened, the bulls bucked and cameras rolled to capture footage that would position the sport the next few years, two young bull riders were getting thrashed and thrown. In front of klieg lights and unfamiliar expectations, the lower-level riders were being schooled. It's hard enough to stay on a bull for eight seconds. The pressure of making sure the cameras caught a great ride was proving overwhelming.

In six outs, the bulls thoroughly dominated.

Among more than three dozen PBR cowboys on hand for the barn party, one watching the evolving exercise in futility was growing itchy.

Sitting in front of the band with his pals Keyshawn Whitehorse and Taylor Toves, Texas cowboy Ezekiel Mitchell saw exasperation in the eyes of director Cory Kelley, PBR on CBS's video storyteller and mastermind of the opening. "With due respect to these guys, the job wasn't getting done," Mitchell later said.

Mitchell, who'd been shaking his butt to the bands, succumbed to his cowboy tendencies. On went his serious face, and he disappeared for a few minutes. To the delight of the more than 250 fans invited to the broadcasted shoot/barn party, he'd next be seen in excuse-me/pardon-me mode, rushing to the chutes in his chaps, helmet in one hand, rope in the other, dragging his cowbell through the set's tight confines toward the night's final waiting bull.

All Kelley and his crew needed was one good take. Ezekiel Mitchell—with more than $100,000 at stake along with enough points

to rocket into the Top 10 in the official bull riding—was going to risk injury to give them what they wanted.

He mounted a bull named Colt 45, wrapped his hand, nodded his head, and then hung on for dear life. There were no judges, no timekeeping, no whistle or buzzer, only cheering fans drowned out by Black Stone Cherry rocking out to "Be Brave! Be Bolder! Be Cowboy!"

It was a good ride. Kelley and his cameras got what was needed.

As Woody Allen, who once claimed to be allergic to the outdoors (making him an unlikely source for Western words of wisdom) famously said, 90 percent of success in life is just showing up. Did the young cowboy from Houston ever show up. Now he was going to be the face of the PBR on the CBS opener.

"I love riding bulls. At the end of the day, I'm a bull rider," Mitchell said. "Doesn't make a difference to me if there are cameras or money on the line. They needed someone to get on that last one, so I did it. Do you put Michael Jordan on the court with a basketball and tell him not to shoot?"

No one was happier than the director who had his bull ride in front of an explosive rock show.

Mitchell stepped in to knock down the bull ride needed. (Dean Allen)

"Zeke's passion and love for the sport really impressed me," Kelley said. "He'd never been to a big shoot before. You could see he was intrigued by it. It really helped to have one of our top riders get out there, and it was pretty cool having that ride right in front of a band whose energy was off the charts."

The secret barn party was Kelley's brainchild, conceived as he sat on his porch right outside Leiper's Fork, Tennessee, sipping morning coffee and pondering the encore to the popular Steven Tyler opener the sport had been using the past two years.

The Tyler segment, shot on a parched desert floor outside Las Vegas, also used a song PBR expressly commissioned for the campaign. "Hold On (Won't Let Go)" was a perfect soundtrack for the man vs. beast desert showdown. Tyler liked the tune so much, it wound up on his rootsy solo record, "We're All Somebody from Somewhere."

The "Be Cowboy" theme is about everyday values and inclusion. The hat and the boots don't define a person; live a certain way, and you're a cowboy. Feet up and mental gears spinning, Kelley got to thinking about his surroundings.

Leiper's Fork is home to country and pop music megastars such as Justin Timberlake, Chris Stapleton, Miley Cyrus, and Carrie Underwood. It's the kind of place where secret barn parties happen all the time. Kelley, who has also shot openings for the SEC on CBS and NASCAR, pictured a drone above the rich rural pastures and fields, swooping toward Kenny Chesney's big, old barn hosting the raging PBR party.

"The vision considered PBR as a metaphor for society," Kelley said. "You'd have the familiar riders and cast of characters mixed with everyday people from different walks of life who are living PBR values and therefore embody the whole 'be cowboy' concept."

Kelley pitched the idea to PBR CEO Sean Gleason outside of STAPLES Center when the sport was making its Hollywood debut. Gleason loved the idea and added that the spot should cast everyday "cowboys." The duo decided on a firefighter, schoolteacher, mechanic,

Jess Lockwood and RaSandra Daniels (Author photo)

businessman, painter, barista, surgeon, and even a skateboard punk to be featured in the long-form area video and added in two faces familiar to fans from the initial Be Cowboy creative: Zoel Zohnnie (the mechanic) and RaSandra Daniels (the painter).

Daniels, who has started a film production company, paints, and is also a substitute teacher in New Mexico, said it's uplifting to be part of PBR's campaign theme. "I try to inspire my students, and this is such a great message of being strong, loving one another, and lifting people up," she said. "'Be Cowboy' is everything I'm about and live for."

Like Daniels, Chevel Shepherd, who at sixteen years old won *The Voice*, sang the national anthem for PBR in Albuquerque, and has performed on Toshiba Plaza at World Finals, is a bubbly cowboy ambassador quick to come to love the sport. "I really appreciate the fans and the culture, and guys like Chase Outlaw who are super tough and overcome so much," she said. "PBR is a place where everyone comes together."

For one night in Nashville, down at a drab loading dock turned into a rollicking barn party, different folks came together around PBR. The secret party is now being shared with the world to open every CBS broadcast, and the magic will be seen for quite some time.

Until Kelley sits on his porch and dreams up the next PBR opener that may just require another bull rider to grab his rope, cowboy up, and save the day.

9

ONE JUMP AT A TIME

(Author photo)

Guests staying in the Sheraton Four Seasons Greensboro in mid-October 2019 during PBR's local stop on its race to the world title saw a small, compact man in a cream-colored cowboy hat, riding bulls. There in the hotel, the gentleman with an eager smile and gleam in his eyes was trying to "make the eight."

There were no real bovines involved.

The giddy cowboy was "riding" couches and chairs with creased Wranglers spread wide as if a strong bovine were underneath, left hand balled in a tight fist above his lap, holding an imaginary rope he'd just carefully wrapped, free arm in the air, demonstrating to fans the proper technique for syncing in a balanced rhythm to dance with a thrashing beast fifteen times his size.

It had been more than thirty years since he had last commandeered a real, hot-breathed bull. But he was still technically sound in his movement.

"I don't think anybody in the PBR has gotten on more 'bulls' all season long than I did here this weekend," joshed Charles Sampson, who, for a short period of time in the 1980s was the most famous bull rider in the world. "But

(Author photo)

to be serious, I see this as my job. I love doing it. I promote the PBR, help kids, and try to win fans over, one at a time."

Bull riding's legendary, cheerful, wisecracking, indefatigable, one-man "Be Cowboy" promotional machine was in Greensboro to lead a seminar for local youth, teaching deserving kids about his sport.

But Sampson isn't shirking fandom. His mission is more important. He's speaking about life, which he tells the kids to take "one jump at a time." And if anyone has the chops to counsel youth about how to make it in a perplexing, often upside-down world, it's an eternally optimistic sixty-four-year-old man who was once a wide-eyed, glass-half full kid from Watts who set his mind on a goal, tried his guts out, and went on to become one of the all-time greats.

"It takes a lot of courage to be a bull rider ... and you're going to be seeing a lot of courage tonight," Simpson told the youngsters about to attend the Wrangler Long Live Cowboys PBR event. "And it takes courage, preparation, and hard work to be successful at whatever you want to do."

Sampson admitted to the kids that there's no fright quite like being in the bucking chute sitting on top of a quivering bull about to explode, but fear comes in many shapes and sizes. "Yeah, there's fear and nervousness on that bull. But there's fear and nervousness in a lot of things we all deal with. When I'm in that chute, the fear and nervousness tell me I can do this. Because *this is what I do*. They didn't pull me out of the audience. I trained hard for this. I dreamed constantly of this. It took me years to get to this moment. And when they call your name, you better be ready."

The Los Angeles native implored the kids that they can be cowboys, too. "Cowboys can come from anywhere. You don't need the hat or belt buckle. You just need courage and determination, and, above all, friendship."

Sampson's message makes a mark on youngsters who might be scared, angry, or confused, because it comes from a very unlikely bull rider, let alone a world champion. The young man from Watts was crowned the world's best in 1982, becoming the first Black cowboy ever to capture one of the most difficult and punishing titles in sports.

Growing up in a tough urban neighborhood, Sampson didn't have the same background and pedigree as other bull riders. But he did share one thing in common with them: a simmering desire to want one thing in life more than anything else. He wanted to ride bulls.

"I just loved the horses and ponies as a kid and that helped me stay out of trouble and find a healthy passion," he said. "I wasn't big enough to play football and I wasn't smart enough to be a doctor. I just wanted to be a bull rider."

As a young kid in Watts, he joined the Cub Scouts and discovered horses. He found a horse stable near his home and got a job there. He would often stay at the stables until 2 a.m., sometimes even sleeping there. With friends, he'd take the hay out of a stack, carve out a virtual castle and wake up the next morning. "We didn't have the money or means to go camping. This was our camping, peaceful and beautiful."

Sampson lived near the railroad tracks off the freeway about a mile from the stables. It wasn't a long walk, but the young boy didn't want to miss one minute of time working at the stables. He'd often jump on a freight train to get to the horses. Sometimes a slow-moving train would become a fast-moving train. "That's when you knew you'd have to jump off. Get off, or you have no idea where that train would wind up," said Simpson with a twinkle in the eye that didn't go away all weekend in Greensboro.

Heading for the stables, picking up speed past the lingering street gangs, the boy known as "Pee Wee" would have to leap from the train. Even if an athlete can accomplish one of the hardest feats in sports—staying on a bull for eight seconds—he has to get *off* the bull. Those train dismounts were early training for Sampson's eventual career as a professional bull rider.

That career started at fourteen, when he got on his first bull. The cowboys who took him under their wing at the stables brought little Charlie to a rodeo in Oklahoma for a two-week trip. Pee Wee entered all the bull riding events, figuring that he could win enough money to pay for the gas to get everyone back to Los Angeles. He won that money and was hooked on bull riding.

"What really helped me was going down the road with older, more experienced bull riders," Sampson said in an interview with *Cowboy Lifestyle Network*. "I would help them pull their bull ropes and watch them ride. I learned from that, then I just decided I was going to do it. The first year I rode with just my natural ability. Then after that, I went to a bull riding clinic and learned the fundamentals—what it takes to ride bulls. Once I learned the fundamentals, I applied myself to that and things really started taking off."

One Jump at a Time

At fifteen, he began competing in high school rodeo. Sampson would rope and become an all-around rodeo athlete as well, earning a scholarship at Central Arizona College. (In fact, at sixty-four, he is still roping.) He traveled throughout the Southwest competing in college rodeos, and after two years he turned pro, as a member of the PRCA, winning for the first time in

Anthony Pittman honored Sampson with this painting.

Lovington, New Mexico. He tried to be a student of the game, intently watching every bull rider, making mental notes on why some made the whistle and others got bucked off. As much as he paid attention to the fundamentals, guts and determination were as important. He calls his personal style, "Never give up."

Charlie had his supporters. And some in an insular sport walled off from the rest of the world tried to discourage him. He wasn't from a ranching background. He didn't have a recognizable family name. He had no rodeo connections. He listened to the positive voices and tuned out everyone else. He would simply enter one rodeo at a time and often win.

Sampson, an outsider, wasn't alone. Another unlikely cowboy, Bobby DelVecchio, a colorful, cocksure Italian from the Bronx, swaggered onto the scene from the opposite coast. Each man was initially suspicious of the other interloper. But they'd form a very close friendship. (In fact, it's the subject of a movie, *Money or Mud,* now in development.) Similar to Sampson earning his cowboy stripes by mucking the horse stables in Watts, DelVecchio got into Western sports by riding horses with his dad on Pelham Parkway, not too far from the family's apartment on 182nd Street where he would take his bull rope out onto the fire escape to practice his riding moves. DelVecchio started riding bulls in rural New Jersey. When he was sixteen, he left home for a rodeo in Texas and never returned.

"Charlie and me, we weren't traditional cowboys who would grow up in the culture," DelVecchio said. "It was odd to have two guys, one from one coast, one from the other, going into the middle of the country. We rodeoed together and developed a great friendship. We showed up from different parts of the country and started kicking ass. And the rest of the guys didn't like it. Especially when we started taking their money."

There have been lingering questions in rodeo circles about whether Sampson, in a judged sport, had it harder than the white riders. He says he was so focused on staying on his bulls he never noticed unfair treatment.

DelVecchio remembers it slightly differently, but cautions against drawing racial battle lines: "In this sport, if you can ride, you're in. That's all that matters. I know the world would like to hear about more of a racial divide. It wasn't there. Now in terms of scoring, were there maybe a few times both of us should have been a few points higher? Sure. I remember having words with one judge once who didn't give Charlie the points he deserved. I was more outspoken than Charlie was. I'd seen it one too many times. And then he never did it again. Over time, we just made them love us. We just wouldn't go away. Charlie kept fighting, especially. Rodeo fans love fighters, they don't care what you look like."

Bobby was built bigger and stronger than Charlie and was an outlier in another way—he largely avoided injury in a bull riding career that lasted more than two decades, only breaking a few ribs, though he did have both hips replaced when he retired.

"To be successful in this sport, you can't hold back; you need to give it all you got," DelVecchio said. "Charlie gave it his all every time. I wanted to flirt with the girls; Charlie wanted to ride bulls, and he wanted it more than anyone. He had his tough streaks with injuries but kept bouncing back. It felt like every time I looked over at him, he had a cast on somewhere. I would always say he's the smallest bull rider with the biggest heart."

On Championship Sunday in Greensboro, Sampson sat in the front row and watched two-time World Champion J. B. Mauney get on a bull with a broken fibula. Holding the "PBR Daysheet"—a print-out listing the rider and bull lineup for that day's round—and keeping score, Sampson nodded and smiled when the first bars of George Thorogood's "Bad to the Bone" rang from the additional loudspeakers that PBR brings in (the usual arena PA isn't loud enough), indicating that J.B. was in the chutes. His grin was one of approval and distant kinship, for back in the day, nobody cowboyed up more than the kid from Watts, breaking fingers, nearly his entire face, his leg (four times), and his sternum. Despite the beating, his professional career spanned an incredible twenty years. Charlie and J.B. may not look alike, but they're brothers in a small fraternity, both tough as John Wayne's boots, who can compartmentalize and block out physical pain, and not let the foreknowledge that more pain is coming stop them from competing.

Mauney's feats of toughness are legendary. Lesser known, Sampson probably should have been killed in Nebraska in 1979, before the invention of the protective rider vest. He was hung up on the bull and, in the parlance of rodeo announcers, "dragged into the well" and stepped on. The force of the bull's jack hammer leg on Sampson's chest snapped a rib right into his lung.

DelVecchio recalls another time he feared the world would lose Charlie. The Bronx cowboy, his buddy from Watts, and four other riders were picked to perform for President Ronald Reagan. The bulls, an ornery group brought up from Florida, were new to the riders. "Charlie had a big white bull, who jerked him down, hit him in the head, and knocked him out," DelVecchio said. "I didn't know what to do. I stuck my hand on top of his forehead, where it was bleeding. They had a center out gate, and I hunkered down, thought I'd get kicked, too, by the bull who was still in the arena."

Sampson would stay in intensive care for a week, treated by President Reagan's doctors. "He had had that mental capacity to almost die and then come back and ride bulls again," DelVecchio said. "Just an incredible, determined athlete. That's why I say he's got the biggest heart. He continued to rodeo for several more years and qualified for NFR several more times."

Sampson would win big events in places like the Houston Astrodome and make eleven trips to the prestigious NFR (National Finals Rodeo). His success came at the highest rate in his championship 1982 PRCA season, beating even the great Donnie Gay—just about every fan's hero at the time—and becoming the first Black cowboy to win a World Championship title.

He'd appear on the *Today* show with Bryant Gumble. (Sampson says it was Gumble's first interview on his first day with the program.) After missing the first chance to meet President Reagan following his brutal wreck, a private meeting with the president was arranged at the White House. Sampson appeared in advertisements for Timex watches and Coors beer, for the latter promoting inner-city programs and scholarships while riding for the brand in lending his name and fame to compete in the new Bill Pickett Invitational Rodeo, formed in 1984 by entertainment impresario Lu Vason, who wanted to create opportunities for black cowboys and cowgirls unable to compete in traditional rodeos.

The impact of Sampson shown as a real cowboy in national advertising in the 1980s can't be diminished. Commercials, like television shows and films (and now social media content), were a primary way American youth were educated. Lessons on black cowboys, however, were few and far between.

"For most people—here and abroad—the image they have of a cowboy is an actor, like John Wayne, playing the part of a cowboy in a movie," said Keith Ryan Cartwright, author of *Black Cowboys of Rodeo*. "John Wayne was a movie star who knew how to ride a horse, yet so many people who are unfamiliar with the West, beyond what they never saw on television or the movies, cannot imagine there being Black cowboys, because far too often they were not portrayed as anything but servants."

Now, here was Sampson, a Black cowboy, riding bulls in national ads promoting the products of mainstream American brands.

For Timex, whose commercials were a regular presence on network TV in the 1970s and 1980s, Charlie sported a watch with a cowhide strap.

"Timex knew I kept getting beaten up to the gills," Sampson said. "I took a licking and kept on ticking."

That's surely an understatement for the 5'4" cowboy who might have more plates in his body than your grandmother has in her cupboard.

Sampson's role as an ambassador for the sport of bull riding had begun decades ago. In the late 1980s, he was invited to Brazil to hold a riding clinic. There, he met future PBR legend Adriano Moraes, and convinced him to come to the U.S. to ride bulls. Moraes would win the first PBR World Championship and became the first rider to win three PBR world titles. There's a good case for putting his face on the proverbial "Mount Rushmore" if choosing the best four bull riders of all time. In fact, when PBR was erecting a statue for their Pueblo, Colorado, headquarters, the organization chose Moraes riding legendary bull, Little Yellow Jacket. Sampson was proud of "discovering" Moraes, and his impish personality seemed to shine brightest when he hung out with the rugged, muscular Brazilian.

In one memorable incident stateside, a TV crew wanted to interview Adriano, who didn't speak a word of English. Sampson was asked if he spoke Portuguese and could translate. He said, "Yes," and stepped in to help. When the reporter asked his first question, Sampson merely shouted it slowly and loudly to Moraes, in English, repeating every word in the language Adriano couldn't understand. Even the crew was laughing as the interview was brought to a halt.

Sampson is still fast with a joke. As a Rodeo Hall of Fame and PBR Ring of Honor member, he remains grateful to a sport that provided a lifetime of opportunities. He still loves horses and the sport of bull riding. And now, driven by a passion to educate young people to be whatever they want to be no matter the obstacles, he is paying it forward.

Inspiring young people to realize that the PBR event they're about to witness is possible because of trailblazing rodeo pioneers from diverse backgrounds is an obligation bringing him great joy. In giving back, he gets as much as he gives. Sampson knows the power of real encouragement when others are putting up barriers. He's there to just help young people to see what's possible.

Comparing Charles "Pee Wee" Sampson to the comparatively humongous bovine beasts that he conquered, any kid can realize nothing is impossible when putting head and heart into it.

Love & Try

For sports pioneer Charles Sampson, the pleasure in serving as a great PBR ambassador, telling his story, and maybe changing a life or two on a Saturday afternoon is all his.

Because how many of us can legitimately claim *"I was first."*

10

FUNERAL FOR A FRIEND

(Andre Silva)

On a raw, gray January morning, they started arriving at the church in Boonville, Missouri, as a fraternal order, mostly pulling up in American-made pickup trucks with shotgun racks displaying bumper stickers advertising Harley-Davidson and Jack Daniels, local rodeos, and American flags. They moved through the early day's misty rain in the stiff shuffle of still-stunned friends, in the dull light slowly making their way across the muddy parking lot toward the Open Bible Prairie Center. They walked arm in arm with wives and girlfriends, proud cowboys in jackets embroidered with the logos of the American Cowboy Association, Great Lakes Circuit Finals Rodeo, Central Bull Riders Association, and the PBR World Finals.

There was no rush. Nothing could change that which would formally be acknowledged.

Inside the chapel, pew after pew revealed a phalanx of wide brimmed hats. The sounds of cowboy church music played over speakers set alongside the altar. Songs like "This Little Light of Mine" and "Go Tell it on the Mountain," first heard in Sunday school, now a somber soundtrack backing the quiet weeping of a young widow on shaky legs, led to the altar where her husband's riding gear sat.

Every seat was taken. Everyone sat at attention, waiting patiently. Not a person was peering into a phone. Nobody was going to disrespect the soul being laid to rest: their good friend; a fine man who could be a generous pillar of the community by day while cutting loose at night; an iridescent personality; owner of an impish grin once seen never forgotten; the humble, fun-loving, unassuming kid next door; the most famous face in town; the professional bull rider Mason Lowe.

Mason had died eight days earlier riding in Denver Coliseum at the National Western Stock Show, and even though the passing of a man in his profession is not a freak occurrence, the news cut to the bone. The subsequent outpouring of love and support from all corners of the Western sports community was so large and unexpected, Mason's family asked for the services to be made available globally on a digital stream.

He was blessed with the kind of personality often described as infectious. Every time PBR made a video, Mason wanted to be the guy featured. He may not have been ranked in the Top Five but was the proverbial home run hitter, riding some of the world's toughest bulls, and he made the World Finals three times in his twenty-five years. Beyond these very respectable on-the-dirt stats, Mason's irrepressible likeability surely justified inclusion as a face of the sport.

"Mason wasn't one to rip his shirt off and show the Superman logo; he was low-key, often in the shadows, and therefore didn't get as much TV time as other riders projecting bigger personalities for the cameras," longtime PBR and CBS sideline reporter Leah Garcia would later observe. "But if you sat down for a beer with Mason, you'd absolutely fall in love with his sly, sarcastic sense of humor. He was more like Cool Hand Luke. He was a tough gladiator and a cocky daredevil full of ambition and aggression, spitting in the face of danger, and at the end of the day—and I mean this in the most respectful way—like a little boy who'd jump up and celebrate when he was happy and get angry with himself when he wasn't doing what he knew he could."

When he's gone, it is our nature to try to find words quantifying and weighing a man's life. In the church, Pastor Tom Levin set the stage for reminiscing by saying, "In sorrow, we find hope. Grief and memory live side by side in our hearts."

Amid the sniffling and quiet sobs, memories of Mason shared by the familiar voices of PBR arena announcers Matt West and Clint Atkins, by turns hilarious and heartfelt, brought more tears. In a world casually throwing around the term, "cowboy," he was the real deal, "a genuine cowboy," they said: a tough, fun-loving American original who loved life and wanted those around him to love it, too. He made his friends laugh until their faces hurt. He never met a stranger, they said. He was humble and generous—not a pretentious cell in his body. (Those kinds of cells must have been replaced by whatever protein and mitochondria trigger generosity. Mason frequently paid the contestant entry fees for cowboys who'd been a little short that week.)

The words of Lowe's brothers in the PBR locker room were read aloud to warm the chilly stillness of the Missouri church.

Derek Kolbaba said Mason brightened every room he walked into.

Stormy Wing attested to no dull moments with Mason, every one of them to be cherished.

J.B. Mauney said no matter how hurt he was, whenever Mason took that rope, he would try until his head hit the ground.

The judges in Tulsa had it differently, but Chase Outlaw swore that Mason Lowe, then eighteen years old, rode Bushwacker when nobody else had.

Koal Livingston pointed out that Mason had more heart than anyone he knows. Even in his final moment, he got up and took a few paces and nearly made it off the dirt after being drilled in the chest by that final bull.

That awful night in Denver, Mason Lowe died, the cliché goes, on his terms doing what he loved. Sometimes clichés aren't boring, lazy bromides. They paint a picture of truth.

The sport the riders love can be a bitter-sweet curse. Nothing feels better, nothing brings more blissful clarity in making life's distractions, problems, and disappointments disappear faster than hurtling through the air attached to a raging storm of bovine muscle. Bull riding will put a man squarely in the moment like no other pursuit. For some, the escape is an ever-present itch to be scratched. And because this addiction lives on the outer envelope of extreme athletic pursuits, it is unforgiving.

Mason's boots were cut off his legs at the hospital. PBR asked for the leather. The league would make crosses with a piece of Mason's boots inside. Each year, one of those crosses would be given to the rider with the highest-scored ride—the Mason Lowe Award—because Mason always went big.

PBR fans rallied to donate more than $200,000 to Mason's family. His funeral stream was viewed that day nearly fifty thousand times. PBR renamed its premier series event in St. Louis that would take place in mid-February, *The Mason Lowe Memorial*. Wisecracking Mason would have had a lot of fun with that one.

Following The Mason Lowe Memorial, a group of Mason's friends including fellow Missourian and former rider turned stock contractor LJ Jenkins, came together to create "Ridin' with Mason Lowe," an event in Cassville, Missouri, bringing together two of the things that the Missouri cowboy will always be best remembered for: riding bulls and helping others.

All proceeds from ticket sales for the now-annual event go to St. Jude's Children's Research Hospital. Ridin' with Mason Lowe has raised tens of thousands of dollars to help sick children.

"As talented and tough as Mason was in the arena, I will always remember who he was outside the arena, with a smile on his face," said Matt West, who donated his services to announce the event. "What stood out about Mason was he was always super positive and was all about helping others. Now, to come back to Cassville and extend that helping hand to St. Jude's … that would have made him really happy."

When I'm at a PBR event and hear something interesting, I jot it down, often on whatever scraps of paper I can find. When returning to the office, I throw the notes in a file. As I began writing this book, rifling through this collection for ideas, information, and inspiration, I found a quote from Mason Lowe, scribbled on what appeared to be a piece of flimsy white cardboard ripped off a laundry delivery box. The smart blue logo on the flip side said "Bibbentuckers," a dry cleaner that operates in the Dallas-Fort Worth area; the snippet of conversation must have happened at one of our February events at AT&T Stadium in Arlington, Texas. I don't remember exactly where we were, but I could tell from the erratic handwriting that it must have been late, after a few drinks. The Dallas location and scrap note's place in the file indicated this must have been about eleven months before Mason died.

Mason had said this:

"*There's no time to think in bull riding. Not a lot's going on in your head. Not a whole lot scares me. If I were scared, I wouldn't be doing it. You know what, maybe I am a little scared. If you're not at least a little scared, you're f-cking crazy.*"

Love & Try

PART III

THE SHOW MUST GO ON

At soft-hand office jobs, there are lots of meetings. Therein, it's smart and fashionable to declare that nobody works harder than your team. Is there a better bone to throw? Everyone will nod, most wondering, "What time is lunch?"

My profession—public relations—offers nice rewards for expertly blowing smoke. But it is with wholesome hand-on-the-Bible sincerity that I declare that *no team works harder to do more with less than those at Professional Bull Riders.*

We've learned how bull riders must have the fire down below, or they'll never succeed in staying on their bulls and making some money. Similarly (well, without the occasional ruptured organ), the surprisingly small staff of employees of PBR have their own inner blaze burning to transform arenas, get the bulls in, and pull off hundreds of high-quality events each year. The organization is indeed "the little engine that could."

Let's visit with a few of the characters—including one fan you'll never forget—whose inextinguishable passion brings the big show to fans all over the country.

11

LIVING WITH DANGER INSTEAD OF HIDING IN FEAR

(Bull Stock Media)

"That was America. This was the first major sporting event indoors with spectators. They prayed before the event. They sang the national anthem. I was proud to be there. This was the perfect example of what makes this *country great. These people were athletes, and they wanted to do what they were good at. And it reminded us all how special this country is and how important our liberties are."* —South Dakota Governor Kristi Noem, after riding her horse onto the dirt, ushering in the return of fans to indoor sporting events in July 2020.

Dener Barbosa took seven stitches in his free hand and then took the event buckle in Duluth, Georgia, after a ninety-one-point ride on a bull named Bullseye.

That part of the Professional Bull Riders (PBR) Unleash The Beast—the sport's premier series featuring the world's top thirty-five bull riders—was standard. A cowboy rode through injury and downplayed it by saying that slicing up the hand that doesn't go in the bull rope is no big deal. Barbosa stayed on all three of his bulls for the required eight seconds, showing he can win at the top of the sport and starting to believe this was his time. The toughness hook was a nice story line but one that emerges nearly every weekend in PBR.

In that respect, it was a routine weekend in professional bull riding. Everything else on Sunday March 16, 2020, felt like an episode of *The Twilight Zone.*

There were no cheers when Barbosa released his rope and leaped off Bullseye, sticking a perfect landing. The arena was silent when the wiry twenty-five-year-old Brazilian, beginning to realize his potential, accepted his second elite series buckle for winning the event. That's because this was a PBR event like no other. It was played in an empty arena. And it was the prelude to one of the strangest and most difficult stretches of, not only Barbosa's up-and-down career, but also that of PBR Commissioner and CEO Sean Gleason and just about everyone in the sport.

Across North America that Sunday, every major sport except a televised bowling tournament had been canceled. PBR's top executive, watching his crew break down a half-mile of steel panels and begin to scoop away 750 tons of dirt they had brought in three days earlier to turn a hockey arena into a bull riding mecca, planned for his sport to soldier on. But from the time Gleason left the Infinite Energy Center for his flight at Hartsfield-Jackson International Airport in Atlanta to when he landed in Denver a few hours

Living with Danger Instead of Hiding in Fear

All hands on deck: Commissioner Gleason wiping down the Lazy E's bucking chutes (Bull Stock Media)

later, new, even tighter restrictions for being in public were announced. The world had changed ... for him and everyone in the "mass gathering business."

Prior to all the planning going into that weekend's bull riding gathering in Georgia, a mysterious, dangerous virus from abroad was beginning to infect people in communities across the United States. Urgent health guidance was issued, prohibiting public events of 250 or more people. The world's most prolific consumers went into panic mode and did what they usually do when large-scale disaster is forecast, making a run on toilet paper and, in this situation, anything in a bottle that could be poured or sprayed on household surfaces to kill germs.

With the PBR season's tenth premier series event on tap in Georgia, Gleason did the math. Factoring in all the riders, stock contractors, and event and TV production crew, he figured PBR could conduct the bull riding in a closed environment—with no fans. Counting essential operations personnel, production and TV crew, judges, bull stock contractors, sports medicine, and the bull riders, PBR could hold the event for TV with 150 people in the building.

The live event team contacted ticket holders. Due to unforeseen and unprecedented circumstances, this would be a closed event. They'd get refunds and could watch the 2020 Gwinnett Invitational at home on CBS Sports. No one outside of essential participants would be permitted in the arena.

The event began with an eerie scene: the usual roar of the fans was replaced by clanging gates and grunting bull riders echoing across the cavernous arena. It was raw and unfiltered, must-see in an odd, intimate way, like being a fly on the wall in the world's rankest practice pen. While Rod Serling calling out the rider scores wouldn't have felt out of place, when Barbosa's name was placed at the top of the leaderboard late Sunday afternoon, it did feel normal. PBR had done it. The league had pulled off a closed event.

Gleason is not an epidemiologist, but he couldn't imagine the virus going away instantly. "PBR Unplugged," available on TV and the RidePass streamer, looked to be the way forward for a while. The term hadn't been coined yet, but this would be PBR's "new normal."

It was a short-lived plan.

As the league's commissioner, a formidable presence at 6'5" with a long gait in his alligator-skin cowboy boots, deplaned in Denver, public gathering guidance had tightened to a maximum of one hundred people. Monday morning, as Gleason steered his Ford F150 to the office parking lot next to the Pueblo Riverwalk, permissible gatherings were reduced to groups of ten.

Everything had *really* changed. All sports were now shut down.

Gleason grew up in a small town in Eastern Washington state, the son of a Washington state patrolman. He had been a heavy-metal fanatic in high school, even "playing" in an air band. But from when he was ten to when he began college, he had also spent more time on a horse than a car. Working for ranchers and farmers, Sean pulled calves during breeding season, and inoculated and branded hundreds of these animals then moved them to pasture.

Gleason would move onto college then wind up sitting in an office desk chair instead of in a saddle, yet he remains a dedicated student and ardent evangelist of the cowboy credo that helped build the Western part of his country. He is known to lean into reason, logic, data, and common sense in making important business decisions. He is not a man to be pushed around. Once, he came within one minute of canceling a PBR elite series prior to rider introductions when the Charlotte arena manager would not allow the U.S. Color guard into the premises because they were armed. Gleason argued these were federal law enforcement officers presenting the American flag. The arena manager said she wasn't willing to risk a shootout in her workplace. Gleason drew a line in the sand. The Color Guard, performing their job as they do across the country, would come in with their weapons, or

PBR would pack up and go home. One minute before he planned to give the crew the signal to bug out, a compromise was forged: local Charlotte police would escort in the armed federal officers allowing them to participate in the opening ceremonies with their armaments. No, you can't make this stuff up.

Gleason's tendency to circle the wagons, dig his boots in, and go to battle can be traced to when he was a young man, unfairly targeted by the humorless establishment during his heavy-metal high school days.

It all started harmless enough. Sean and a fellow rocker had started a music concert review column in the school newspaper. Gleason had no agenda other than to share music he loved. Yet for promoting a passion, he wound up stirring up a hornet's nest of trouble among parents and school officials. He would be called a "devil worshiper." Rather than put down the pen, his music reviews became more colorful. School board meetings were held to decide if he'd be expelled for peddling songs and a way of life allegedly corrupting local youth.

That youthful battle over free expression and a successful refusal to back down to an agenda-driven mob made a permanent mark on Gleason. His fighting spirit would come into play when uncontrollable outside forces again came crashing down on his greatest passion—running a professional bull riding league that he believes represents a way of life. This time the battle began with a perplexing health crisis bringing absolute all-or-nothing edicts in the name of public health.

The country was locking down, and Gleason was thinking about stubborn cowboy resilience when meeting with his leadership team in "Murray," a cowboy-themed conference room at headquarters named after PBR cofounder Ty Murray, where he told them: *"We have a choice in front of us: We can go hide in fear, or we can learn how to live safely with danger and keep our business going."*

This bold decisiveness is what had helped make Gleason successful in leading a dirty, brutal sport—maintaining its rough and rugged edges while courting corporate respectability (and dollars). Years ago, it also made for some rocky times when the cowboys who founded his organization first began taking orders from a man so sure of his decisions yet he'd never even gotten on a bull. "I went from wanting to beat the shit out of him to saying he's the best commissioner in sports," said PBR cofounder Cody Lambert, who, as director of livestock, picks all the bulls that get to compete in PBR and has worked with Gleason for nearly twenty years.

Lambert and the PBR executive team are a group who believe the world owes you nothing. Opportunity is equal and you make your own way. They didn't have to debate the binary choice offered to them. They knew the direction Gleason was leaning. Self-reliance was a trait throughout the room. Without hesitation, they chose the deal-with-danger option: Get up. Dust yourself off. Climb back on the horse. Use your smarts and intuition. Find a way to do the job you love, to sustain the people you love.

This response to the dire situation was born of necessity. Sidelined athletes in other big-time professional sports would begin to get busy searching for the latest Zoom workouts. Most had guaranteed contracts, and their sports enjoyed lucrative TV deals providing a financial cushion. They could take a break. PBR, however, is a live-event business dependent largely on ticket sales. The virus was an existential threat to cowboy athletes and bull stock contractors who are independent operators without the luxury of a steady paycheck. The crew who build and break down the bull riding arenas, from "the dirt doctor" (yes, PBR has an expert ensuring the best conditions to maximize the bulls' performances) to the real physician, Dr. Tandy Freeman, who helps save riders' lives, are also largely independent contractors. (You'll later read about both.) Without ticket revenue, and well-attended events to deliver value to brand partners, these hard-working people and—eventually, if the lockdown lasted—the sport would be in dire straits.

"This health situation was so new with so many unknowns," Gleason said. "There was no playbook for what to do, and it was clear that nobody was going to give us one. We could have easily closed the tent and waited. We could have packed up to ride out the storm from the safety of our homes. But we were driven by the desire to put on events, keep our industry working, and bring fans the sport they loved."

PBR had always been "the little engine that could," formed by twenty rodeo cowboys who broke away to create their own bull riding-only league and achieving a level of growth and near-mainstream status that's admirable considering its relative infancy compared to other major pro sports that began before television was even invented. Sensing the greatest threat in the sport's twenty-six-year history, Gleason immediately formed a crisis committee that was dubbed "Red Dawn," named for the 1984 film featuring a group of intrepid youth in Colorado fighting off a Soviet invasion. Meeting first thing every morning—including weekends—until Thanksgiving, the team felt like they were banding together to fend off an invasion to save their business. The Red Dawn team didn't set out to do anything to be first. They simply felt a responsibility to figure out a way to get back to business safely and responsibly.

"The goal was always to get our people back to work," Gleason said. Once shut down, someone had to step up and chart a path back to normalcy. The prevailing wisdom was to lock down and wait it out. If bull riding were to return, it would be under intense public scrutiny. Any sport returning to play would face enormous risk.

Optics and bad press notwithstanding, of course nobody wanted anyone to get sick. The Red Dawn team under Gleason spent hours learning about how airborne viruses are transmitted to write comprehensive protocols that would allow PBR to become the first major sport to resume competition in late April in closed events at the Lazy E in Oklahoma, a mere forty-one days after mass gatherings larger than ten people were banned.

During the first broadcasts showing empty stands as the backdrop, the new stripped-down experience from Duluth continued. Nobody was there, outside the riders, stock contractors who raise and handle the bulls, and crew. But since PBR is a collision sport, it wasn't exactly like watching golf. Inside barren, empty arenas, clanging metal gates, grunting cowboys, and chants of "Hustle! Hustle! Hustle!" from cowboys in the bucking chute replaced the usual noise of raucous, often well-lubricated crowds.

The first pro athletes seen on television wearing facial masks turned out to be professional bull riders. The ubiquitous masks were as essential as the riders' protective vests: requisite for continuing to compete. Sensitive to removing PPE from crucial front-line and health care workers tapping a tenuous supply, PBR would even make its own respirators for the crew, an idea hatched by IT Director Brandon Reeves using the league's 3-D printer.

In the fall, many arenas across the country would draw big crowds again—but as election polling places, not to host games. Four months prior to that, led by South Dakota Governor Kristi Noem riding Old Glory into the Denny Sanford PREMIER Center in Sioux Falls for the new team tournament championship in July, PBR broke down the barrier for inviting fans into arenas with new safety protocols in place. The sport had to go where governmental gathering regulations allowed, setting a completely new schedule for a ten-city second half swing to complete the regular season. New events came to cities such as Ft. Worth, Texas; Bismarck, North Dakota; Lincoln, Nebraska; and Des Moines, Iowa.

On the dirt, twenty-three-year-old phenom José Vitor Leme appeared to be Krazy Glued to his bulls, winning seven events and fifteen rounds. Undoubtedly, many Americans were getting out of bed each morning with a harder landing than the way Jose was dismounting his bulls. It was a joy to witness. The former Brazilian soccer star was riding at a sizzling 70 percent, including eight ninety-point rides, removing his helmet to punt it after every big ride, then sinking to his knees to thank God for making his dream come true. Soft-spoken Texan Cooper Davis came back from a broken neck at the season opener in New York to win in Lincoln, Nebraska, propelled by scoring 92.5 points on a bull named Hocus Pocus. The 2016 World Champion, who won that title after Lambert observed he was too fat, driving Davis to lose thirty-five pounds and transform into a lean bull riding machine, was back in prime form as a championship threat. In August, the next last American hero, Marlboro-smoking, Jägermeister-swilling, rebel throwback cowboy, and two-time World Champion J.B. Mauney returned from his longest-ever stint on the injury shelf, hanging on until his head hit the dirt to win a few rounds, notch three straight top four finishes, and rocket 157 places in the standings to ride into his fifteenth consecutive World Finals.

And so, a twisting, turning, challenging season came to a climax for the first time in twenty-seven years outside of Las Vegas, which was still dark due to the virus. When the cherished gold buckle was presented to Leme after he knocked down a massive 95.75-point ride on a bull named Woopaa to clinch the title ("the equivalent to a walk off grand slam!" shouted PBR on CBS voice Craig Hummer), it marked an audacious accomplishment that seemed unreachable when the lockdowns began in March. PBR had delivered its 2020 season to fans. And nobody got sick.

How PBR wrote the initial return playbook for sports and live entertainment is ultimately a story of—you called it—love and try. The virus had created a fog of fear and paralyzing uncertainty. Someone had to step up to implore the country to chart a path to normalcy in a bold yet sensible way, without taking the virus into a community, or bringing it home afterwards. It makes sense that a group of optimistic, determined cowboys led sports back to business, trusting their intuition to drown out voices of doubt, negativity,

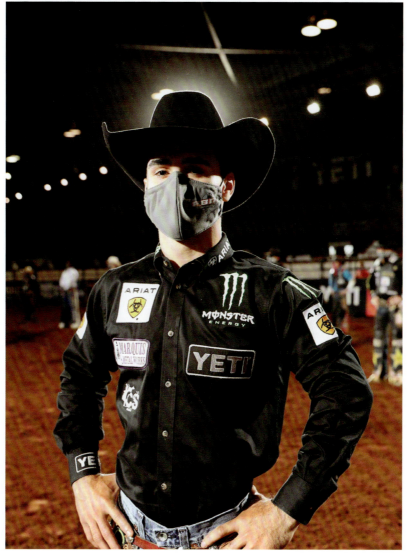

The first pro athletes on TV wearing masks were PBR riders. (Bull Stock Media)

and skepticism to get back to work and help open up cities. Cowboys, after all, are accustomed to adversity. They settled the West by battling through harsh conditions, constant danger, and incredible odds.

PBR's boss may have claimed the goal wasn't to be first. Yet by virtue of forging ahead when others waited, an example was set. It's easy to forget that seven months prior to Leme's coronation, as every bull rider was living in a socially distanced RV in the lot of the Lazy E Arena in Oklahoma, self-isolating instead of staying in hotels with others, the ship was sailing into completely unchartered waters. No other sport had committed to any concrete timetable for coming back. Speeding ahead in its return, the PBR organization had been second-guessed—not a surprise when everyone was still learning about the virus and one pervasive school of thought was to stay completely shut down.

Personally, friendly reporters and former colleagues were privately saying, "We usually support what you guys at PBR are doing, but this is stupid. You're gonna kill people."

But this was no reckless, half-baked venture. The team had done their science-based homework to create common-sense protocols approved by the authorities with oversight. It was just a matter of responsibly executing the plan. In being brave yet disciplined, the sport demonstrated a path forward. Six weeks after the country shut down all live sports, PBR began bucking bulls.

The canary would make it out of the coal mine. PBR would go on to safely hold twenty event weekends, thirteen with fans in the stands in 2020. And when other pro sports finally came back, all the big leagues outside of PBR and the UFC saw their television ratings plummet, some at record-setting drops. PBR's TV audience would increase 8 percent.

None of this should be lost to sports fans. Or anyone who wants their old life back.

Of course, our lives *have* changed. Questions and uncertainty remain about when things can fully return to "normal." With variants emerging, health guidance flip flopping, and honest questions about the vaccine (which PBR strongly encouraged for all staff and competitors) discouraged, will full normalcy ever return? But there is one certainty for those following the cowboys and bulls. After Leme rose from his knees near the fifty-yard line where the Dallas Cowboys usually play on Sunday to gratefully raise the 2020 championship cup, long after the back pen, bucking chutes, and fences came down and the dirt was vacuumed up and hauled away, the significance of what PBR accomplished during the first year of the virus will endure.

For when confronted with the daunting and potentially deadly challenges of a scary invisible threat and hearing the discouraging voices of skeptics who said, *you can't,* a group of stalwart cowboys answered, *yes, we can.*

They rose together, bold and brave, like our country's early pioneers slowly rolling west on a caravan of wagon trains, leading us toward faint light at the end of a very long tunnel.

Love & Try

12

HEAVY IS THE CROWN

(Bull Stock Media)

In its mash-up of sports and entertainment, deadly serious bull rides and clowning riffs, hard hits and funny bits, there is no sport quite like PBR. And there's one passionate, complicated man at the center of its unique presentation, who has arguably done more to shape the experience of attending a PBR event than anyone else.

His role truly is unusual. Play along and imagine this:

You're at an NFL game—a series of violent collisions with down time between plays worthy of the nightly highlights reel. For months ahead of this outing, you had been told to keep away from people. Now the cabin fever has subsided; you're finally allowed back into your favorite stadium. You're in the stands, surrounded by other lock-down parolees, having a grand time because you're out free among other human beings in a sporting arena again, and even more so because during breaks in the frenetic action, out on the fifty-yard line presides an Entertainer. He is part stand-up comedian, part game show emcee, He's in a uniform, shorts, and a jersey with brand logos on his chest and back, strutting around the playing field, bantering with the crowd.

"Breaking news! I want to alert you to a new study," he declares. "It has been determined that strangers in the actual physical presence of one another, without masks on, are much more likely to have a good time."

Very few people with a public platform can joke about a deadly virus in the course of their employment and get to keep their jobs. But the crowd loves it.

The Entertainer has now locked in on a group of young men a few rows off field level. The in-house camera zooms on the motley group, now seen on the Jumbotron, grinning with beers in hand. Each is wearing a hair style instantly recognizable as a mullet.

"Guys, I had that haircut back in 1979 ... and I wore it a lot better," The Entertainer says. "And this is what you have to look forward to."

The Entertainer rips off his cowboy hat, revealing a bald spot the size of an IHOP pancake.

"A solar panel ... that powers your love machine! We're talking Green Energy!"

The chorus of laughter from real people enjoying a live sporting event sounds louder than The Entertainer remembered it. He is pumped. He is still filling the commercial break. For another minute or so, the floor is his.

"Folks, let me tell you one thing, and don't you ever forget it: There's only one Saturday night a week. Let's not screw it up!"

Loud toe-tapping fiddle music comes up over the stadium loudspeakers. He does what appears to be cross between a happy Irish jig and a suggestive twerk. Then the music segues into "Billie Jean." His body has straightened up, and, out of nowhere, there's a fedora on his head. He's floating backwards into a perfectly executed moonwalk, as if infused by the ghost of Michael Jackson. The crowd is cheering, louder and louder. The music fades and all eyes go back to the action beginning to resume.

This wasn't an exercise in imagining a weird new way to watch the NFL. It's exactly what happens in the PBR every weekend. There's nothing like

Pilfering David Lee Roth's electric blazer. (Bull Stock Media)

it. No sport combines punishing unscripted athletic competition with full-on comedy. In PBR, it's brought to fans by the sport's wisecracking, twerking, moonwalking, mullet-loving, solar-panel flashing, bachelorette-party aficionado, and exclusive entertainer Flint Rasmussen.

Since 2005, the master of ceremonies, on-dirt quarterback, sultan of sarcasm (that manages not to feel sarcastic), and chief instigator of both the mischief and the unfiltered musings playing out across events showcasing the height of athletic daring and subsequent broken bones (how's that for a challenging backdrop for making people laugh) has been a fifty-one-year old former school teacher done up in clown makeup, patrolling the dirt as if it's the maple wood stage floor of Carnegie Hall and making jokes that sound like Eddie Murphy crossed with Larry the Cable Guy.

If nothing else, PBR is one darn fun time. It is Rasmussen who sets the tone and moderates the mood. Former PBR CEO Randy Bernard has said that Flint has been as important to the sport's growth as any single cowboy or bull. What Flint has said about fan-favorite riders like J.B. Mauney, Jess Lockwood, and Chase Outlaw on his show *According to Flint* on SiriusXM applies right back to him: He's good for business.

Fans have said they'd buy a ticket to see Flint even if they didn't much care for the bull riding. It's hard for any fan to imagine what the premier series would feel like without him. Maybe that's why so many ask him about his heart; Rasmussen suffered a heart attack when he was only forty-one years old. He tells them, "It must be OK; it was beating when I got up this morning." Flint had two stents put in, went on blood thinners, was told not to get rammed by a bull, and only missed less than forty days.

He still thinks about his heart every day and, as he's gotten older, has had to depend less on physical comedy and dancing. Yet when PBR began to host fans in the arena following the for-TV events during COVID, Flint was doing cartwheels in the arena. Not metaphorically. At fifty-one, he was performing actual cartwheels. "I am in very good shape and can still shake it pretty dang well," he said.

But this is not a one-man show. Flint considers himself a spoke in a wheel, as he plays off arena announcers Clint Atkins and Matt West with Richard Jones providing the musical soundtrack all under the show direction of Dan Hickman. He likes a rock and roll band analogy Atkins uses, where if the bass player has an off night, the other band members pick him up, and nobody really notices.

Before he joined the gold standard for entertainment in Western sports, Flint had always been funny, but unlike so many bull riders who knew exactly what they wanted to be from the time they could walk, he didn't grow up planning for life clowning in the rodeo, let alone reinventing the job in the transformative way he would. In his hometown of Havre, Montana, he wasn't a show-off or the class clown. But he liked to have fun and get a reaction. (A collection of his mother Tootsie's old Christmas letters sent out annually in the late 1970s has a recurring theme: "Flint still entertains us.") He was a regular in school plays and sang in the choir, getting a taste of adulation from an appreciative audience. There was a constant "pull" to be in front of crowds performing. Growing up in the Western culture, there was always a place drawing crowds eager to be entertained: rodeo.

When Flint was nineteen, during the summer, first on a dare, he began working amateur rodeos in Montana, getting nervous like he did playing high school football (making All-State), but having an absolute ball in making people smile and laugh. He was no longer an athlete. But being out on the dirt performing in front of people during a rodeo competition was scratching an itch. It felt good. It was *fun*—an emotion he tries to remember when sixteen years later, body parts he didn't know he had ache, the airport food court is closed because no one wants to go to work anymore, and the airline has canceled yet another connecting flight.

Flint treated rodeo like a summer job. The plan was to get through college and then teach. After graduating from the University of Montana Western, he would get a job teaching high school math and history. But he kept getting phone calls. Rodeo organizers who had caught his act saw potential. Promoters know their crowds, and he was busting them up. This Flint Rasmussen character just might make a name for himself if he gave it a chance, they said. He quit teaching school at twenty-five and began performing at professional rodeos.

"I was single and didn't owe anybody anything and didn't own anything. I thought, 'I'll try this for a couple of years,'" Rasmussen told *Tulsa World* in a January 2021 profile.

During one slow period in the fall, a rodeo in Hibbing, Minnesota called. Their regular rodeo clown couldn't make the event because his trailer caught fire on the highway. Could Rasmussen come?

Flint did his thing, impressing one of the stock contractors, who recommended him to rodeo promoter Jerome Robinson, who happened to be planning a few winter shows. Robinson was producing PBR's first events in the 1990s and used Rasmussen there as well. One man's very unlucky trailer fire lit the fuse for Rasmussen's rise, so to speak. But truth be told, there was a lot of simmering powder already in place. It's hard to imagine he would not have been "discovered" to play much bigger stages.

Music is a big part of Rasmussen's appeal, and he's benefitted from PBR's emphasis on contemporary music and investment in expensive, high-clarity, high-power sound systems hauled city to city. With PBR Music Directors Richard Jones and Brad Narducci playing off Rasmussen's lead, every event is loaded with singing and dancing to get the crowd going. Leading fans through Journey's "Don't Stop Believin'" and Neil Diamond's "Sweet Caroline" is a staple. Flint still hits the high notes every show on "Your Love" by The Outfield (changing a few lines for comic effect). On Saturday nights, near nine o'clock, he's known to break out a harmonica and sing Billy Joel's "Piano Man."

Flint claims to not be musically inclined but don't tell that to Bernie Taupin, the lyricist and musical partner of Elton John. Taupin used to own a few bulls, including being a partner on legendary Little Yellow Jacket and one called Rocket Man. He's been to a number of PBR events. At one of them, Flint pretended to play piano on a Billy Joel song piped in over the PA.

"You really play the piano, don't you?" Taupin later asked him.

His daughters, Paige and Shelby, are talented musicians (in addition to rodeo athletes; as a Montana State University sophomore, Paige won the College National Finals Rodeo all around championship in 2021), but Flint had to confess he can't play a lick of piano. Faking out a legend, who has partnered on selling more than three hundred million records and written the words to fifty Top 40 hits, was a pretty good compliment.

The bit that fooled Taupin shows the range of Flint's talents as he modernized the role of traditional rodeo clowns, previously confined to baggy outfits, telling a certain style of corny jokes, and participating in silly skits. The only "clown" thing about Flint is his exaggerated circus makeup, which

Flint signs Holly Holm…and the UFC superstar returns the favor. (Bull Stock Media)

he held onto as a salute to rodeo tradition and to distinguish him from the U.S. Border Patrol cowboy-protection team of bullfighters he works with.

Makeup on, Flint has transformed the role to be more like stand-up comedy with singing, impromptu bits, and physical performances. Because he is so much more than a clown, PBR decided to call him their official entertainer.

Instead of channeling previous rodeo clowns, his inspirations are athletes, comedians, and musicians. His favorite basketball player was "Dr. J." Julius Erving, who was "a great player and great entertainer all in one." He watched Michael Jackson wow crowds of every age and believes he's the greatest entertainer of all time. Musically, Billy Joel, Bon Jovi, and Garth Brooks are revered influences, and he has studied the comedians Eddie Murphy, Howie Mandel, and Jerry Seinfeld for their timing and masterful ability to hold an audience's fickle attention.

It's not always all fun and games on the dirt. Rasmussen has been hit and hooked by bulls.

"Most people probably look at my job and say, 'I could do that,' because it looks like I am just out there goofing around. But there is a lot going on," Flint said in an interview with *This Week in New York*, prior to the season launching at Madison Square Garden in New York in 2020. "If I'm not paying attention at any given time, I could get hurt very badly. But as far as the bulls go, I think people in cities don't understand that most of us grew up in a rural, ranch-type setting. We have grown up either around, or directly involved in, the large-animal industry. This lifestyle exists in a strong way in this country. It is how people eat! Yes, bucking bulls are different. But they aren't bucking because they are pissed off. They are bucking because their bloodlines tell them that is what they are here to do. Not every horse runs fast. But the ones in the Kentucky Derby are bred to do it, so they do. Bulls are not rare, exotic circus animals. There are millions of people in this country who are around bovines every single day to provide food for this country and to make a living for their families. So, when anyone in the PBR is face-to-face with a bull, they aren't really thinking; they are reacting in the way that their body and mind have been conditioned to over the years."

He's not done yet in what is a Cowboy Hall of Fame career. There have already been plenty of accolades and awards: he's an eight-time Professional Rodeo Cowboys Association Clown of the Year and eight-time Wrangler National Finals Rodeo Barrelman.

While influencing a generation of new Western sports entertainers, Rasmussen remains the perfect man for the biggest job—holding court in PBR arenas. While the "show" is helped by his dancing and jokes, the sport is unscripted, raw, and dangerous. Amid the mayhem on the dirt, Flint's heart is right on his sleeve as he pushes the envelope, including sneaking more and more social satire into his act, especially during COVID-19. He found a way to dance around the absurdity of the situation at a time when questioning one-size-fits-all health mandates is verboten. A half-year after PBR's super spreader of joy publicly set the tone for spotlighting the day-to-day absurdity of life during a virus that now appears to be laboratory-engineered, partially funded by your tax dollars, comedians like Jon Stewart and Bill Maher then followed Rasmussen's lead in their acts to joke about what the nation has been put through.

When PBR came back from the shutdown and was first to welcome fans into the arena, in Sioux Falls, South Dakota, Rasmussen was at his best. During the outset of another one of the sport's milestones in scratching and clawing back to normalcy, he again found a way to articulate what everyone was feeling.

Flint looked up at the crowd and said, "This is almost like ... Life. This is almost ... America. I want to thank every fan tonight for coming out and letting us do our jobs for you."

Love & Try

13

DOCTOR OF THE DINGED UP COWBOYS

(Bull Stock Media)

Madison Square Garden was rocking like a panel van on lover's lane on opening night of the 2016 season as Silvano Alves busted out of the bucking chutes on Cochise, a big, rank bull the color of Mississippi mud with devilish, downward-pointing horns.

Cochise hopped out straight, taking two quick jumps. He veered to the left, jumping twice more. Alves, who already had three PBR gold championship buckles, tying fellow Brazilian Adriano Moraes for the most in the sport's history, was on him like white on rice. Forget the bull's powerful gyrations. Alves was master of this ride, ready for a high score. Or so it appeared. On the third jump, as if Cochise were greased with oil, Alves slid off onto the ground. The bull kept bucking, Alves down on his side. A hind leg blasted down onto his helmet, snapping it off his neck. Silvano was out cold. To punctuate who was the real boss, Cochise kept thrashing and stomped on Alves's back before being lured away by the three bullfighters frantically working to protect a defenseless rider in serious trouble.

Soon as Alves went limp, fans in the building, who can get loud enough to shake the entire edifice, went completely silent. The bullfighter protection team was still managing Cochise, and the walk-off gate next to the bucking chutes shot open. A man in sharply creased Wranglers, starched denim shirt, slick boots, and black cowboy hat who'd been standing next to the side of the bucking chutes sprinted out to Alves. Dr. Tandy Freeman dropped to his knees, positioned so the rider's head was square between his legs. Boring his knees into the dirt, Freeman bent forward, cradling Alves's head, making sure it was stabilized, and began to assess his condition. In three decades as a Western sports doctor, he had seen many bad wrecks like this and was mentally flipping through a checklist to make a diagnosis and determine next steps.

In the media moat by the fence maybe ten feet from where Alves laid, I was watching PBR's doctor, now surrounded by his sports medicine team. It was my first time managing PR for a bull riding event in this dream arena, my favorite structure in the world, thirty miles from where I grew up on Long Island, magical home of my Rangers and Knicks, the beloved circus as a kid, then McCartney, Elton John, The Who, Billy Joel, and Bruce. And now one of the greatest dream-come-true nights in my life—finally working an event in this *sports cathedral*, an All-Access badge dangling over my chest—had become panic time. A sheen of sweat worked its way down my back. What adequate words can you possibly write to announce the death of a legendary athlete on opening night of a new season?

I was a rookie with PBR events but instinctively stared at the doctor for any body language clue signaling how bad this was. Graying at the temples, Dr. Freeman is immutably stoic; he doesn't telegraph much. During the triage, however, Alves began communicating with the staid doctor. His legs moved. Great sign. Soon, the rider with the thick crop of black hair was sitting up, then on his feet. As he was slowly led to the locker room by two members of the sports medicine team, the Garden crowd broke into howling applause, rows of astonished fans now standing, egged on by the arena announcer shouting about "the toughest athletes in sports." New Yorkers may not always know exactly what they're screaming about during a great bull ride, but they certainly can identify exceptional toughness, and these athletes they came to see were displaying uncommon levels of that quintessentially New York trait.

Tending to bull riders like Alves, whose injuries can be grizzly, was the proverbial "'nother day at the office" for PBR's so-called "doctor in the dirt."

At every PBR premier series event, Dr. Tandy Freeman sets up shop close to the athlete locker room, operating what is akin to a small emergency room in a hospital off the side of a freeway on an icy New Year's Eve. Then he stands next to the chutes, often holding a Styrofoam cup of coffee, closely observing the world's most dangerous organized sport—the only one in which a lightweight goes up against a heavyweight. Injury is ever present. Tandy has estimated he has medically presided over more than one hundred thousand bull rides, and with studies showing one in fifteen rides ends in some type of injury, that means he's attended to more than fifteen thousand injury situations.

He grew up in a Texas ranching community, but he has never mounted a bull. Yet his presence at PBR events is essential in making sure the competitors stay healthy, are treated promptly for the injuries that are a grim certainty, and, more importantly, can have a future beyond the few years of an average elite level bull riding career.

It's been said that Dr. Freeman is not your normal doctor, because his patients in PBR are not your normal athletes. Sure, he's seen his share of trauma. His orthopedic residency was at Parkland Memorial Hospital in Dallas, one of the busiest trauma centers in the country, which had treated John F. Kennedy after he was shot, along with the president's alleged assassin, Lee Harvey Oswald, two days later. Plenty of doctors see gore. What makes Freeman different is his holistic, realistic approach in counseling his special risk-taking patients after the trauma. He understands and appreciates the unique hard-headed mentality of bull riders. Attending to their frequent, serious injuries, the standard physician would simply advise riders to stop. Tandy realizes that in his sport, this is impractical, useless, and counterproductive advice. It completely dismisses the riders' cowboy core. It devalues what they do and how they feed their families. It overlooks their purpose. Bull riding is their essence—*who they are.*

Love & Try

As much as diagnosing and treating physical trauma, Freeman's job is to find a balance in treatment and recovery so the riders can be themselves without killing themselves. And, when they do stop competing, be left in a physical condition to go on with a relatively normal life.

Freeman may tell bull riders it's not the world's smartest idea to tape up a broken wrist or ankle or ride through a painful dislocated joint to be popped back in after he hits the ground. But after explaining the risk, he won't stop a

Dr. Freeman (left, pale blue shirt) a

rider with non-catastrophic injuries from competing. Sometimes, he'll even help to ensure ride-on decisions don't maim them.

This rider-friendly approach to keeping the boys competing helped Luke Snyder set a record that may never be surpassed: competing in 275 consecutive PBR events. That would be a pretty good run for showing up to play darts let alone *bull ridings*. During nine years of not missing an event, Snyder battled through a torn rotator cuff, a broken right hand, a groin pull, and a broken fibula.

"The streak would have stopped any time Tandy had said, 'You shouldn't be doing this.' He didn't," Snyder said. In fact, when the Missouri cowboy broke his leg, Freeman created a makeshift cast allowing him to ride on.

Oh, and Snyder also broke his neck during the streak, which would end in 2009, but the injury coincided with a pause in the schedule, so he didn't miss any events. "As far as broken necks go, I couldn't have done it better, because it was a hairline fracture of my C7," he said. "When you mess around with your neck, it's no joking matter. But it didn't require surgery."

As special as Snyder is as a stubborn, tenacious athlete (with a good sense of humor: he calls his

Stormy Wing on the dirt inside the Sprint Center in Kansas City. (Bull Stock Media)

record "the perfect attendance award"), he's not an outlier among his peers in tuning out pain in order to "get on bulls to feed your babies," as Chase Outlaw says. Freeman cites an unpublished pain tolerance study from the 1980s in which athletes from different sports took a test—immersing their hands into a bucket of ice water and timed for how long they could stand it before pulling out. All of the participating Western sports athletes kept their hands in the ice the whole time, Freeman said. The only athletes who had a similar off-the-charts level for tolerating pain were hockey players and race car drivers.

"This sport is different than others," Freeman said. "You can't drive the lane in the NBA with a torn ACL, but you can ride a bull with that kind of injury. If these athletes don't compete, they don't eat. There's a lot of pressure to ride. The 'cowboy up' mentality is do your job, and don't whine about it. There's a grit-your-teeth-and-bare-down mentality. The guys who make it here to this level have the talent and ability to deal with injuries."

A badly banged up knee or cracked ribs is one thing. Attempting to play through other more serious injuries is another and won't be tolerated by Freeman. When it comes to internal organs or head and neck issues, he has the authority to put riders on the shelf, and he will exercise that power.

"The bull rider has a mentality that you go do your job, even if you're hurt. But sometimes we need to be saved from ourselves," Mauney said. "Bull riders trust Tandy and will listen to him, because he understands our mentality and our situation."

How much does Mauney trust Freeman? Following one dismount gone awry, he was dragged, flung, and stomped—knocked out cold. Or "taking a nap" as bull riders call it. Mauney's rotator cuff was torn completely off the bone. His arm hung to his body only because of his skin. Mauney trusted only one doctor to save his career: Freeman. Freeman operated on the shoulder, putting in thirteen anchors and a screw.

"[Tandy] knows what you can deal with and what you can't deal with, what can hurt you more," Mauney told writer Matt Crossman who wrote a superb feature on Freeman in *Cowboys & Indians*. "You put a different doctor in it who's never been around it and never seen anything like this, they'd be like, 'Holy s---'."

Freeman sees just about every common injury in sports—ACL tears, muscle strains and tears, ligament injuries, joint injuries, and broken bones.

But what makes his makeshift trauma center in the bowels of the arena not unlike that side-of-the-icy-freeway ER is treating what can amount to gruesome injuries like those caused by high-speed motor vehicle accidents, such as liver lacerations, brain bleeds, bruised kidneys, spleen ruptures, intra-abdominal injuries, and spine injuries.

"This is not a contact sport. It's a collision sport producing high-energy trauma," he said. "When you've got a seventeen hundred pound bull, and an individual competing more or less against an opponent more than ten times their size, it's a mismatch not seen in other sports. There is more energy involved in the injuries. But it's still a matter of taking care of athletes, educating them to the risks so they can make the right choice, and getting them back in competition as soon as it's safely possible."

The joke used to be that rodeo and bull riding sports medicine was "a bottle of aspirin and a six-pack of beer." And if that didn't work, you doubled up on the beer. Like most jokes, there was a lot of truth to the quip when Freeman first got involved in treating cowboy athletes.

As a young doctor out of medical school, he had developed a friendship with the physician, Dr. Pat J. Evans, who would professionalize Western sports medicine and modernize rodeo athlete wellness. Freeman first met Evans during his Dallas residency, after receiving his medical degree from University of Texas Southwestern Medical Center. Evans had been the team physician for the Dallas Cowboys and the Dallas Mavericks for decades, while cofounding the Justin Sports Medicine Team for rodeo athletes. Freeman had studied the way Evans dealt with his patients; the elder doctor became his orthopedic surgery mentor while shaping Freeman's bedside manner. They developed a close, lasting bond, and when Dr. Evans was approaching retirement, Freeman, who respected the blood, sweat, and tears Evans had put into the nascent rodeo sports medicine program, was the logical choice to take over this program.

Traveling with and observing Evans, who was popular and trusted among the cowboys, helped Freeman gain credibility with riders very happy with who they already had and wary of a new doctor, according to Crossman. Evans's endorsement helped win the riders' trust.

"I remember the first time J. Pat brought him around," Ty Murray told Crossman. "You're always a little skeptical. 'Who's this new guy?' It's pretty weird looking at it from this side now. We feel pretty darn lucky to have him.

It's important when you're talking about a sport like this that you have a doctor that you really believe in."

For more than two decades, Freeman has also served as PBR's medical director. Seeing riders week to week, and often fixing their broken bones and torn joints in his office in Texas, he has developed a profound patriarchal fondness for young athletes he wants to protect but knows will eventually get hurt. During an interview in New York with the respected documentary filmmaker and investigative journalist Mariana van Zeller, sitting on a stool above a pool of dried blood on the floor of the Sports Medicine Center, Freeman emotionally admitted he'd like nothing more than to remove all the catastrophic risk from the sport and provide the athletes an impenetrable armor of protection. But knows he can't do that. Heavyweights will always get the better of lightweights. And sometimes it will be ugly.

"These are professional athletes, and a lot of them are still kids," Freeman said, his voice breaking up. "They could be *my* kids. If I could make them all safe, that's what I'd do. I feel a great responsibility to do what I can to help them make good choices. I've been doing this nearly thirty years, twenty-seven with PBR. I'd like to think the things I've done have had a positive impact on people I take care of. I care about these athletes. I want them to be successful and healthy. I want them to leave this sport and have a future and the best possible options for their life ahead."

Despite his powerlessness in preventing serious injuries, Freeman has helped PBR take significant strides in its most significant advancement in athlete care: diagnosing and treating concussions, which was the injury Silvano Alves suffered in New York City.

Concussions make up about 15 percent of the injuries in PBR. Recognizing their long-term threat to any athlete's well-being, in 2012 PBR created concussion protocols to diagnose and treat head injuries. At the core of the program is creating a concussion baseline, which includes cognitive, balance, and ocular tests, as a screening tool. At the beginning of each season, riders visit Sports Medicine to record their baseline, including the cognitive tests, which Mauney called "The Idiot Test." Despite the joke, J.B. was all business in racing through exercises like repeating back five words read to him ("candle," "sugar," "paper," "sandwich," "wagon")—backwards—as well as the same with a series of numbers read to him in rapid succession, such as "718462." Mauney attacked the questions as if they were an IQ test given to him by a bull who had humiliated him with the results to be broadcast on the evening news.

I asked Mauney why he motored through the exercise so intensely and competitively without even considering going slowly to set a low baseline that could easily be passed.

"'Cause I don't plan on getting knocked out much," he said.

Yet even world champions occasionally "go to sleep" on the dirt. Following such a blow to the head—knockout or not—riders must be retested following physical exertion on an exercise bike, which serves to bring out any symptoms. Riders who don't come within 10 percent of their baseline are not allowed to compete in PBR until they are symptom free (including no headaches or nausea) and then pass the test against baseline.

The system is reliant on the bull rider athletes being honest in how they're feeling. If they meet their baseline test, there's no way PBR can stop them from getting on a bull. "The bull riders are independent contractors who have the right to make a living," Freeman said. "Riders have to self-report symptoms and then would be referred to specialists who they'd see voluntarily. Visiting the specialist is their choice. That said, the tests do motivate an athlete to be honest, and we've had a lot more discussions about head injuries throughout the sport creating more openness to seek out specialists when recommended."

Freeman notes that science is still unclear on when a person has fully recovered from a concussion. And contrary to popular belief, loss of consciousness is not an indicator of the severity of a concussion. The duration and severity of the symptoms of a concussion determines how bad one is. PBR's response has been to focus on carefully diagnosing head injuries, relying on riders to share any problematic symptoms they may be feeling, then staying stringent to testing against individual baselines before any rider diagnosed with a concussion can return to action.

"The best method we have for this injury is for a person recovering from a concussion to undergo physical and cognitive tests that are compared to their baseline results when normal," he said. "We also focus on educating athletes on the risks of concussions, particularly in going back to competition before the brain fully heals."

PBR's concussion protocol, which was developed in 2012 and has been updated several times along with new advancements, is now among the most stringent in professional sports. Freeman is not a neurological expert; he'll refer riders to neurologists. He points out he is an expert at identifying when a rider has had a concussion, and he will err on the side of diagnosing one. Once that determination has been made, riders automatically enter the concussion protocol and will be held out of competition until medically cleared.

Alves, incidentally, passed his concussion test the day after getting pummeled by Cochise. He was back in the draw at Madison Square Garden to compete the rest of the weekend.

Meanwhile, other safety advancements in the sport, including mandating riders wear a protective vest as well as helmets required for those born after October 15, 1994, have helped make a difference. While helmets won't do much in preventing concussions—which, in bull riding, are more often the result of what happens inside the skull not outside it—they do help prevent facial fractures, skull fractures, and intracranial bleeds.

"I've seen more than one bull rider manage to avoid a head injury because he was wearing a helmet, and I'm pretty sure that at the very least he would have spent time in the intensive care unit and probably would not be riding any bulls anymore if he hadn't been wearing a helmet," Freeman said. Vests have also reduced the number of major intra-abdominal and chest injuries, according to Freeman.

Yet there's only so much protective equipment a cowboy can wear. And the bulls, overall, are getting stronger and more athletic. More sophisticated bull breeding is continually refining their bloodlines, producing more rank bulls in any given round today. But counterintuitively, that doesn't necessarily translate into more rider injuries.

"Getting on a bull who's not very good can be just as dangerous. You can get hurt getting off a bad bull," Freeman noted. In fact, bull riders have the same frequency of injuries today as two decades ago, according to statistical analysis. "Any sport where you can be potentially incapacitated or killed is a dangerous sport. This is one sport where every time the athlete goes out, he is taking a chance."

One thing isn't left to chance. When those athletes are thrashed, flung, smashed, and stomped, each one is personally assured that the man who rushes to their side is their advocate, ally, and one heck of a skilled physician. The rest is in God's hands.

Love & Try

14

FIRST RESPONDERS

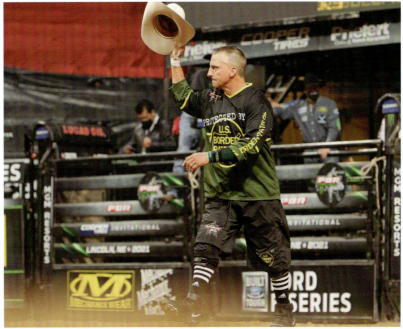

(Bull Stock Media)

In October 2021, veteran bullfighter Frank Newsom broke his leg on the dirt in Lincoln, Nebraska, a week before his sport's biggest event—PBR World Finals.

Mere mortals doing a job reliant on highly functioning legs to divert rampaging bulls from fallen riders, dashing time and again into the eye of a raging storm, would consider their already long season officially over. *It's a broken leg*! Pack it up. Head home to enjoy the off-season with the wife and kids.

That's just not Frank Newsom. His nickname is "Fearless Frank"—a spot-on descriptor of legendary toughness and grit. Few men who have entered a bull ring have fought off bulls as skillfully, valiantly, and with such fiery determination, for such a sustained period.

Throughout a quarter century of fighting bulls professionally, Newsom has sacrificed his body for the riders he's charged with protecting. Once kicked in the face by a bull, breaking his jaw, Newsom was visibly irked he put himself in that position—every injury is *always* his fault, never the bull's. Forced to sit out a day, he was livid. Another time, in Anaheim, stepping in to save Kaique Pacheco, he was completely smoked by a bull, concussed, and back-boarded from the arena, missing the next event. He was drilled from behind in Springfield, flipped like a flapjack, and reluctantly sent to the hospital. He's broken his scapula and every one of his ribs.

During his career, Fearless Frank has kept countless less-conspicuous injuries to himself. While a busted leg would put the usual bullfighter on the shelf, Newsom was raised a different way. Buckle down, suck it up, and get the job done. If there were any way to join his U.S. Border Patrol Protection Team partners, Cody Webster, Lucas Teodoro, and Jesse Byrne, on the dirt at the 2021 World Finals—the final one in Las Vegas before the five-day competition moved to Fort Worth, Texas for 2022 and beyond—Frank would find a way.

Beyond its pomp and spectacle, the black carpet arrivals, and wall-to-wall TV coverage, World Finals held an even greater meaning for the forty-six-year-old bullfighter. Twenty-one years earlier, he had been scheduled to be working the sport's most prestigious event. But that time he was out of commission. It wasn't due to injury. It was the consequence of addiction. Newsom was sitting in an Oklahoma jail cell.

His life had spiraled out of control—the result of the convergence of his new freedom, money in his pocket, and an all-or-nothing personality that was no match for chemical temptation. Through it all, as crazy as it sounds, Newsom was committed to being a better bullfighter. It didn't mean much to the arresting officer that he was only using the methamphetamine to stay up to drive all night to the next bull riding where he'd take more to get jacked up to do the best job in making sure nobody got hurt.

Newsom was born in Oklahoma and raised in Texas as a churchgoing kid by his dad, a ranch worker and animal nutritionist with a degree from Texas

A&M, and his mom, an elementary school teacher. Now, all that freedom gone, he was sitting in a dank jail cell wondering how his life got to be so messed up to be here instead of inside a Las Vegas locker room strapping on his gear to be among the bravest protecting the toughest athletes in sports in a globally televised championship. He cried out to the Lord for help.

"I really wanted Jesus," Newsom said. "And He showed up."

Straightening up his life would take hard work. But that was okay; Frank had always been around hard-working men whom he looked up to. "If you wanted something in life, you worked hard for it," he said.

Fortunately, the right people would show up as well. A good friend, Rob Smets, a fellow World Championship bullfighter, introduced him to rancher Randy Stalls, who put Newsom to work on his ranch in the Texas panhandle, a place where Newsom didn't know anyone. He got up early and worked until the sun went down. He attended AA meetings. He put in the work to pull himself up and get his life together, clawing his way up from the bottom to make it back to the top of the PBR.

Despite the gruff, tough exterior, Newsom is soft-spoken and reserved. He is quiet about his faith. He's not a preacher. He's not out to convert anyone to anything. Still, when called by churches or other organizations, he shares his story.

At first, he wasn't comfortable talking about himself. It was difficult to open up. As with everything Frank Newsom does, he worked at it. He's open about his past, his struggles, the pain he saw in his wife Dea's eyes when relapsing, and his blessed redemption. He believes the Lord wants him to share his story of mercy granted and accepted to help others trapped in addiction. God continues to have a job for him to do, and every job deserves your all.

Now in November 2021, back at his nineteenth World Finals, Newsom's head and heart were in the right place, but his left leg wasn't. There was already a plate in that broken leg from a previous bull mishap, and he limped into PBR Sports Medicine at T-Mobile Arena to shore up his body. On the table amid shirtless bull riders being pulled and stretched and massaged, he was given a thorough tape job and air cast to the top of his calf muscle. "It felt pretty good and strong," he said. "A few times I'd step the wrong way and it would hurt, but it was pretty stable. They made me as strong as they could, and I was ready to be there."

Love & Try

Early in Round 1 on the first of five days of competition, Brazilian rider Leonardo Lima charged out of the opening gate on a dark brown bull named Liston. Some bulls head right to the back pen when the rider is thrown, and their job is done. Liston was one who wanted to taste some more action.

The bullfighter's job is like a first responder: automatically, instinctively rushing in. Newsom was near the steel fence, and he hesitated just a bit. In a split second, Liston veered toward Newsom, planted into the dirt, and crushed him into the metal wall. Frank's blue eyes shot wide open in shock and pain. He was stunned, but he never went down, staggering like a boxer taking a big shot in the fifteenth round.

He appeared to be done.

But first appearances are incomplete assumptions with Frank Newsom. He gritted his teeth, caught his breath, pulled his cowboy hat down, and got mad. It was vintage Newsom—when hurt badly, just bear down even harder.

"I hesitated a little bit and paid for it," he said. "At that moment, I was so frustrated and pissed, plus the pain was bad; it was a bit of a turning point for the week. The rest of the Finals, I was hurtin' worse. I couldn't sleep well. But I put on a more aggressive mindset. Some bulls test you. That one did. You battle on. Either you're all the way in, or you're out. We got through it."

Newsom says "we" because bullfighting is a team endeavor. Without the three or four bullfighters on the dirt operating as one—knowing each other's

Frank Newsom coming to the aid of Keyshawn Whitehorse (Bull Stock Media)

First Responders

Newsom with his protégé Cody Webster. (Bull Stock Media)

moves and tendencies, able to anticipate where their teammates will go before they've stepped in that direction—a lot more bull riders would get hurt. Those riders are comfortable putting their lives in the hands of bullfighters, who are called "the secret service" of PBR for the way they, as a matter of training and duty, throw their body in front of the proverbial assassin's bullet. In this job of ultimate service and sacrifice, the bullfighters, too, are a unit protecting one another. Newsom's closest teammate is his protégé, a thirty-year-old bullfighter named Cody Webster, who is like a son to him.

Webster, who was at his sixth World Finals in Vegas, was a scrawny kid when he showed up on Newsom's front porch at his place in Paoli, Oklahoma, in the early 2000s.

Little Cody, who lived five miles away, hadn't been much of a student. In fact, he disliked just about anything that had to do with school. One day in the library, he found something he liked a lot—a rodeo book. In those pages, he saw a bullfighter called "Fearless Frank," a former high school football captain now in a sport centered on bulls rather than a pigskin and putting his body in harm's way to save fallen bull riders.

Bullfighting was brave and cool. Saving cowboys. Now that was something a superhero would do.

Cody just about wore out that book. He wanted to be just like Frank Newsom—saving bull riders from rampaging bulls.

When young Webster showed up at the house of the man he was studying, he didn't want a photo or an autograph. He was lugging along cleats and a bullfighting dummy: he was there to convince the great Frank Newsom to teach him to fight bulls. He was eleven years old.

It didn't take long for Newsom to see he was dealing with a wild colt full of vast potential. The kid had *that look* in his eye—the expression of someone who wants something he's gonna get, and nobody's gonna take it away. He wasn't about to coddle the youngster.

One time, Cody was in the practice pen fighting bulls, smack in the middle of the action, where he always was. A bull caught the kid, hit him in the head, and flipped him. Cody landed against the bottom rail of the fence, and his arm went through the slats. The bull got on top of the defenseless boy and snapped a few of his ribs.

"Being a little kid ... man," Webster remembered when recounting the story on Flint Rasmussen's *According to Flint* podcast. "It hurts now!"

His ribs hurt so much he could barely breathe. He couldn't cry if he wanted to.

A young girl on the side had been videotaping the training. Newsom called out to the injured boy, "If you're hurting too bad you can go video this, and she can come fight bulls."

Newsom walked off.

This is the way a kid learns. Frank had seen the fire in Cody's eyes. So how bad did he *really* want it? It was time for the kid to decide.

The answer came quickly.

"I look back, and Cody's there gritting his teeth. He's not gonna leave. He bears down. I'm thinking, '*Lord please don't let us kill this kid today.*' That bull ran over him pretty good. You could tell he was hurt bad, but he kept wanting to go on. And you know what, he finishes the day out."

It was as if Newsom were watching a younger version of himself, a kid who understood beyond his years the importance of a job to do. You're not done until you're done. Even if you're hurt, you finish the job.

Hearing Newsom tell the story, Webster acknowledges it was a turning point in his life. "I knew then this is what I was set out to be," he said.

Webster became a constant fixture at Newsom's ranch. In an unofficial apprenticeship, he learned from one of the greatest bullfighters to enter a rodeo ring. The hardest thing was holding Cody back, away from the meaner, older bulls.

"He always wanted to go in there and do what the older men were doin'," Newsom said. "I could see all that talent. It wasn't like I was feeding him to the wolves. He was always bugging me so much. *'C'mon lemme get in there!'*"

As a bull fighting team, Webster and Newsom are good for one another. "He gives me a slap in the head when I need it and I do the same with him. We pick each other up," Newsom said.

Webster would first make it to World Finals in 2014, getting there through the ultimate sign of respect. Bullfighters are voted in by the very bull riders whose necks are on the line. Webster was only twenty-three when first chosen for the sport's most prestigious event alongside his mentor, Newsom, who had missed a few Finals years earlier but then turned his life around and remains a man every rider wants running in when he's down.

That rodeo library book is still checked out. Nearly twenty years later, Cody Webster is still learning from Fearless Frank Newsom about honesty and toughness, sacrificing for others, and finishing the job you started. Yet the most valuable lesson is also the hardest for any of us. And that is, for a man to save others, he must first be saved himself.

Love & Try

15

MISS CINDY'S PLACE

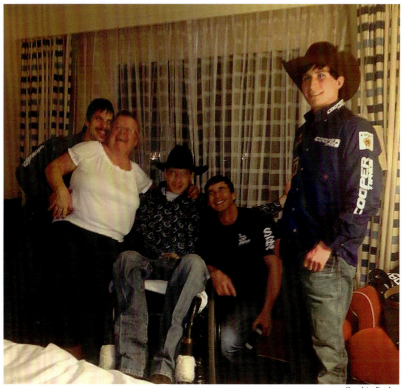

Cynthia Becker

It was just after 3 a.m. in Cynthia Becker's cluttered Charlottesville hotel room when the party had finally cleared out. She collapsed into the queen-size bed in the ground-level room with a view of the parking lot. She didn't mind being so low in the building. It was preferable, considering the massive haul of food and drink that had been brought in: more than a dozen coolers of beer and chicken and pork and seafood, trays of lasagna, and plates of cookies, along with crock pots and buffet tins, and the cans of Sterno underneath.

"Miss Cindy," the name she was affectionately called by all those who'd dropped by earlier, had barely killed the light and closed her eyes when she heard playful knocking on the sliding glass door facing the parking lot.

Miss Cindy, who was in her late fifties, grabbed her eyeglasses and sprang from the bed. She tugged the scratchy curtain aside to see a couple of jaunty young men in cowboy hats, kicking out booted legs sideways while raising their arms. Then they started doing loose-goosey jumping jacks. Variety Hour—albeit a late one—had come to the Hilton parking lot. Miss Cindy knew these guys. It was Luke Snyder and L.J. Jenkins, performing a ridiculous version of "The Freddie," a dance fad from the 1960s made famous by Chubby Checker.

Miss Cindy was about dying with laughter. The boys were hungry, and still thirsty, and every nearby diner and watering hole was closed. There was, really, only one place to go—to the fan who'd become every rider's favorite crazy aunt with a sense of humor as nutty as theirs and a tantalizing spread of homemade grub, cold bottles of beer, and plenty of wine. Miss Cindy slid the door open, still laughing, knowing she was joining the kind of fun daylight doesn't discourage.

The gallivanting cowboys knew the location of Miss Cindy's room because it was common knowledge, a valuable piece of information shared with all the riders, crew, and staffers. Whenever Miss Cindy was at a bull riding, her room number was posted in the locker room and blasted over text messages. Miss Cindy wanted it that way. Anyone on tour—riders, crew, TV—was encouraged to visit.

In Charlottesville, the late hour didn't matter. Miss Cindy's was never off limits. During bull riding weekends, sleep was time wasted. Luke and L.J. weren't the first or last PBR cowboys who would rouse Miss Cindy out of bed.

Miss Cindy has been running a veritable bar and grill out of her hotel room at most PBR events east of the Mississippi since 2006. Entering the 2022 season, however, COVID-19 continued the pause put on a scene that's hard to imagine occurring once, let alone for fourteen years, in any other professional sport. Before the act of human beings jamming into limited indoor arenas became verboten, she had fed the world's top cowboys more than one hundred times.

How Cynthia Becker's ambitious operation came to fruition can be said to be a story of necessity mothering invention.

It started with a camera. She took pictures at as many bull ridings as she could get to. "Wiley Peterson called me 'Paparazzi' because I'd sneak up on him and the guys," she said. The photos were for scrapbooks, which she donated to the Rider Relief Fund, raising $10,000 at an auction to help pay injured bull riders' medical bills.

One of the best places to play paparazzi was the hotel lobbies where riders would congregate, especially late at night. "At the time, there were about ten riders who were underage," Miss Cindy recalled. "These kids couldn't get anything to eat because they weren't allowed in the hotel bar."

One eighteen-year-old cowboy had caught her special attention: up-and-coming cowboy Brian Canter, who stood 5'3" and weighed 115 pounds but acted like he was 6'5", 250 pounds. Canter was a riding partner of fellow North Carolinian, J.B. Mauney. At first, the cocky SOB got on J. B.'s nerves. But Mauney's dad had given him sage advice: you'll only be as good as with the guys you rodeo with. Mauney asked Cantor to go on the road with him. They weren't exactly peas and carrots, but they sure became close. At the time, a determined cowboy in North Carolina could find bull ridings any day within a three hundred-mile drive. Seven days a week, Mauney and Cantor hit rodeos, jackpots, open bull ridings, practice pens, you name it. Canter was otherworldly. Riding every day, he fell off fewer than a half dozen bulls the entire year. "Just about every event I was sucking hind tit behind Brian," Mauney had told Flint Rasmussen on his podcast.

Years later, the rider many called the GOAT (or Greatest Of All Time) would say that Canter, who was initially taught to ride by PBR cofounder Jerome Davis, was the best bull rider he'd ever seen live in person.

Up at PBR, Canter would qualify for World Finals four straight years from 2006 to 2009, all the time getting physically punished. Miss Cindy remembers a time Canter was too hurt to walk. Two bull riders picked him up and lowered him onto the bull in the chutes. Canter rode for eighty-five points and had to crawl off the dirt. Nobody had more heart, but the physical punishment tore the kid up, and Canter's career was cut short.

Two other eighteen-year-olds, Jenkins and New Mexican Travis Briscoe also caught Miss Cindy's eye. The boys looked like they were starving. She wanted to help.

"You don't bitch about stuff in life. You do it. I started feeding them," she said.

At the next event in Charleston, South Carolina, in the hotel lobby, Becker began serving late-night sandwiches (sliced home-cooked ham, tuna, and ham salad) and light appetizers including deviled eggs, meat, and asparagus rolls, and a cheese and meat platter. She kept bringing food to events. Finally, hotels had had enough. The late-night lobby parties would relocate to her room.

"That's when I started making real meals," Becker said. "My formula was a poultry entrée, a beef, maybe New York Strip and the meatloaf that the guys loved, a pork, and a seafood like Thai shrimp, along with a vegetarian dish. There would be mac 'n' cheese and lasagna. I always made smoked BBQ—two full days in the smoker. Some vegetables, but the guys weren't too keen on that. I couldn't get them to eat anything green until Cody Nance came along."

The appetizers grew to include stuffed mushrooms, spinach artichoke dip, and spinach soufflé. And, of course, a full bar—beer and wine. "I used to go through a case of wine a night back when Versus was televising PBR. That TV staff would come by and really enjoy themselves."

On busy nights, more than a hundred people worked their way through. There were superstar riders coming in like Justin McBride, Ross Coleman, Rocky McDonald, and Snyder, sometimes bringing along NASCAR drivers. Chris Shivers, who had won the World Championship in 2000 and 2003, once strolled in wearing his cowboy boots tucked into little boy print pajamas.

It was like a contest to see who could make Miss Cindy laugh the hardest. The guys were unfiltered and comfortable in letting loose because Miss Cindy made it safe by setting two non-negotiable rules: no pictures and no autographs.

She never had a room trashed and was only kicked out once. That was in Philadelphia "the King Pin of them all," as she dubbed it, when Snyder brought up a group of Eagles. A suspicious little security guard saw the massive football players mingling with bull riders limping into Miss Cindy's room. He assumed bad behavior was brewing, when only a harmless good

Miss Cindy's Place

Miss Cindy (lower right) with her PBR crew. (Cynthia Becker)

time was transpiring. He called city police, who wound up posing for photos faking that they were cuffing Miss Cindy.

There were a few other close calls early on, like when Miss Cindy brought in a large microwave along with electric crock pots and hot plates.

"I had all the stuff plugged in, and the whole room goes dead," she said. "Brian Canter is running back and forth shouting, 'I'll fix this! I'll fix this!' There must have been twenty cowboys in the room. They didn't know me that well at the time and had expected me to get upset and explode. I came out with a bouquet of electric plugs. I hold them up and say, 'You suppose this is the way you start hotel fires?'"

The cowboys were quickly learning that half-crazy, perpetually lovable Miss Cindy was one of them. Word continued to spread.

After the blackout, she would switch to Sterno cans, adding more hot food. Her legend grew.

In New Orleans, there was a knock on her door at 4 a.m. She opened it without a thought. (She'd survived Woodstock after all!) "There's [bull rider] Douglas Duncan. I'd never met him, and he's all sheepish, just the cutest thing I'd ever seen. The first words he said were, 'Sean Willingham said you never go to sleep!'"

Next thing she knew, Rocky McDonald led in a line of cowboys toting their gear bags. With 6 a.m. flights, they'd stay with Miss Cindy until heading right to the airport.

Snyder claims the badge for leaving the latest—staying one Sunday morning in Atlanta until 10:30 a.m. when he split for his flight.

"Luke was one of my favorites," Miss Cindy said. "Him and guys like Mike White. I just loved those guys. They treated me not like an old lady but a big old clown ... they'd do such funny things to make me laugh. If you laugh at Luke, he just can't stop clowning around."

She remembers when Luke Kaufman brought his guitar to a party in Greenville, South Carolina, that wouldn't quit. At 5 a.m., the hotel manager moved the gathering to the lobby. "Luke Snyder says, 'Give me the guitar. I need to play something I learned in jail.' He takes the guitar and starts running a beer cap up and down the neck, so it sounds like a file—as if someone were trying to cut their way out of a prison cell!"

Laughs like that made the time and labor-intensive work worth it—all the dishes Miss Cindy cooked and froze, along with preparing salads, hors d'oeuvres and desserts. Each cooler (sixteen in all) weighed up to seventy pounds and was crammed into her Subaru Baja so tightly a single nickel couldn't fit between the canisters and the car's wheel wells. Then, add travel. During one stretch in 2016, Miss Cindy set up at five events in five weeks, driving nearly five thousand miles to and from her home in Pennsylvania. And factor in the cleanup, too, since Miss Cindy leaves every hotel room in better shape than when she had arrived.

Bringing so much joy to so many didn't come cheap. It was only after the grandmother of five blew through her inheritance that a tip jar came out. "The jar wasn't very profitable, but I always said, 'Jesus is my cohost.' I always seem to find the money," she said. (In 2015, to say thank you to a fan like no other, PBR CEO Sean Gleason paid to bring Miss Cindy to World Finals in Las Vegas, complete with chute-side seats.)

"Nobody told me to do this," she said. "It was my own idea. I took the initiative and did it. It worked because the riders and crew didn't have to be in *a fan's* room. Those guys got to know me first. I became their friend. Even the guys who have gone off and retired I'm friends with to this day."

So many friends and memories made, and then a terrible virus put Miss Cindy's Place out of business. "A couple lab scientists don't hose off properly when clocking out and the whole world is turned upside down," she joked.

Miss Cindy is as playfully mischievous and energetically industrious as ever. She's seventy-one now, but when the world stabilizes and the time is right, she'll be back. She'll set up at fewer events—four or five total hours sleep over a weekend ain't easy. The menu will scale down—sandwiches and fewer hot items should make for fewer coolers. The slow-cooked BBQ will be missed. But make no mistake, Miss Cindy's Place will be back.

As soon as it's deemed safe, bull riders will again be knocking on Miss Cindy's door. At any hour.

And it will always be open.

Love & Try

16

VOICE OF PBR IS AN EXTREME ATHLETE TOO

(Lois Schwartz)

"Chase Outlaw tossed like a human Frisbee!"

"Bruiser puts a bruising on Tanner Byrne!"

"Lockwood locked in ... and Rising Sun helps him to a fourth qualified ride here in Las Vegas!"

"Medicine Man trying to send Lucas to the hospital!"

"*Barbosa runs into the Right Stuff ... at the wrong time. He's down in 3.7!*"

"*Dracarys! Leme lights up the Pit here in Albuquerque!*"

Every PBR fan instantly recognizes these patented calls ... and the exuberant man behind the CBS mic they come from, one of the most under-appreciated play-by-play voices in sports.

What fans may not realize is that Craig Hummer, the voice of the PBR on CBS, is also an extreme athlete with serious street cred. Better yet, make that ocean cred.

The Emmy-nominated veteran broadcaster grew up an accomplished swimmer in Columbus, Ohio, winning his first medal when he was five years old. He was a three-time high school All-American, and the top Ocean Iron Man for most of the 1990s. Hummer competed in the professional Australian Iron Man circuit, considered the pinnacle of surf lifesaving, combining swimming, running, kayaking, and paddle boarding, virtually owning the ocean scene for close to a decade. At one point, he won the King's Race in Honolulu, Hawaii, four straight years. Ultimately, he won more than forty national and international lifesaving titles, including six consecutive International Ironman and nine straight Run-Swim-Run titles.

Hummer was as dominant on the Pacific Ocean as the championship bulls he now so colorfully describes are on the dirt.

He retired from being a full-time athlete in 1996, moving directly into broadcasting. But the competitive experience keeps Hummer inside the mindset of a "passion athlete," which he defines as those who'd compete in a grueling sport for no money at all. PBR has paid out nearly $200 million since its founding; some say the cowboys would still get on the rankest bulls on earth even without that kind of purse. Hummer was able to make a nice living on the spectacular shores of the Southern hemisphere of the world but admits he'd probably have done it for free.

Tapping into the experience as an aqua-sports extreme athlete gives the former swimming sensation from Columbus, Ohio, a unique perspective for covering pro bull riding. While he's never been on a bucking bull, Hummer can think like a rider.

"Even though my sport was not as extreme, going through a chaotic ocean break with twenty-foot surf plays into the mindset of a professional bull rider," he said. "At the PBR, I truly appreciate every single rider who has crossed my path, whether a world champion or someone who only got one qualified ride in his career. This is the top level of the sport in the world—we preach that on CBS week in and out. It's one of the biggest reasons I love my job. I'm around the greatest athletes of the sport. There might be many different paths on how they got to that level of greatness. Even though the riders might not know I'm an athlete, it fuels me. It makes me eager to come to work, and, while it's an overused word, it makes me very *passionate* about these telecasts and my part in getting it right."

Hummer won more than 40 championships on the water. (Craig Hummer)

Hummer may have started in broadcasting by happenstance, but his second career was the by-product of preparation. In the mid 1990s, he was at a race in Hawaii, finishing a weekend of lifeguard racing on Waikiki Beach. He approached event organizer Tom Kiely and shared that he was starting to plan for the next phase in his life. He asked for any opportunity Kiely might have. Not more than five minutes after the conversation, Kiely walked over to Hummer on the beach, handed him a microphone and asked him to interview the winner of the Waikiki Rough Water Swim, the world's largest open water swim drawing competitors from all over the world.

If Craig did well, Kiely said he'd keep him in Hawaii, all expenses paid, to host his show for the Diamondhead Biathlon for ESPN the next week. Hummer wasn't an outright ham, but he never saw the camera as an enemy, either. In the television program *Baywatch*'s first year on NBC, the hit show featured a young character based on Hummer's life story. Hummer was a featured extra in a few episodes and would play himself, though his name was curiously changed to Scott Hummer. On Waikiki Beach, Hummer nailed his rough ocean interviews and biathlon hosting duties by drawing on his experience as a successful athlete accustomed to answering questions. "It wasn't hard for me to flip that script. I tried to plan as best I could for whatever I'm covering," he said.

Sports announcing is a lot like free-ranging improv; it's a skill that can be developed, and Hummer has worked very hard at the craft. Competing in surf lifesaving and working for nearly thirty years as an ocean lifeguard prepared him for the serious responsibility of describing the aftermath of violent bull riding wrecks in which riders don't always get up and walk away.

"I have to be in the moment, completely adaptable to take the broadcast in any direction, including when someone is injured, sometimes horribly," he said. "One of the unique aspects of calling PBR is to be willing to lead people through a life-or-death scenario, live. Going through all the training and treating people on the beach, seeing the look of horror on a parent's face when their child is brought back coughing up water gives you a small window into how bad things can be. On the broadcast, I always try to be respectful while leading people down a comforting path."

Over the course of his career, Hummer has called more than sixty different sports, including five different Olympics on NBC, and the Tour de France for nine years, as well as adventure racing, swimming, diving, figure skating, volleyball, and UFC at Mohegan Sun. Bull riding came to him instead of him seeking out the sport.

He was in Sestriere, the NBC mountain bureau in the idyllic Italian Alps as a field reporter covering the 2006 Winter Olympics when he received a call from an executive at the Versus network asking what he knew about bull riding.

It wasn't much. In 2004, Hummer had tuned in when the championship battle between Adriano Moraes and Mike Lee came down to a final ride. The telecast on NBC was running long. The broadcast had to switch from live on NBC to OLN, shades of the NFL's infamous Heidi game when the Sunday movie cut off a New York Jets – Oakland Raiders thriller. Hummer didn't have the OLN cable package; he admitted to the executive he had no idea who won because of the programming switch. (Lee won, becoming the first man to win the World Finals event and the World Championship in the same year.) That was the extent of Hummer's knowledge of PBR. Didn't matter. He was asked about coming on board full time. Hummer, then forty years old, booked a flight from Venice to Reno, Nevada. "I saw a career opportunity for something I thought could be an amazing thing to be a part of … and I've never regretted that decision for one day in my life."

The learning curve was quick and steep. Hummer started as PBR reporter, and, by late summer 2006, took over the PBR play-by-play duties.

He asked PBR CEO Randy Bernard if he could address the riders at one of the periodic all-athlete meetings. "I got up on the dais and said, 'Look, guys, you may think of me as not of your kind, but the only reason I'm here is to make you look good and tell the stories to help you be understood and appreciated.' That's my job. There are other people on our broadcasts to be critical. My job is to pull out the criticism from those guys. I am a storyteller. That doesn't mean breaking down, it means building up."

Hummer wasn't a cowboy. But he fit right in.

"Craig would show up in his slacks, fancy shoes, and designer shirts. He didn't pretend to be who he's not," said Leah Garcia, who had spent a dozen years as the PBR on CBS sideline reporter teed up by Hummer. "I'm always so tickled when someone is out of their element but in their element. Very few people can be part of the clan when they're not part of the clan. Craig is one of them."

Hummer (center) with ace color analysts Justin McBride (left) and Ty Murray (right)

PBR on CBS: Hummer, Harrison, and McBride (Bull Stock Media)

Hummer would report on Chris Shivers and J.W. Hart finishing their storied careers and get to build up a chunk of two-time PBR champion Justin McBride's dominant run. He'd call Silvano Alves's three championships, nearly the entire blazing career of J.B. Mauney, and the emergence of new world champions like Cooper Davis, Jess Lockwood, Kaique Pacheco, and José Vitor Leme, still early in an already stunning career that, if his body holds up, may outshine every other cowboy who's wrapped a hand in a bull rope. In August 2021, Hummer got to call the highest-scored ride in PBR history when Leme rode the bull Woopaa in Tula for 97.75 points. Four riders had scored 96.5, most recently in 2004, and this ride far surpassed that mark. Then Leme put up a 98.75 on that same bull, Woopaa, on his final out of the 2021 World Finals in T-Mobile Arena—breaking the mark he had set three months prior. The place exploded. As did Hummer. For the rider portion of the score, Jose was marked a fifty. The "perfect ride" was a first in PBR history.

"My goosebumps had goosebumps," Hummer said. "If you can take a magician, an escape artist, and a bull rider, and combine all three of them, José has the best qualities of all three. José's moment was in my top three sports experiences, not only as an announcer but as a fan. It was cool to witness."

The 2021 season was Hummer's sixteenth as the voice of a sport that's grown steadily. From 2010 to 2020, PBR's fan base grew by +22 percent (from sixty-eight million fans to eighty-two million, according to ESPN Sports Poll). Live attendance increased 69 percent from 2014 to 2019. He is on point for a broadcast that on some Sundays has been second only to the NFL, on those days attracting a larger audience than traditional stick-and-ball sports, which get more mainstream media attention. CBS is pleased with its bull riding broadcasts; in 2019, the network again renewed and expanded its contract to remain the home of PBR until 2028. In 2021, *PBR RidePass* on Pluto TV launched, bringing Hummer's patented calls to fifty million people across the world using the leading free streaming TV service.

Each fall, when bull riding is telecast in the prime Sunday afternoon NFL lead-in spot, the broadcast draws a significant number of potential new fans who have never seen the sport. Hummer navigates a tricky balance—going deep enough into strategy and world title implications for avid fans while keeping it simple for those sampling for the first time something foreign and intriguing.

"The biggest challenge is balancing the macro and micro story lines—within the event, telling the story of one rider in a short time span to hook someone," Hummer explained. "How do you catch someone's interest? That's the constant creative struggle. I happen to do it live with words I can never get back."

Taking himself outside of the broadcast in trying to view the product objectively, Hummer praises the extraordinary talents of his main color analyst Justin McBride, who deftly dissects subtle technical components of each ride in a way that's accessible and interesting to both hard-core and new fans. He's disappointed that their show has never received accolades like an Emmy Award. "We may be the most unique sports programming on television in our storytelling."

A qualified ride takes eight seconds, but before the gate opens, as the riders settle in on their bulls, Hummer has about sixty seconds to serve up what his producer wants, tee up his analyst (along with Justin McBride, Ty Murray, and J.W. Hart who sometimes joins the broadcast), and keep sideline reporter Kate Harrison and one of the mic'd up bullfighters in the mix as well.

McBride says Hummer could call any marquee sporting event today because of the diligent way he prepares, allowing him to stay in the moment and effortlessly quarterback the chaos on the dirt. Fusion GPS has nothing on Hummer's dossiers. Each week, he creates a book on more than three dozen riders—everything from hometowns and family member names to their best rides and buck-off streaks. On the road, he's up late poring over a list of dozens of bulls—their tendencies, their high-marked rides, who's ridden them, and who hasn't. For an event like World Finals, the list reaches 145 bulls.

Even with all the preparation, the patented punning calls and imaginative alliterations are spontaneous.

"I'm calling at least thirty-five rides a show, and they need to look and sound different, with characters who can hold people's interest," Hummer said. "Going down the pun avenue is more to emphasize the bull's unique name and the cowboy pairing. I'm not trying to be a comedian or funny; I'm just trying to distinguish the moment and if people have fun with it, and are entertained, all the better. Chris Berman was doing this with NFL players a long time ago. If you said, 'He's trying to 'Bermanize' the bull out,' I'd laugh and say you're probably right."

Hummer's unconventional ride as a championship athlete, face on *Baywatch*, and accomplished broadcaster shows the range of things that can be accomplished if a person has the right attitude and work ethic, is adaptable, and, no matter the task or opportunity, dives in headfirst ... just as he did when handed that microphone on Waikiki Beach and when taking a phone call on a snowy mountain in Italy to hear about the opportunity to go cover bull riding in Nevada.

"Everyone wants to celebrate the big achievements and success stories," Hummer said. "Anyone who's studied success knows it starts with the small steps and each decision we make. Every day I try to take small steps to set me up for success. If you do that enough, by the end of the day, the week, the month, you're going to make progress. Big wins aren't achieved instantly. There's no book called, *Miracle: This Is How You Do It*. Our biggest struggle is to motivate ourselves, get on the path, and keep pushing ahead."

Hummer's prescription for success mirrors the evolution of the sport he calls. A standalone bull riding sport wasn't an instant hit. The organization formed by the breakaway rodeo cowboys had to scratch and claw for respect, recognition, and reach. But through the hard work put into each seemingly small incremental step, it's now seen in hundreds of millions of homes around the globe, and the lead voice on those broadcasts is a former extreme athlete who understands there is no glory without a heck of a lot of try.

Love & Try

17

DOWN IN THE DIRT

(Author photo)

PBR's growth over the past three decades can be chalked up to any number of contributing factors.

There are the daring, dirt-tough cowboys any kid can look up to, courageously riding beautiful bucking bulls, who continue to be bred to get more powerful and athletic.

There's a world-class television production, combining artful storytelling with the arresting visuals of big-time rides and spectacular wrecks.

Fans coming in person get a fun, high-energy experience captained by Flint Rasmussen, an entertainer referred to as a "national treasure." Creative marketing and social media programs do their part to put the sport in new places.

And then there's the dirt.

While the pre-show pyro is great, Flint's banter hilarious, and the beer seemingly colder and more refreshing when consumed in the company of salt-of-the-earth fans, it is the eight-second bursts of bull riding mayhem that are at the core of the PBR experience. The sport is wholly contingent on the performance of the bulls, frantically bucking with primal power, wild abandon, and hard-to-fathom agility. Beyond a rider who can give them a good battle, the bulls need one more very important thing to put on a great show: good dirt. Without the right dirt, they can't do their jobs. They'd be, at best, mediocre.

Before every PBR event, a crack team hauls in and creates the optimal bull riding surface. The guru of the ground responsible for sourcing, loading, transporting, spreading, maintaining, and picking up that dirt when the show is over is Randy Spraggins, otherwise known as "PBR's Dirt Man."

Spraggins, owner of Special T-Tracks, Inc., based in Akron, Ohio, has spent thirty-six years "putting dirt where it doesn't belong" in arenas coast to coast for PBR as well as rodeo and motorsports events.

"In PBR, everything revolves around letting the bull do his thing," Spraggins said. "If the dirt is too soft or slick, the bulls will check-up and not buck as hard. It's like walking on an icy sidewalk. Your confidence level depends on your shoes and footing. The bull is like that. He needs to be comfortable and confident to push, turn, jump, and twist at the highest level."

To ensure the bulls feel good about their footing, PBR's Dirt Man uses a sandy-clay mix. The best dirt is clean—free of debris, fresh, and consistent. Eight inches of the locally sourced material is spread across PBR arenas. The top two to three inches serves as a cushion, giving the bulls a feel for the surface as they push into the firmer base.

Since two athletes participate in every ride, Spraggins must consider the cowboys, too. The dirt must be forgiving enough to allow the human athletes to walk away from rides gone bad. "You can't have it too hard, because the cowboys get drilled into the ground," Spraggins said. "There needs to be a little give in it."

While Spraggins has been around long enough to recognize good dirt by smell and feel, he still uses scientific tests to ensure the proper particle size—a distinct ratio of fine vs. coarse grains. "A good composite dirt mixture with different sized materials makes for better compaction and workability," he explained. "If there's too much clay, you blend in more sand."

Take an arena like Madison Square Garden in New York City. The dirt for PBR's annual Friday night weekend opener arrives on 33rd Street in midtown Manhattan late Thursday night each year.

It's a busy venue. Since the New York Rangers' ice surface stays in place for the entire hockey season, before the dirt goes down, a team of carpenters builds a subfloor comprised of six hundred sheets of ¾" plywood that is dropped over the ice. Hockey clubs around the country like when PBR comes in. It's counterintuitive that 1,800-pound bulls jumping five or six feet in the air to land with tremendous force on a temporary surface put above the ice would be welcome, but the PBR setup makes the ice very hard, which then makes it play faster.

With the subfloor down, the crew adds a layer of six-millimeter black plastic to act as a vapor barrier. The "cowboy court" at MSG—750 tons of dirt—comes from Lyndhurst, New Jersey, on a massive convoy of forty-five dump trucks. Once the trucks arrive in midtown Manhattan, it takes about six hours to move the soil up into the arena, dump it, and have sponsor Caterpillar's trucks push it out evenly.

In a city of iconic skyscrapers reaching for the clouds, it is fitting that "the world's most famous arena" sits on the building's fifth floor. At any time during the load in, three trucks are moving dirt piles up a spiraling ramp to the arena floor. Meantime, thirteen more trucks are lined up downstairs on 33rd Street waiting their turn. It's a nearly ten-hour dance choreographed to the minute.

Each year, typically on Friday afternoon, the Wild West meets the concrete jungle when PBR's bovine athletes parade up the same ramp in what's known as the "running of the bulls." The trip can take forty-five seconds to a few minutes, depending on the mood of the bulls.

With the dirt down, the load-in crew—typically twelve crew members from PBR and up to thirty local hires—spends the next four hours building bucking chutes, fencing, and corrals. The steel that makes up the back pens and encircles the dirt surface collectively weighs 130,000 pounds and would be one mile long if lined up straight. Nine fifty-three-foot PBR trucks visit each arena: five production trucks, two arena trucks, and two TV trucks, one that costs fourteen million dollars and the other six million dollars.

For nearly twenty years, the entire arena load in, as well as the break down for dashing to the next city, was overseen by PBR Production Manager Jim White, a wisecracking jokester who'd turn stern in an instant in his job, making sure the proverbial set-up clocks run on time.

Jim White oversaw the arena load-in for nearly 20 years. (Author photo)

White, a formidable man with a closely cropped white beard, was usually seen in a black blazer, blue jeans, boots, and gray cowboy hat, wires snaking past his collar to earpieces set in both ears, a two-way push-button radio draped across one shoulder as if he were a state trooper presiding over a bull riding. He is a gregarious quipster who'd sneak up and goose me from behind every time I went to an event. Yet with the weight of the arena transformation on his shoulders and the responsibility of overseeing a team battling an unforgiving clock ticking down to when the pyro is set off to start each show, White would turn on a dime into a blunt, no-nonsense, task-master shooting what he called "death stares" at anyone who dared to slow down the load-in.

(It goes without saying, I cluelessly wandered onto the freshly manicured dirt before White even knew my name.) If any single element of the setup were delayed, a cascading domino effect throws the entire set up into disarray, making White's life a veritable nightmare, especially on nights when TV was set to go live at the top of the hour to begin an event. Indecision was Jim White's greatest enemy. Quick, creative contingencies were his best friend.

The wired-up man overseeing PBR arena production would retire at the end of the 2021 season. He needed to go home, sleep in his own bed, and give his wife, Joyce, a break from mowing the lawn at their place in Bethany, Missouri. In eighteen years, he'd only missed four PBR events—three for medical reasons and one for leading a church trip to Africa.

White was more than a boss to a staff of twelve who, pound-for-pound, man-for-man, woman-for-woman, might accomplish more than any live event production team on earth. He took a group of disparate individuals and made them into an unstoppable, us-against-the-world team that would lead the sports world back to competition during a global health pandemic.

For the chosen few who can handle a rigorous job with long stretches away from home, White's MO was tough love, which he learned as a youth pastor and then Pentecostal missionary for seven years traveling to places like Macedonia, Kenya, Uganda, and Rwanda. "Some people do very well in this environment, others don't. The crew spends a lot of time on the road away from our families, working long, hard hours. I loved every person who came onto my crew. We ran through walls for one another."

He's not exaggerating about the time on the road. Take Jack Gardner, who drives one of PBR's nine semi-trucks, hauling everything from the sixty-five tons of steel that make up the arena fencing and back pens, to sponsorship signage and T-shirts fans buy on the concourse. For thirty to thirty-five weeks a year, Gardner doesn't see his home in Bolton, Connecticut. He drives a PBR truck from one event to the next, works the event, and then it's off to the next city.

"Jim taught me everything I know about production," Gardner said. "He gave me a chance. He believed in me when others didn't. I don't have a big brother. Jim took that place."

White not only taught his crew how to accomplish the virtually impossible, considering the unforgiving turnaround times for PBR to move from city to city let alone doing so during a pandemic. The former missionary who was virtually driven from his ministry for being too progressive in his methods ("which are now being used all over the world today," White claims), would lend an ear to listen, a shoulder to cry on. He would counsel anyone facing family and personal challenges. If a crew member needed money to make a car payment, he'd quietly give it to them.

"It's not a loan," White said. "It's a blessing. And if you're blessed to be able to pay it back, that will be your opportunity to give me a gift."

Under White's supervision, the PBR crew rigged up video, audio, lighting, and other equipment. Loud music and booming yet understandable arena announcers are essential to the PBR experience. Therefore, in most arenas the team brings in its own sound—sixty speaker cabinets rigged to crank up to 384,000 watts. "This system would blow grandma's wig off if we turned it all the way up," White said. "We like an in-your-face sound, and it has to be crisp, clean, have a lot of low-end, and be intelligible. If it sounds like mud, I start looking at my audio guy and asking, 'Where are you going to be working next week?'"

And when it comes to real mud, all things dirt-related are left to Spraggins's expertise. PBR's Dirt Man oversees prepping, grooming, and maintaining the all-important surface. If it's too dry, he'll add water. If it's too sticky, he'll cook out the moisture by adding hydrated lime.

"It's like cooking in the kitchen. You deal with it when it's in front of you," he said. "In New York City, Sacramento, and some other cities, PBR bucks bulls for three days, and on Sunday night, after the event champion gets his buckle, we collect the dirt. We're really renting— it all goes back for reprocessing. When we find good dirt, we want to keep it for future use. We've got PBR dirt stashed all over the country."

The best material PBR's Dirt Man has ever seen was in Bakersfield, California, from a carrot grower. "When they washed the carrots, all the dirt went into a sediment pond—and then that dirt got dug and stacked up. It was super clean with the right consistency, the most awesome dirt you could ever imagine!"

New York may have a reputation as being a very dirty city, but an abundance of good-quality, fresh dirt is hard to find in and around New York City. PBR's soil savant goes to "the Garden State," and he gives Jersey dirt high marks. When his team pulls up the plywood and plastic sheath below, just about every crumb will be caught, removed, and brought back across state lines.

"Good old-fashioned elbow grease: we take away what we bring," Spraggins said.

Or as White noted, "By late Sunday night, you'll never know we were here except for the flies."

After opening the season in New York, Spraggins, White, and the PBR crew would head to Chicago for another clockwork load-in. On the crowded island of Manhattan, five floors above a busy train station, a bull riding mecca was broken down and transformed back into a bright clean sheet of ice awaiting the New York Rangers' return. Not a morsel of Jersey dirt was to be found. All 750 tons were being carried away on a caravan of dump trucks, leaving the world's most famous arena and heading across the Hudson River. The dirt will be back—along with fans who'd cracked out their cowboy boots and hats to fill the Garden's corridors—in a year's time.

Love & Try

18

DENNIS AND DANA

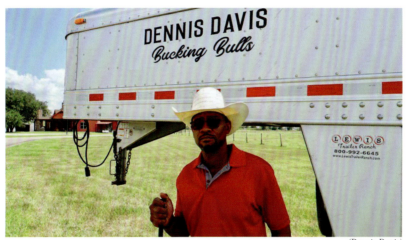

(Dennis Davis)

Dana White's bucking bull is a lot like him—not the biggest, but compact, muscular, and fiery with lots of heart.

The UFC boss is very proud of the bull. No matter his mood, mention F Bomb and he'll stop midsentence to whip out his phone to show the latest video of his prized animal athlete.

F Bomb, named after White's favorite go-to word, is an up-and-coming, four-year-old bull managed and trained by Dennis Davis, a former bull rider with a knack for recognizing potential in the animal athletes he used to mount.

"There's no quit in that bull," Davis said. "It's a matter of time, having F Bomb compete and see where he goes. That's not just this bull, that's any young bull. He's not quite mean, he doesn't have the size. But like Dana says, he has the heart."

As professional bull riding grows, experts with a niche specialization have come to the fore, developing successful businesses that help the sport improve. Davis, fifty-two years old, has become one of the industry's premier bucking bull trainers.

Call him a bull whisperer if you want. But Davis rejects any inference of fuzzy spiritual mysticism to explain how he identifies future greatness in an animal, then does the hard work of training him to deliver the goods. "To get the maximum performance out of a bull, you need to know the bull," he says. "It's like a relationship with an employee—you need to know them and be around them to get the best performance out of any person."

Davis's program democratizes the bull side of the sport. Anyone with a healthy checkbook can become the owner of a bull that competes in PBR. The rest is then up to Davis, who made his bones with the "Jaynes Gang," which created the pioneering futurity blueprint programs under the company Billy Jaynes of Exclusive Genetics/ Bucking Bull Games.

His role is akin to training racehorses. As one of the sport's premier trainers, Davis is essentially compensated for housing, feeding, and caring for the bulls. He hauls them to events, too, and gets into the chute to prepare the bull for each out. Davis is entrusted with every important element of care for the animal, who, hopefully, will begin generating winnings. Each bull owner pays Davis a monthly fee and collects 20 percent of the bull's earned prize money.

Dennis Davis Bucking Bulls has about thirty-five bulls, owned by regular Joes and guys named Dana. He manages the bulls and the owners. White, for instance, once dialed up Davis to ask about how his bull was doing ... immediately before addressing millions of Americans at the 2020 Republican National Convention.

Davis also personally owns five bulls. He comes from a rodeo background in South Texas. His father was an all-around cowboy who bucked horses competitively at backyard rodeos in the 1960s and 1970s near their home in Eagle Lake.

Davis's parents separated when he was three years old. He'd see his dad from time to time, and his family on both sides rodeoed. Every day before school, Davis, up before dawn, would go to his grandfather's ranch, checking on the cows and often getting on the calves. "He'd hold one down and let me get on one," he said of his Grandpa Tucker, the man he credits with teaching him the value of hard work, discipline, and responsibility.

Davis would work his way up to bull riding as a freshman in high school in Hallettsville, Texas, outside of Houston. "It was scary at first, and I have to say I was still a little bit scared on almost every one of them after that," he said. "It was like being on the back of a car holding on. Bulls showed you a whole different power."

In addition to becoming a top rodeo athlete in high school, Davis was playing basketball and football, and he became a standout in track as one of the top long jumpers in Texas. He took a break from bull riding and attended Texas Southern University in Houston on a track scholarship.

One day after graduation, Davis went to a practice bull riding. Beers were passed around and jokes exchanged. "There was one bull nobody wanted to get on," he remembered. "It wasn't like a big-time bounty bull, but he was said to be mean. I rode him; turned out to be a flat spinner, nothing special. But I'd forgotten the feeling of how amazing this felt. It lit a fire, and I went full-time."

Davis entered various rodeo events, and as he was finishing up his career, the PBR was founded. He also competed in the PBR Touring Pro division, a feeder series for up-and-coming riders.

There were several Black cowboys touring at the time, and Davis traveled with Ervin Williams of Tulsa, an accomplished NFR cowboy who took Davis under his wing. Donald Goodman, who despite once breaking his neck won several Bill Pickett Invitational Rodeo championships and excelled in bareback events, was his roommate at one time.

"I could hold my own and hung with those guys," Davis said.

He was still competing on weekends into his mid-thirties. During the week, he worked at Igloo Products Corp. On weekends, a son and daughter often joined him and his wife on the road.

At a Thanksgiving bull riding—the John Nash Bull Bash—Davis was turned upside down by a wild jump kicker. The bull stepped on his back and broke his scapula. "The doctor said, 'You have two children now and want to think about what you're doing. Break it again, and you can lose the mobility of your right arm.'"

Right there, he knew he was retiring from bull riding. Still, after healing, he competed in calf roping at jackpots around the South.

Davis had known Billy Jaynes, the PRCA stock contractor, and in fact had passed his ranch—the Jaynes Gang Place—every morning going to work at Igloo. He had heard Jaynes was involved with ABBI (American Bucking Bull, Inc.) futurities, which begin with two-year-old bulls bucking dummies in their development to become full-fledged bucking bulls and knew Jaynes would be hauling bulls to Las Vegas.

"I had always wanted to go and be in that atmosphere, so I stopped by to see if he needed a hand and had an opening," Davis said.

It turns out Jaynes was doing a fair amount of embryo and artificial insemination of cows, and he needed a database built to house and manage his genetics information. Davis was hired to build the system, and, as the project was being completed in 2012, the Jaynes Gang's trainer quit.

"Billy asked me if I had ever thought about training bulls. I said, 'Heck yeah that's what I'm here for! Not to mess with computers.'"

Davis, now head of the Jaynes Gang's training program, could focus on bulls every day. When Exclusive Genetics/ Bucking Bull Games shut its doors in 2018, the torch was passed, and Dennis Davis Bucking Bulls was formed.

"I still wanted to play the game, and by that time I felt I had a knack for the bulls," Davis said. "I'm figuring them out, they're just like people. I knew I could do this on my own."

Davis had already "flipped the switch" on a bull for $500,000—meaning he raised someone's bull who at the end of the futurity won the jackpot. The success of that bull, Miss Kitty's Peace Maker, who went on to buck in the PBR Pendleton Whisky Velocity tour, boosted his confidence.

"I got it right. What happened was what I thought would happen. So, I started Dennis Davis Bucking Bulls."

In announcing his retirement news, Billy Jaynes said, "I encourage all my customers to leave their bulls in the capable hands of Dennis Davis. I am so sure of the future success of Dennis, that I am offering my training facilities for him to work his magic."

Davis, who is a member of ABBI, began courting his own customers, including UFC boss, White. The two had met in 2016 when White was traveling the country to discover new MMA fighters as part of his reality show, *Dana White: Lookin' for a Fight*.

Davis with PBR cofounder Jerome Davis (Dennis Davis)

Wherever the show set up to recruit fighters, it followed a prevailing local theme. In Houston, the motif was rodeo and bull riding. Okay, predictable, but White knows show biz. His mastery of marketing and promotion is one reason UFC has more than a quarter billion fans worldwide.

How could he *not* show someone from his crew getting on a bucking bull?

But how could that person be him? Dana White had a company and an entire sport, let alone his own family, relying on him going back to his hotel in one piece.

Sure, the risk was real and considerable. But White, known to tackle any challenge, and appreciating a dramatic hook for his show, decided to attempt a bull for the cameras.

"I always thought bull riding was absolutely insane," he said. "And it's literally the most dangerous sport in the world. I'm not really afraid of anything, including death. That was the first time I felt *legit* fear. I was scared."

UFC's wild-man boss hung on for 3.07 seconds. He skidded across the dirt and the bull came within inches of seriously stomping him. He called it, "the fastest, scariest, craziest three seconds you will ever have in your life."

In learning about the bucking bull business during the filming (the YouTube video of the episode has nearly two million views), White decided to purchase a bull. And then he would buy another. And another.

F Bomb is his favorite.

White is known to post F Bomb bucking videos on social media, reaching millions of new potential PBR fans. He's always interested in how F Bomb is doing and will reach out to Davis to ask about him, even when half a world away at Fight Island off the coast of Abu Dhabi.

Davis monitors all his bulls very closely. For White's bovine pride and joy, he has his eye on future Velocity Tour events, where Davis's bull team competes.

The business motto of Dennis Davis Bucking Bulls is *"You can own a bucking bull."* There's no truck, trailer, or ranch needed. Davis takes care of all that for yearling (one year old), futurity (two year old), derby (three year old), and classic (four year old). He'll hook potential owners into breeders or buy the bull himself.

He's generally on the road forty-eight weekends a year, doing what he loves, for customers who can share in the thrill of a sport that's always been in his blood.

Unlike Dana White, nobody has to "test drive" a bull. Fans who are interested in bull ownership can find Dennis Davis on social media.

19

MADISON AVENUE COWBOY

(Author photo)

In January 2021, PBR stormed into Madison Square Garden in midtown Manhattan for the fifteenth time. Years earlier, when twenty bull riding cowboys broke away from the rodeo in the early 1990s to form a standalone bull riding league, they had no idea they'd one day be competing in "the World's Most Famous Arena."

In fact, when PBR first began hauling 750 tons of dirt, a half mile of steel corrals, and dozens of bucking bulls up to the fifth-floor arena above Penn Station, there was ample skepticism.

During those days of doubt, a bull rider named Pistol Robinson was caught up in a terrible wreck. The bull stomped him, breaking both his legs.

Pistol was transported to the hospital, where an ER doctor asked him, "How did this happen?"

"Riding a bull," Pistol said.

The doctor didn't believe him. "There's no bull riding in New York City!" he said.

Pistol pleaded his case. He swore he was telling the truth.

The doctor, along with nurses attending to the rider, was wondering if this banged-up guy in cowboy boots was drunk.

Finally, Pistol capitulated: "OK, OK. I got hit by a cab. Can you please fix me up?"

There are no longer doubters that cowboys ride bulls in the Big Apple. The sport regularly sells out The Garden and other big arenas coast-to-coast and is seen in hundreds of millions of homes globally through its CBS broadcasts. It could be argued none of this would have been possible without a man very few cowboys or fans have heard of: Barry Frank.

The man who received the prestigious Jim Shoulders Lifetime Achievement Award at the 2018 PBR World Finals has had a significant, if largely unnoticed impact, on professional bull riding.

"Barry helped put the spotlight on our sport like no other at a time when to most fans PBR stood for 'Pabst Blue Ribbon,'" said former PBR CEO Randy Bernard.

Back in 2001, Bernard was in a pickle. He wanted to bring the eight-year-old bull riding organization's television rights back in house, allow the cowboys to control their own fate, and go mainstream. At the time, the sport was carried on TNN. To revert those rights back to PBR, the entity that owned them was demanding an exorbitant fee. A colleague at NBC suggested Bernard call Barry Frank over at IMG.

Frank was already a legend—one of the sports industry's most influential and prolific content creators, television rights negotiators, and talent representatives. (Years later, in receiving a Lifetime Achievement Award at the thirty-ninth Annual Sports Emmy® Awards, the committee would proclaim,

"It's safe to say that no one man shaped modern sports television more than Barry Frank." He passed away in November 2019, a year after being inducted into the PBR Ring of Honor.)

Frank read the league's broadcast rights contract, quoted Shakespeare, dropped a funny expletive, and told Bernard he'd take care of it. And he did. True to his vaunted reputation, he won back the PBR's television rights at less than half of the original asking price.

Frank pitched CBS to cover pro bull riding. He presented it like a big-league sport—real athletes with interesting personal stories battling in riveting life-or-death competition for a World Championship—rather than a sideshow spectacle. The band of maverick cowboys riding wild bucking bulls joined a powerhouse portfolio including the NFL, PGA Golf, SEC football, and NCAA basketball. Bull riding has entered the big leagues and now sometimes pulls Sunday ratings second to only the NFL.

"Barry was a tremendous matchmaker who put the two of us together," explained Dan Weinberg, executive VP of sports programming, CBS. "With Barry's help, guidance, and passion, a marriage happened that is still together in large part because of his original vision."

"I didn't do it just for the money," Frank said. "I got involved in the sports I like and admire."

Frank had done deals for all the major leagues and is credited with launching Olympic rights into the stratosphere after his seismic deal for the 1988 Calgary Winter Olympics. Yet he'd always been drawn to sports perceived as off the beaten path. He especially admired unsung athletes outside the traditional stick-and-ball games.

"In PBR, these cowboys are the toughest athletes in sports," he told me about a year before he passed. "They take a terrible beating and get back up every time. If I can help their [financial] means, I'll go do that. It's been a pleasure and privilege to work with the PBR."

In a truly illustrious career, Frank said negotiating PBR's TV deals has been "one of the things I'm most proud of."

Looking back, the legendary executive characterized his long career as a fortunate accident. He grew up in Dayton, Ohio, fondly recalling smelling the gasoline and hearing the squeal of rubber at Indianapolis Motor Speedway as a five-year-old boy. He loved open-wheel auto racing but wanted to be an actor.

He was drafted into the Army but rejected due to a heart murmur. After earning degrees at Carnegie Mellon University and Harvard Business School, Frank wound up in Chicago.

Unable to land any acting roles, opportunity beckoned at the ad agency J. Walter Thompson in Detroit, working with Ford, then the biggest advertiser in sports. "I never thought I'd wind up in sports or TV, but I fell in love with it," he said.

He was fortunate to join ABC Sports and learn at the knee of geniuses like Roone Arledge, the creator of *Wide World of Sports* and *Monday Night Football*, and smart enough to soak in all the wisdom circulating in a hothouse sports programming era predating bloviating talking heads and cringeworthy reality TV.

"Roone Arledge keenly understood what audiences wanted, even if they didn't know it themselves, and he taught me everything I know," Frank said. Observing how Arledge created masterful emotional drama and "up-close-and-personal" sports storytelling, Frank developed shows that resonated across America like *The Superstars, The Skins Game, The Tiger Woods Primetime Challenge,* and *World's Strongest Man* for CBS, the longest running sports show on TV.

"People like to see others doing things they can't do," he said. "It's why *World's Strongest Man* has been successful for forty-one years, and I think it's part of the success of PBR. Riding a bull is one of those things you and I can't ever imagine doing."

As PBR grew to operate tours in five countries and sold-out arenas across the US, Frank envisioned additional growth. "People really like cowboys. They're considered good people, honest guys, tough as nails," he said.

Even at eighty-six years old, and until shortly before his passing, Frank could be seen several days a week in his office on Madison Avenue, wearing a splendid suit, a spiffy pocket square and a broad smile. The advice he gave newly minted agents packaging and selling media rights was more Main Street than Harvard Business School: everything starts and ends with relationships. Always be honest and upfront with people. Con or hustle someone once, and they'll remember it for a lifetime.

His brand of old-school relationship building was built on a genuine concern for others, creating real human connections rather than spamming contacts on LinkedIn. His motto was "always take the long plane ride." No phone call can ever replace meeting in person.

"Barry truly cared about people and did not have one single enemy," said his wife, Elizabeth.

After hundreds of often tense, high-stakes negotiations, that's no easy feat. At the negotiating table, Frank was a wizard. His secret strategy: you don't want to slaughter your opponent. In fact, he always tries to lose the last negotiation point.

"I want the guy on the other side of the table to know he beat Barry Frank," he said. "I want him to go home to dinner to his wife and kids knowing he had a good day."

Today, and for years to come, anyone having a good day in the PBR—from the fan on a Sunday afternoon enjoying the sport on CBS to the cowboy standing under a storm of fake million-dollar bills raining down from the arena ceiling while he prepares to accept the real check for his World Championship—can thank the man they probably have never heard of, the one and only Barry Frank.

Love & Try

PART IV
HEROES AMONG US

The Love & Try that motivates the bull riders, stock contractors, and tireless crew who travel together to produce a sport enjoyed by millions also regularly inspires others to use their talents, determination, and try to make the world a better place. The nurse. The sculptor. The boilermaker. The police officer. The PR rep. The U.S. Army helicopter pilot. They're everyday people with connections to bull riding who are doing extraordinary things. Next, their remarkable stories of grit, grace, and gratitude.

20

THE GREAT BULL GIFT

(Bull Stock Media)

Sports fans celebrate the big wins, and deal with crushing defeat, each to their own. We all mourn the big loss in different ways. Fans, for all their lovable quirks and foibles, are similar in one predictable way. Pick a sport, and they will eventually engage in the same basic argument, one that attempts to identify "The GOAT."

Making the case for the "greatest of all time" is a highly subjective undertaking. Consensus is difficult to reach because even with refined statistics, comparisons across generations of athletes can never really be apples-to-apples. Can today's dominant apple be compared to an orange who couldn't be beaten from decades ago? The opinionated debate can go sideways when one person is basically in the produce aisle and the other is yelling from frozen foods. You know what I mean. (If not, you may express your befuddlement on Twitter to @LoveAndTryBook).

PBR is no exception. Apples, oranges, or whatever the statistical comparison, anointing the best all-time bull rider will generate spirited debate. However, on the bull side of the equation, it's virtually a closed case. No deadlocked jury here. To the vast majority, the top bull, the biggest star, the bull first associated with the sport, the greatest and most famous of them all, is Bushwacker.

After all, when *ESPN The Magazine* broke new ground to put an animal athlete on the cover of its annual "Body" issue, they chose the ripped chocolate brown bull—a mighty, ultra-competitive heavyweight, who gave up one qualified ride, early in his career, then went on a dominant buck-off streak, forty-two consecutive cowboys unceremoniously thrashed, dumped, and ejected, until finally conquered by a swaggering Carolina Cowboy who refused to believe any bull, even the great Bushwacker, could be unridden.

J.B. Mauney, the loose-limbed, narrow-waisted, try-until-your-head-hits-the-ground cowboy topping many a GOAT list, may have had a plan—keep picking Bushwacker until he rode him—but Bushwacker never had one. With J.B. or any rider. There was no book on this bull. He was wildly unpredictable; probably didn't even know himself which way he'd go until the moment the gate opened, and he'd blow out like a hurricane then change direction. Or he wouldn't. But don't assume Bushwacker was irrational or out of control. He was completely in tune with the physicality of the vaunted "dance" that is a bull ride. Those who have been around the sport and can detect and describe elements of the ride invisible to the rest of us said Bushwacker could feel when a rider was in control, and the realization of someone getting too comfortable on his back only made him twist and kick harder, turning up the heat until the unwanted human passenger was summarily dispatched.

Gentle bulls unload at the arena and put on their game face, turning into mean, all-business SOBs on the weekend. During the week, back on the ranch, away from the cameras and crowd noise, they'll act sweet as pie. Here, Bushwacker never changed things up. This wasn't a bull to go and pet. He was a surly character in and out of the arena. He'd have to be separated from the other bulls. He didn't get along because he was never going to be the one to stand down. He knew he was a star—the only bull with full-time private security during his retirement tour—as much as he could *feel* a

The Great Bull Gift

cowboy's rising confidence to go harder and rid him from his back. He also realized when cameras were trained his way, and he'd pick up his head and puff up his shoulders and make eye contact—each photo a declaration of what Bushwacker knew, and what he sensed we were hip to as well, which is that he was *The Bull*.

Still, when the otherwise disorderly bull stood in the bucking chutes, he'd stay dead calm. "This was one smart bull. He loved what he was doing, and he wanted to give you the best shot every time," said 2001 Rookie of the Year Luke Snyder, who picked Bushwacker six times in championship rounds, once making it as far as five seconds on him in Kansas City. "He knew your motor was running, and he knew he was going to go from zero to sixty in about one second, and he wanted to heighten the anticipation and make your motor run even harder."

Bushwacker transcended the sport. Yet for all the accolades the legendary bull received, all the lofty comparisons to the likes of Seabiscuit and Secretariat, two racehorses who became bigger than their sport, Bushwacker isn't necessarily a household name beyond the world of PBR.

One bull, however, did make that grade. He's far more famous and one of the world's most recognized and photographed animals. He's about four times as big as Bushwacker, weighing three and a half tons, and was born not on a farm or ranch but in New York City in an audacious act of guerilla art committed by an Italian immigrant, a young artist of great talent named Arturo di Modica.

This bull is an inanimate sculpture, and his name is "Charging Bull."

Like every great bull, and every great piece of art, he has a story, too.

This one starts in 1973 when di Modica, the artistic prodigy, arrived in New York from Sicily. Arturo was virtually penniless, even though his outsized talents with marble had led to his nickname "young Michelangelo" back in his home country. He found a few patrons and was able to set up a studio in SoHo.

In late October 1987, the stock market crashed. With a studio not far from Wall Street, di Modica was deeply affected by the crash. He loved America because it was a place where you could do whatever you wanted, say whatever you wanted, and create whatever you wanted. The artist who had to run away from home to pursue his dream was very appreciative of everything he'd received in New York. For di Modica, whose country was liberated by

Allied Forces not long after he was born, America was in every sense the land of golden opportunity. And lower Manhattan was its heart and soul. Grateful for his opportunities in New York, after the market crash, di Modica began breathing life into a symbol connected to Wall Street that would represent all that he valued most in his beloved adopted home—a formidable bull sculpture that would project feelings of power, strength, determination, freedom, optimism, and confidence.

The bearded artist, who appeared to have been plucked from Central Casting, worked on the sculpture for two years, starting with wood and metal then pouring clay into molds … along with more than $350,000 from his own pocket. Finally, a defiant, fearsome bull, who looks a lot like a snarling Bushwacker and appears to be moving even when he's not, was cast in bronze at a foundry across the river in the largely Polish enclave of Greenpoint, Brooklyn.

The bull needed to be set free. In the dead of a cold night in mid-December 1989, Arturo and a group of friends put the eleven-foot by sixteen-foot, seven thousand-pound sculpture on a flatbed truck and hauled him down to the New York Stock Exchange. They left Charging Bull under a Christmas tree on Wall Street. There was no better place for one heck of a gift to the city. The market had finally, fully recovered from the October 1987 crash two months earlier, but that was irrelevant to the intention of Arturo's bull art, now a throbbing presence on the financial district's main artery.

The next day, when the artist was having lunch, the unauthorized oversized present was hauled away by the authorities.

Designing the world's most famous bull (Arturo di Modica)

For the city's soulless, grim-faced bureaucrats, however, it was too late. The *New York Post* had put Charging Bull on that morning's cover and a citizenry had fallen in love with the powerful beast. Hearing that the "illegal" bull was being removed from Wall Street, the tabloid masses went berserk. The resulting uproar matched the loud, emotional era of Mayor Ed Koch.

Arthur Piccolo, head of the Bowling Green Association, was listening to the populist explosion while envisioning the larger promise of Charging Bull. He navigated the city's bureaucracy to bring the statue a few blocks west of the stock exchange to the North Plaza of Bowling Green, the site of a cattle market in the mid-1600s. And that would be the bull's home. He's stood on a small triangle-shaped plot of land off Broadway for more than thirty years.

"Charging Bull represents the strength of America and optimism for its future; it's for all of America," Piccolo said. "The bull makes people think of strength and power, but it is also an animal everyone adores. They touch it. They photograph it. For children, it's a magical creature they're endlessly drawn to."

Honored at MSG (Bull Stock Media)

Charging Bull has delighted millions of visitors of all ages. Today, it's as much an irreplaceable part of the cityscape as the Statue of Liberty and Empire State Building. Visitors usually pose for a photo, and the most popular vantage point is at the rear of the bull, where people can smile in front of two big bronze ones. They may not know it, but it's a good match for the spirit of di Modica's gift—displaying a giant pair, pursuing the audacious, and thumbing one's nose at silly rules of authority blocking the greater good.

Di Modica's bull drew on his own experience of scratching and scraping to make it in the big city along with his encouragement for an ever-resilient metropolis to rebound no matter the crisis. Another one, bringing unimaginable horror, would happen mere blocks from Bowling Green on September

The Great Bull Gift

11, 2001. And again, gut-punched New Yorkers stood back up. When things get bad, they unite, work harder, get stronger, bear down, and make it better. That resilience was exactly what di Modica has immortalized in 7,000 pounds of brass bovine bravado. The generous outlaw spirit in which his daring gift was created, its rebel-Robin Hoodish dead-of-night delivery, and everything Charging Bull represents feels ripped from PBR's "Be Cowboy" brief.

So, when reading in the *New York Post* that a deranged man from Texas had attacked Charging Bull with a steel-reinforced banjo, opening a gash in the bull's head the size of a cantaloupe, what could I as the sport's publicist possibly do but call the *Post*'s reporter with an offer from PBR to pay for the damages to help repair the bull?

Arturo di Modica would see the resulting story, and I was invited to discuss the matter with him over lunch at the only place he ate—Cipriano's, where once a year the artist settled his tab with a new sculpture. Sicilian pride precluded di Modica from allowing PBR to pay for the repairs, estimated in the low five figures. However, we agreed on other measures to consummate a beautiful new relationship. To open the 2020 season, the Sicilian artist—now an American citizen—would be acknowledged on the dirt at Madison Square Garden three-and-a-half miles north of Charging Bull's home. Even better for fans, the artist created a trophy just for them—a mini replica of Charging Bull. The new trophy for the annual

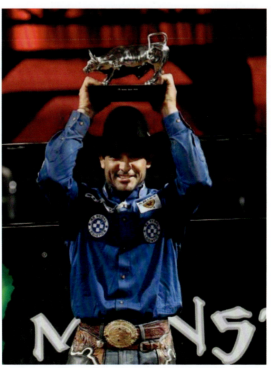

Joao Ricardo Vieira raises a special trophy (Bull Stock Media)

event winner in Gotham City debuted at Madison Square Garden at the 2020 season opener.

While di Modica is world famous for his connection to a stunning bull statue, he had never seen the planet's top bucking bulls in action. When PBR celebrated di Modica's life in the season-opening press conference and then on the dirt at the Garden during a break, he would get that experience. The seventy-five-year-old artist, walking slowly and easily tiring from an ongoing fight with cancer, came early before doors opened to fans. He was as excited to tour the locker room and meet the badly mismatched cowboys as he was to get up close to the snorting bull athletes in the back pen.

"I have always appreciated those who understand and value the power and the majesty of bulls. In my entire career as a sculptor, nothing has given me more pleasure than creating Charging Bull," di Modica said in his thick Sicilian accent. "I have a deep appreciation for the talented athletes who ride bulls. They experience and embody the power of bulls in ways I have tried to express in Charging Bull."

After that weekend, PBR's next scheduled event at the Garden would be canceled due to COVID-19. The arena stood empty and locked in January 2021, and the season began in an outdoor rodeo arena in horse country in Central Florida. A few weeks later, Arturo di Modica passed away at his home in Sicily.

As a young artist pursuing his passion in the hopes of developing a career that could sustain him, Arturo di Modica had to run away from his home in Sicily and hop a steam train to Florence to defy his father's wishes and become a sculptor. He had a dream. Nothing could stop him from the try of its pursuit. He went for it. No compromises. No excuses. No regrets.

To end the memorable weekend that had started the 2020 PBR season, when di Modica was honored by a sport he had just been introduced to—on a gray, chilly Sunday afternoon in a city that has over the years taken tremendous body blows, always rising stronger—after a punishing three-day event, João Ricardo Vieira, who had been born and raised on a farm outside of Itatinga, São Paulo, triumphantly raised a silver Charging Bull over his head, right about where Joe Frazier broke Muhammad Ali's jaw, the Pope

The Great Bull Gift

once led Mass, and Marilyn sang "Happy Birthday" to JFK. The exhausted Brazilian cowboy had a lot in common with the defiant, uncompromising, grateful, and giving man who created the special trophy he held, a tribute to the world's most famous bull, one who will live forever.

Love & Try

21

A COMPASSIONATE FAN NEVER FORGETS

(Lisa Twinde)

In early October 2018, fans who attended the Milwaukee Invitational saw a rascally couple cruising the concourse of the Fiserv Forum decked out in colorful peacock attire.

The sparkly get up was not a Halloween test run. Or a ploy to get noticed by PBR Official Entertainer Flint Rasmussen to nab "Cooper Tires Fan of the Night" honors.

Actually, there's a serious story behind the festive outfits, which serves as a great lesson in *Love & Try*. It starts with a woman with extraordinary compassion.

Lisa Twinde, a mega-PBR fan and decorated registered nurse, founded the Acres of Hope and Aspirations—a rehab farm in Wisconsin, assisting special needs children and veterans with brain and spinal cord injuries. With catastrophic injuries, every step of rehab is an opportunity to reinforce each advance forward, which Twinde calls "Proud as Peacocks" moments. She created programming branded "Proud as Peacocks of PBR." The RN who earned her graduate degree in rehabilitation at University of Wisconsin–Milwaukee says it is an honor, privilege, and her life's calling to care for gravely wounded soldiers facing daunting odds for a full recovery.

Such was the case with one veteran who'd been shot in the head in the Iraq War in 2006. Sgt. Winlom Woods came back to the U.S. on life support with his skull flap removed and the bullet still embedded in his brain.

"Winlom was known as 'Noah' because he loved animals," Twinde said. "He also had a very big heart and would give you the shirt off his back."

Noah was not expected to live. If he did, the prognosis was to exist in a vegetative state. But Noah fought hard and was weaned off life support and placed in a nursing home. He couldn't walk or talk. Chances for a full recovery or anything resembling a normal life were miniscule. He was thirty-two years old.

He had gone through a divorce while in Iraq and had no home to return to. His loving grandmother and other family members didn't have room or resources to take him in. He needed significant medical and skilled nursing care.

Enter Twinde.

She comes from a loving, strong family. Her father, grandfathers, uncles, and cousins all served in the military. "I knew this man needed hope, empowerment, and a purpose to live," she said.

Noah was now part of her family, living at the rehab farm under her nursing care in collaboration with physicians among the peacocks, mini horses, donkeys, pet deer, pot-bellied pigs, ducks, rabbits, dogs, tortoises, and a parrot she trained to ride the farm's 110-pound tortoise as if he were a bull.

The bullet couldn't be removed from the middle of Noah's brain. Cadaver bone was used to rebuild his skull flap. He had multiple cognitive and physical deficits and faced life-threatening complications. He wore diapers that Twinde changed for him.

Twinde worked with Noah for seven and a half years, nursing him through multiple surgeries and serious infections. Feeding off this love and support, Noah gained strength and courage. Learning to walk and talk again with a true "angel of mercy," the soldier had many "Proud as Peacocks of PBR" moments.

With Sgt. Winlom Woods, a.k.a. "Noah" (Lisa Twinde)

For nearly two years, Noah's brothers in the Iraq War had believed he had died from the head wound. Twinde helped locate his buddies, producing more Proud as Peacocks of PBR moments at soldier reunions she hosted at the farm.

Noah's brothers from the service marched in the local parade behind the car that transported him. She took him back and forth from VFW meetings and to his grandmother's for family events.

Love & Try

Noah always wanted a dog. Lisa got him a little therapy pooch, who walked Noah through his first steps, then a big Italian Mareeba Sheepdog as a service dog to help his recovery.

She brought Noah to the PBR event in Milwaukee in 2011, along with two other soldiers with brain injuries rehabbing at the farm.

"He had never seen bull riding but was so encouraged by the cowboys and these gigantic beasts," she said. "This soldier was a lot like these bulls, full of strength, and a lot like the cowboys, full of guts and courage, and a spirit that never gave up."

Noah was paralyzed on one side of his face. Nevertheless, his goal was to sing the national anthem again. Eventually, at a VFW picnic at the farm, he walked in carrying the American flag, then sang "The Star-Spangled Banner," using cue cards due to his brain injury. It was Lisa's finest Proud as Peacocks of PBR moment.

"Peacocks are a symbol of beauty and strength," she said. "When the peacock displays his feathers, he is proud and majestic. That's how these wounded men and women can feel again."

She says these values, which PBR stands for, attract her to the sport even more than on-the-dirt thrills from riders like her favorite, J.B. Mauney. She's seen some of J.B.'s biggest rides, including the biggest of them all on Bushwacker, breaking his PBR-record streak of forty-two consecutive buck-offs, as well as on Pearl Harbor and Air Time. She has also held her breath during very scary moments such as when Bonner Bolton was loaded onto a backboard after shattering his C2 in Chicago.

"This sport has given us great memories and inspires me to continue to assist those who need it most. It brings joy and fun to fans, but also gives the warmth and understanding of family, respect, service, and sacrifice," she said. "I am proud as peacocks for the respect, love and support that PBR gives to the military, to those who serve and sacrifice, as we stand for the national anthem at every event."

She was raised on country sunshine on a small farm in Wisconsin. Her dad had beef cows. Her grandfather ran a large horse farm and owned a Western store. The men put her on a tractor when she was five years old. She grew up watching rodeo legends Lane Frost, Ty Murray, and Cody Lambert, and today, she attends bull riding events with her fiancé Troy Tveitnes. The couple met when she was a forklift trainer, and he was one of her students as an engineer with Snap-on tools.

"Troy is on the road a lot as an engineer, and I'm on the road as a contracted field nurse helping injured soldiers," she said. "Our life story is like *The Longest Ride*. We get together for PBR events, doing seven to nine a year, including World Finals."

She's written passionate letters to Roger Goodell and football players taking a knee, telling the story of Noah and pleading with them to understand that the national anthem isn't the right platform for protest. The letters were not answered, and that only made her more determined to support Noah in his sacrifice, a veteran with no immediate family who could take him in. She simply would not accept walking away and would not prejudge a man who had described himself as a juvenile delinquent raised in downtown Milwaukee among gangs. When she first met Noah, he was lifeless. And now she'd helped give him his life back.

Battling a brain injury, Noah used cue cards to sing "The Star-Spangled Banner" (Lisa Twinde)

"The one thing we can all do more is show compassion," she said.

They prayed together every day. They cried together, for all the things he couldn't do, a physically broken man, now part of her family.

And then came the hardest day of her life, February 16, 2014, when Lisa performed CPR to try to save Noah. She had given him the love. Noah had provided the try. But now it was his time.

"Every day, this courageous man tried and wouldn't give up. His ultimate sacrifice *will never be forgotten.*"

And now in memory of Noah, she hosts groups at the farm to teach compassion. "He was a walking miracle. I want him to inspire people to never give up. I want Noah to never be forgotten."

Twinde has an idea. To tell the story. To keep the memory alive.

"Noah was a proud American who never got the recognition he deserved for the sacrifices and the ultimate price he paid with his life for this country," she said. "He will never be forgotten by me, and he'll be smiling down from heaven knowing that in his memory, a champion bucking bull has been named Noah."

22

THE WATER WARRIOR

(160Over90)

The PBR was storming into Glendale, Arizona, in mid-March 2021, marking an anniversary nobody wanted to celebrate. A year ago, to the week, people in the United States had started to get very sick, many dying after contracting a virus that had originated overseas four months earlier. Dire warnings were issued to restrict the size of public gatherings. Arena events were verboten. PBR complied, telling ticket-holding fans they'd get refunds and holding an eerie-feeling, for-TV-only bull riding in a drafty, empty Infinite Energy Center in Duluth, Georgia.

In the ensuing year, so much had happened. Many had lost loved ones or jobs or a sense of hope for the return of their old lives. After creating the safety protocols that would lead the sports back to business and becoming the first to host fans back inside an indoor arena, PBR's ninth event of the

2021 season would entail another weekend of COVID-19 tests, hand washing, mask wearing, and social distancing. Yet in Arizona that March, it finally looked like the light at the end of the tunnel was not an approaching train.

Three vaccinations approved for use were being administered in every state across the country. COVID-19 caseloads and death rates were dropping. Three feet instead of six would be the new guidance on social distancing. And in the world of professional bull riding, the league had sold nearly 9,500 tickets for the Glendale weekend, the most for any regular season event since the onset of the virus. Considering fans were still in pod seating to keep groups separated, this was considered a big win. You could feel the optimism in Flint Rasmussen's delivery as he thanked fans for coming.

You could feel the optimism in Flint Rasmussen's delivery as he thanked the fans for coming and letting him, the riders, bull fighters, and crew do their jobs. The presence of a bachelorette party in the stands—an entire row of masked lasses spending more time on their feet dancing to the beats of PBR Music Director Richard Jones than in their seats—didn't tamp Flint's great mood, either.

Everyone seemed to be smiling, especially the PBR executives responsible for the sport and the livelihoods of everyone associated with it. In a rambunctious Gila River Arena, they saw for the first time in more than a year the crowd doing "the wave," and, even with pod seating, it worked—well, for those who appreciate this corny form of fan celebration.

The face bearing the broadest, brightest smile belonged to Keyshawn Whitehorse, who had just ridden Lil 2 Train for 90.25 points in the championship round of the first part of the weekend—the conclusion of a weather delayed event in Del Rio after historic storms swept across Texas and halted the event midway though. It was a career-high moment for Whitehorse, a long time coming. Even though the compact rider was only twenty-three years old, he had started bucking calves when he was eight, at his home sitting between four sacred mountains in the high desert of rural Southern Utah.

Some riders bust into the arena, joke around with their pals, put on their gear, and snap into a serious trance only when they get ready to ride a bull. Before that, it's almost as if they're welcoming any distraction other than to consider what might be the most dangerous eight seconds of their lives until it's time to face the music. Others get in the zone much earlier.

The Water Warrior

When Whitehorse enters any PBR arena, he's all business. His preparation is carefully planned and methodically executed. His pre-event routine includes a series of stretching exercises and a prayer ritual blending Navajo tradition and Christianity. Before stepping into his fringed chaps and emerald-green protective vest emblazoned with the logo of his top sponsors Ariat and the U.S. Border Patrol, Whitehorse, who grew up on a Navajo reservation, anoints his body with burnt cedar as he asks for protection and for communion with the bull he is matched with. He prays for a safe, successful partnership with his bull, for while every bull ride is a dangerous and jarring endeavor, when things go right for the rider, it's also a beautifully choreographed dance in which both human and bovine athlete contribute equally to the final score. It takes two to win in this sport.

Keyshawn Whitehorse (Bull Stock Media)

Keyshawn believes that if he stays in the moment, he has a chance to stay on even the rankest bucking bull.

"People try to live in the future and, yet, aren't even there yet," he told *Cowboy Lifestyle Network*. "Most times, people's minds are working overtime to try and predict multiple outcomes without knowing what the actual outcome is going to be. I try to focus on the task at hand, training as hard as

I can, taking care of business, then showing up and riding the best that I can knowing that I've trained my hardest and I've given it one hundred percent. If it doesn't work out, then you can still say you did everything in your power to let that opportunity arise and hopefully it was made for you, but if not, you gave it your best shot."

Whitehorse was crisply in the moment on Lil 2 Train. Their pairing was the best of the night. On the dirt, accepting the buckle for his first career elite series win, he turned more reflective, sharing how he needed to push ahead to fight all of life's trials and tribulations.

Sitting in the socially distanced stands of Gila River Arena watching the post-event interview, Zoel Zohnnie, who grew up on an Indian reservation in north central Arizona, knew exactly what Whitehorse meant.

When the global health pandemic came, it hit the Navajo Nation hard, generating a higher per-capita death rate than any state in the US. Before the onset of COVID-19, the Navajo Nation, which stretches across much of Northeastern Arizona, Northwestern New Mexico, and southeastern parts of Utah (where Whitehorse is from) already had a poverty rate (38 percent) more than twice the rest of the country. During the virus, even essential businesses were being forced to close by 3 p.m.

The pandemic had affected Zohnnie, a part-time actor who many fans were recognizing from PBR's "Be Cowboy" campaign. About a year ago, he had been laid off from his job as a journeyman boilermaker, specializing in power plant maintenance. He could have been forgiven for using these unfortunate circumstances as an opportunity to wallow in self-pity. Instead, Zohnnie asked himself, *"What can I do to help others in need?"*

While he knew several nonprofits were bringing essential supplies to Navajos, Zohnnie noticed one thing some people in remote areas weren't getting—water. Amid severe drought conditions, the Navajo Nation lacks an adequate water supply and is running out of water; Zohnnie observed some families were completely parched. Compounding the situation, the federal government was continuing to neglect Native American communities, where substandard housing and infrastructure make it more difficult to cope with climate shocks. In fact, many residents from Arizona were driving across the border to Mexico to get water. At the water stops, they fed quarters into a coin slot, similar to buying air at a gas station, to fill their barrels before heading back to the United States

The Water Warrior

Without a 9:00 to 5:00 to constrict him, Zohnnie, a broad-shouldered man with arms covered in mystical tattoos, networked with friends, farmers' markets, and community health reps who check in on the elderly to identify those without running taps who needed water the most. He began hitching up a 275-gallon tank to make deliveries to elders in remote areas of the Navajo Nation. At one of the first homes he visited in New Mexico near the Arizona border, an old man appeared, bringing out fifteen buckets. He didn't have a storage barrel. "During my childhood, we didn't have running water," Zohnnie said. "I hauled a lot of water and knew how difficult it must be without even a storage barrel."

He bought the man a barrel, delivering it the next day. His service snowballed from there. Zohnnie would go on to found the nonprofit Collective Medicine and then the Water Warriors United campaign, which paid for hundreds of storage barrels for Navajo families. Collective Medicine also delivered firewood throughout the winter, processing and delivering 131 tons of wood.

As a show of support to several PBR partners, when Zohnnie, now often called "The Water Warrior," needed vehicles for Collective Medicine to traverse the rugged, bumpy dirt roads of the Navajo Nation, he used donations to purchase Ford trucks, outfitted with Cooper Tires.

Zohnnie's initial connection to PBR had come in December 2018, when a casting director called the strapping Navajo, who on occasion acted, to audition for a new commercial being created for the bull riding organization. The point of the campaign was to show that what defines a cowboy isn't the boots, hat, or buckle; all those who live the cowboy code, and espouse values like honesty, hard work, and determination, are cowboys, too. To bring that concept alive, the league turned to 160over90, a sister company to PBR in the Endeavor network, to cast and shoot the kind of people who carry dirt under their fingernails. Zohnnie fit right into the campaign, which debuted in January 2019 on Super Bowl Sunday prior to the big game.

"It's a real campaign—real people who work hard every day, get in there, and get it done. This is what they do. I'm proud to be included," he said.

When Zohnnie appeared in the campaign's official debut with signage plastered throughout STAPLES Center in Los Angeles, strangers noticed him from the posters and TV spot, providing an opportunity to spread Navajo love. "This came out of nowhere; it was pretty nice. The commercial has resulted in so many great conversations. People want to know my background, what's my story?"

Considering how he would apply his cowboy values, it was effective casting. Zohnnie appreciates a role allowing him to cast attention on others.

"When Native American riders do well in the PBR Global Cup (a five-nation tournament in which Native American riders have their own sovereign team as part of the Team USA contingent) or win events like Whitehorse did in Glendale, it creates ripple effects beyond the world standings," Zohnnie said. An entire group of people is inspired, motivated, and even validated. For those raised and now living in hardscrabble circumstances, this is more than a game.

"Here we are as Navajo people, from humble beginnings and with the struggle of growing up in a situation of poverty. Then with guts and determination, these bull riders have success accomplishing something on an international level at an elite stratosphere," Zohnnie said. "Lots of Navajos on the ranch know who guys like Keyshawn and Cody Jesus are. Achieving that level of success turns everyone's head. We rally around them and are very proud of them. The older people will cheer them on as if it's their child. In the past, this kind of success was only a dream, and now it's become attainable to a lot of our cowboys and young kids. We really look up to these guys."

It was a bonus that the campaign Zohnnie was cast for promotes the sport stoking his pride, like when pow wow dancers led the historic all-Native American team into AT&T Stadium in February for the PBR Global Cup. "It gave me goosebumps," Zohnnie said. "That opened a lot of doors and eyes. Everybody was rooting for the Wolves. They came up short but did really good."

Navajo, Cherokee, Sioux, Chippewa, Potawatomi, Northern Cheyenne, and Blackfeet tribal nation bull riders forming the Wolves finished in third place at the international tournament, despite having never before competed together.

Well before the Global Cup, Zohnnie had been keeping a close watch on Whitehorse, a fellow Navajo, and he became a fan of young Cody Jesus when he saw the slight yet fearless rider compete at a fair in Window Rock, Arizona.

The Water Warrior

The mild-mannered, affable Jesus is also a quintessential story of grit and determination, love and try. One of eight siblings, he also grew up without electricity and running water. Jesus would collect pinion nuts and recycled cans to pay for his bull riding entry fees. There were no gym memberships; to work out, Jesus climbed trees in his hometown of Window Rock, Arizona. In one of the many PBR interconnections, the biggest ride of his career was also on Lil 2 Train, the bull Whitehorse rode to win Glendale. Jesus rode the bull for ninety-two points to win Round 2 of the 2019 PBR World Finals.

In Glendale, with Whitehorse triumphant and Jesus returning from a nagging groin injury, the Navajo Nation connections came full circle for Zohnnie and members of Collective Medicine. They were recognized in a ceremony during a break in the action for their courageous, selfless efforts that brought desperately needed water and wood along with precious hope to many.

"I'm more than grateful to be part of the 'Be Cowboy' campaign and represent my people, and to be honored with our organization by PBR for helping others," he said. "The slogan 'Be Cowboy' goes a long way. It symbolizes hard work and just being a good quality human being. That's what my dad and uncle and so many others have taught me. And it's what I hope I can teach others."

Love & Try

23

THE OUTLAW AND THE BIG HEARTED COP

(Tommy Norman)

Tommy Norman was all of thirteen years old when he found his life's calling.

The kid from North Little Rock was hard working and industrious. On weekends, he'd mow laws for good spending money. After one particularly productive workday, Tommy was in his room, watching TV, still sweaty with fresh grass shavings clinging to his skinny legs.

Love & Try

"I turned to 'Feed the Children,' and it just captured my heart," Norman said. "I took the sixty dollars I'd made mowing lawns to my mother and asked her to send it to those children."

On that steamy-hot summer day, Norman knew he wanted to dedicate his life to serving others. For making good on that promise, and embarking on a world-renowned career in law enforcement, he would wind up being honored by PBR at the Little Rock Invitational at Verizon Arena one Saturday night in March 2017.

Now a patrol officer with the North Little Rock Police Department, Norman is a beloved figure making a difference with struggling youth, mending fences with the minority community, and influencing law enforcement strategy nationwide.

Rather than cruising the neighborhoods, he's usually outside his police car, walking the beat, routinely handing out candy bars, snacks, and sodas to children. If a kid needs sneakers, he'll buy a pair. The shoes are put to good use; kids of color run *toward* this white police officer.

Officer Norman will clown with kids and shoot funny videos posted to an Instagram account boasting more than one million followers. In times of heightened tensions among police and minorities, his constant stream of videos, photos, and inspirational words of advice with the hashtags *#CommunityPolicing* and *#StayCommitted* is helping change how people view police and has earned Norman the moniker "the social media cop."

His devoted followers across the world have sent thousands of packages for North Little Rock residents containing clothing, meals, and toys. He even caught the attention of rapper The Game, who started a GoFundMe page that raised tens of thousands of dollars to help local kids.

Before the bull riding in Little Rock, Officer Norman had another set of arms to help dip into the trunk full of food, snacks, and drinks when star rider Chase Outlaw rode shotgun. The duo visited community shelters and stopped by a food kitchen to bring provisions and smiles. "It was fun to see Tommy put smiles on a lot of kids' faces," Outlaw said. "Smiles are contagious."

"I'm not good at much," Norman said. "I don't have many skills. I do have a heart and a connection to people that is rare. I try to capture the community's own heart with trust and respect."

The Outlaw and the Big Hearted Cop

While he's a household name locally and has been covered by national media, Norman's primary responsibility, of course, is to enforce the law. "I know the same people I meet and form relationships with won't think twice about breaking the law," he said. "If there's a reason to take them to jail, I will."

Even when that happens, the results can be surprising. A former career criminal Norman had arrested ten years earlier thanked him for the kindness that helped the grateful man turn his life around.

Before realizing as a thirteen-year-old that he wanted to serve others, Norman had his mind fixed on being the next Michael Jordan. "I tried to walk and talk like Michael Jordan," he said. "But before long, I realized I couldn't play basketball like Michael Jordan."

He would follow the career path of another personal hero—his uncle, who was a small-town police chief in Hot Springs Village, Arkansas. He loved his uncle's uniform, his badge, and his gun, as well as the stories he'd hear on special trips in the chief's cruiser.

The trappings of a modern-day law enforcement office are unfortunately often viewed as symbols of aggression. Norman is turning that all-too common and unfair perception on its head. "This uniform, badge, and gun create so much opportunity to connect with the community," he said. "But it's ultimately not the uniform and badge people see. They look into your heart and see the way you treat them."

One of nine siblings, Norman credits his mother for shaping his selfless disposition and sense of service. "My mom, an extremely loving person, was always helping people, always teaching her children to give back and help those less fortunate," he explained.

In a predominantly Black town where the poverty rate exceeds 21 percent, he says his policing philosophy in North Little Rock "is really as simple as treating people the way you want to be treated. When a police officer gets out of the car and his boots hit the ground, the first mission should be to love, trust, and respect people. When you lead with your heart, they'll respect you even more in return."

He was flattered to be recognized at the local PBR tour stop. But the ceremonial honors and additional publicity were nothing to get too excited about.

"I'm on the inside looking out trying to smash barriers and build bridges," he said. "I don't see what you see. It's a way of life for me so, honestly, I don't see amazing work, and I don't need to see it. I don't want to lose my focus."

24
GRIT AND GRACE

(Bull Stock Media)

Can a group of snot-slinging bucking bulls help unite a divided country?

Fanchon Stinger believes so.

Stinger has spent the past quarter century as a local news star, most recently as the evening news anchor for Fox 59 in Indianapolis. She was exceptional at her job—fifteen Emmy awards on her mantle prove that.

She is a woman of sublime storytelling and communication talents. She's active in the community. She radiates positivity and optimism. She was also professionally beholden to a medium that puts a premium on shock and titillation. There's a saying about local news: if it bleeds, it leads. And there's more blood every day.

Stinger's most recognized career moment is wrapped into one of the country's darkest days—when she rushed to lower Manhattan for her Detroit news station to cover the aftermath of the 9/11 terrorist attacks. Reporters live to be assigned "the big story." But nobody wants to cover genuine horror. Stinger went in with her training, but it was her humility, ability to connect with people, her faith, and her sheer instincts that took over. Reporting from the smoking rubble in the heart of a city reeling and wounded but also swiftly united in a shared grief that seemed to make everyone a better, kinder human being, she was empathetic yet hard hitting, and she won an Emmy Award for her reporting.

The experience changed how she approached news. Conveying a realness of people's stories would mark her reporting since those dark days from "the pile." More than twenty years later, night after night, the job required her to chronicle a litany of crimes, misdeeds, and misfortune exposing her to the worst human inclinations that would dim the sunniest of personalities.

Yet Stinger found light. It comes from her faith, her family, a close circle of friends, two 1,800-pound bovines named Stinger and Lil' Hott—world-class bucking bulls she part-owns—and with her new charitable organization she has founded to share the sport she loves and to equip young ladies "to step into their calling while leading with integrity, grit, and grace in all they do."

Stinger's foundation, Grit & Grace, launched late in the 2021 season. In 2022, she is appearing at roughly a dozen PBR premier series events, hosting middle and high school age girls, and offering them scholarship opportunities to help grow their leadership skills. Stinger also brings in special guests—women personifying excellence who amplify the pillars of her foundation: girl grit, courage, self-respect, selfless compassion, and patriotic spirit.

The most important lessons at events with Fanchon come through hands-on learning about animal care. Her guests learn from the best in the business up close and personal with the bulls who are on the receiving end of abundant love and care.

(AniMotion Photography)

Fanchon's story of transforming from an enthusiastic PBR fan to a bull owner using Western sports to inspire others, which culminated in partnering with Chad Berger, the eleven-time PBR Stock Contractor of the Year, is one of persistence and serendipity, and of course grit and grace.

Stinger grew up in Michigan and spent a lot of time with family and around animals in Mississippi. She adopted a Western style, wearing cowboy boots and hats while riding horses and attending rodeos. The best part was the final discipline: the bull riding, especially the majestic bucking bulls who brought each rodeo to a thrilling close.

"The bulls were always my favorite, and that's why I became a fan from the year PBR began when I started dreaming about owning a bull," Stinger said.

In the sport's early days, she would watch with her dad, admiring the animal athletes and the indomitable spirt of the mismatched cowboys trying to conquer them. The riders slammed to the dirt would often get hurt. But they'd keep getting up and coming back stronger than ever. It was mesmerizing. And inspiring.

The cowboys' oversized courage and stubborn grit was influencing Fanchon to rely on faith, courage, and perseverance. Bouncing back following a setback became a metaphor for her life. She'd get knocked down in her own way but would rise up to keep walking in the purpose she knew God had created her for.

Some of the setbacks were personal. Others professional. One crossed into both areas of her life.

Earlier in her career, she had been one of most popular broadcasters in Detroit but then faced ugly and untrue allegations in the media after a man she was seeing was accused of delivering bribes to Detroit city officials. That man turned out to be an abuser. Stinger was never investigated, had no knowledge of his dealings, and was never involved. Before the truth came out, she found herself the victim of weaponized media and a survivor of verbal, emotional, and physical abuse at the hands of that man. Her career was temporarily derailed; she left the station and the city she loved only to become even more successful in Indianapolis. From that traumatic experience, she now lends her voice to fighting for accuracy, fairness, and balance in media. She also educates people on the realities of domestic-dating violence.

Fanchon says God has used many disappointments, bad decisions, hurts, and hard lessons to build her fierce faith and passion to serve others. She sees it all, especially the hardest of times, as His blessing to help her share her faith and encourage others.

Professionally, even as she managed through these challenges and continued to win accolades and awards, Stinger's eyes remained fixed on bull riding.

"I loved what the cowboys represented in toughness love, honor, determination, and respect," she said. "And at the same time, I found myself cheering a little bit more for the bulls. I'm an animal lover, and I wanted to find a way to be part of a fun sport that made for good, wholesome family entertainment. Of course, I couldn't ride a bull. The next best thing was a dream to be a bull owner. I love the way the animals are honored. They're treated with the utmost respect and the best care. I believe wholeheartedly in that and wanted to be part of it."

Fanchon also appreciated the sport's completely level playing field—a meritocracy grounded in simple rules, along with the bulls who didn't give a hoot where the rider came from, what he looked like, or how much money he had. Everyone is the same on the back of a two-ton animal trying to launch its passenger into oblivion. Hold on for eight seconds, or you don't get paid. Talent was important. Try even more so.

Stinger has always respected those who believe they can accomplish things that are difficult. Riding a bull is very hard. The odds are stacked against every rider, yet every rider goes in envisioning success. Guys get their butt kicked. Yet without fail, they come back to do it again, confident of success.

Plus, in bull riding, there are no time outs. No place to hide. No participation trophies. No victims. No blame. No excuses.

The more she learned about the sport, the more magnetic it became. She'd work for ten years to bring her dream to life as a bull owner.

The journey started at World Finals in 2009, the thrilling wrap to an intense season in which PBR boss Randy Bernard consciously created a marketable rivalry between Coloradan Cody Lostroh, who'd quit college at the University of Wyoming to join the tour, and the hot-shot twenty one-year-old gunslinger from North Carolina, J.B. Mauney. Bernard created a conflict that took hold. He made sure Lostroh was only photographed for promotional materials in a white hat; Mauney would always be in black.

With the rivalry going full steam, Stinger would see two of the greatest World Finals performances inside Thomas & Mack Center off the Vegas strip. Mauney, free arm pinwheeling like Pete Townsend playing power chords on "Won't Get Fooled Again," made history by riding all eight of his bulls, finishing with a monster 93.75 points on a bull named Black Pearl. It turned out to be the greatest World Finals performance any rider ever had without winning a world title, because J.B. couldn't catch Lostroh, who went a near-perfect seven for eight to win the 2009 World Championship.

As good as the title race was, Stinger's goal was to meet Chad Berger. As a fan, she knew Berger was a very successful bull stock contractor with a reputation of being an all-around terrific person. Arriving in Las Vegas for championship weekend, she didn't know a soul but made it her business to find and befriend Berger.

Stalking is too harsh of a word, but Berger will joke that's what Stinger did. Call it uncommon persistence. Through a "divine appointment" she introduced herself to then-CEO Bernard, who appreciated Fanchon's high-wattage zest for the sport. Bernard understood the power of media connections for a sport clawing into the mainstream. He introduced Fanchon to the affable bull stock contractor at a fan experience.

"From there, Chad and I clicked," Stinger said. "We share the same values of treating animals like family. When his bulls retire and eventually die, he buries them on his property. That really touched me. We became friends that day; Randy, too."

Bernard also hooked her into his top lieutenant, Sean Gleason, who'd take over as the sport's top executive five years later and made sure the organization would lend its support to Grit & Grace. It is now the first community-focused foundation to officially align with PBR.

Back in 2010, the time wasn't right for Stinger to pursue bull ownership on her own. Berger wasn't about to offer a fire-sale on one of his rising bulls. The opportunity finally materialized with her dear friends and now partners Daniel and Melissa Brunner. They heard Stinger's vision of using the sport, its animals, and female leaders to promote what she and the Brunners call "The Honor Culture" and jumped on board to pool resources and become partners in two of Chad Berger's bucking bulls.

Stinger finally got the chance to meet her bulls at a tour stop in Oklahoma City in 2021.

"It was like a mom going to meet my own child," she said. "I told Chad, 'I want the bull to know I'm his mom.' When the house lights went down, they said that prayer, and played the National Anthem, all that emotion overcame me, and I was brought to tears. It was an emotional weekend for me. It made my resolve even deeper to honor and help this sport."

Fans may remember Stinger on the CBS broadcast atop the bucking chutes bobbing up and down in nervous anticipation as Joao Ricardo Viera mounted her bull below, then jumping up and down overwhelmed with joy when Vieira rode Stinger for 84.5 points.

Through Grit & Grace, she's promoting fundamental principles of family, faith, and freedom, joined by female mentors sharing their personal stories while discussing goal setting, developing one's gifts and talents, honoring others, and nurturing boldness, confidence, and integrity.

She sees PBR as an "untapped gem" that can bring people together. She had once covered New Yorkers of all backgrounds and places of life putting aside differences and rallying around our common humanity. The threat today is different—warring camps battling in a culture of contempt. Yet today's divisions need not be passively accepted as the national condition of tomorrow. As God's children, we just need guidance and something to believe in.

"I'm watching America lose touch with our core values and become more polarized by the day," Stinger said. "We are losing sight of what makes us a great nation. At the same time, I've grown to love a sport that I sincerely believe can be an antidote to the division and discord I see and reported on every day. PBR is a big, unified, and diverse traveling family, which lives by and celebrates important values. People have a deep desire for faith, family, and freedom that is honored in Western sports and its values. These values are intertwined with the animals who are loved as God's majestic creations. I believe, together, all those components can help quench our thirst for the unity we all crave. I've also recognized that young ladies need a comfortable place to go for family fun where they are also uplifted, honored, and inspired to be all they were created to be. I see this sport as that place, and I'm grateful for this platform the Lord has given me."

And now she's looking forward to watching Stinger and Lil' Hott buck, sharing her love for the sport, and inspiring young girls to work hard, tap into their dreams, seize their potential, and do great things in life.

"I wanted to be part of this sport because faith, freedom, patriotism, God, and country need saving, and those are the pillars of this sport. Those are the values of the cowboys (and us cowgirls), and right now the world needs more cowboys," she said. "I've been welcomed like family from the very beginning. That's a blessing and a gift to me. And now I want to share that gift with others."

25

APPER'S LEGACY

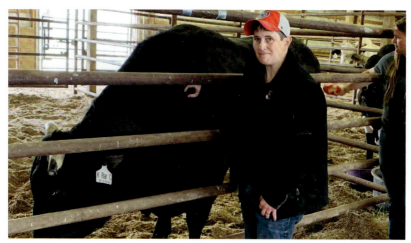

(Mary Apper)

In some ways, Mary Apper was an ordinary PBR fan. In other ways, she was extraordinary.

How many fans have a bull named after them?

How many have PBR fan clubs rallying around them during an unflinching fight through illness?

How many become legendary to a legion who declared in broken-hearted sincerity that, even though they'd never physically met, Mary was like a long-lost sister, a kindred spirit who will continue to inspire them long after she's gone?

The family that is PBR—the fans, crew, partners, and athletes—followed her battle. And then Mary Apper—lover of animals, decorated Navy veteran, PBR superfan, devoted daughter and sister, and stone-faced warrior—was gone.

She passed away at thirty-nine years old on January 14, 2021, just before sunrise in her condominium in Fresno, California, two days before the new PBR season was to start, surrounded by her mother, father, and two sisters, following a valiant three-and-a-half-year battle with cancer.

"Mary will always, and in all ways, continue to be God's loving light in our lives," her mother, Liza, wrote in a CaringBridge forum that had shared Mary's journey in hospice. "She will be shining from a different vantage point, but I know she will be with us."

Hundreds of fans had followed Mary's final days through the online journal. Many shared Mary's impact on their lives. "We are not related by blood, but the love I have for Mary makes her my sister by blood," wrote Rick Storm of Beaverton, Oregon, who had met Mary through a fan group and spent time with her at a horse ranch in northern California. "Mary inspired me and so many others," Storm said. "Just knowing Mary made me a better man. She had more cowboy in her little toe than I ever had in my entire body. She *is* the definition of 'Be Cowboy.'"

Mary's fight had inspired the creation of a "BUCK CANCER" campaign. Homemade signs with that slogan were posted by fans, riders, and even PBR Commissioner Sean Gleason to raise awareness of the second-leading cause of death in the US.

"Cancer is an everyday thing," Mary said in a video thanking fans for supporting the Buck Cancer campaign. "There are ups and downs, highs and lows, good days and bad days. It is an everyday battle—not all of them bad, not all of them good. I want to thank everyone; I love the work you're doing to get the word out."

Mary loved get-togethers, backyard swimming, family game nights, puzzle building, coffee "chitchats," and law enforcement television shows like *Third Watch, Chicago PD,* and *Criminal Minds.* She was especially drawn to the portrayal of the close-knit Reagan clan on *Blue Bloods*, whose weekly Sunday dinners were Mary's favorite part of the show, according to Liza.

"She would often say to me, 'Mom, let's do that. I want us, the whole family, to have dinner together like that,'" Liza remembered. "So, we would make a ritual of gathering together frequently for those 'Sunday dinners' that didn't necessarily fall on a Sunday. It became important to our family to share meals together and end with coffee and chitchat."

With Cody Nance (Mary Apper)

During her last summer in the one hundred degree Fresno heat, the family gathered several times a week for what her sister Meghan dubbed, "Float and Feed!"—swimming before a summer feast, swimming again after their meal, then enjoying coffee and chitchat. When it got cooler and darkness came earlier, Mary would cook barbecued meals on her gas grill under the summer stars.

"It was a beautiful time of shared love, laughter, and togetherness that I now hold in my heart," Liza said. "We created our intimate family of love this summer. Mary loved our Float and Feeds. She would get so excited every time we got together and, before the night ended, she and I would plan another Float and Feed get-together in that same week."

In fall 2020, Mary had planned to travel to more PBR events, including the *PBR Air Force Reserve Cowboys for a Cause* aboard the *USS Lexington* docked in Corpus Christi, Texas, where she would be honored as a military veteran aboard the famed aircraft carrier. However, the masses in Mary's body had stopped responding to chemotherapy and were embedding in her ribs. She was back in the hospital in severe pain.

"I'm a fighter, and I'm trying with everything in me to beat this," she texted me as our PR team arranged her VIP spot. "I hope to be on that ship! My PBR family means the world to me."

Unfortunately, Mary remained hospitalized and could not make the special team event launching the sport's charitable initiative that raised $250,000 for military causes. In a few weeks, she would return home for her remaining days surrounded by her family's laughter, jokes, stories, and gossip, sometimes dozing off and startling them by interjecting a funny comment, and later falling into a deep sleep next to her mother.

"Tonight, as I laid in bed with Mary, her deep breathing and low-key snoring put me to sleep," Liza wrote on CaringBridge around Christmas. "We both woke up a little while later because of my snoring—the mom-daughter sleeping duo in action! It was a funny and wonderful moment to wake up beside Mary, both of us, at first, wondering how we woke up. And later realizing we had both been in synchronized sleep."

Most fans first learned of Mary's fight, which would include multiple surgeries to remove two ribs, her gallbladder, parts of her small intestines, stomach, pancreas, and liver, through her relationship with bull stock contractors Kenny and Cristy McElroy.

Apper, a fan of the PBR since 1996, met the McElroys and their bulls, including her personal favorite, Big Black, when she visited K-Bar-C Bucking Bulls ranch in early 2019 as part of a Premium Experience tour in Ohio while she was in-state to receive treatment for her cancer. Mary was especially excited to meet Cristy, who she'd gotten to know on social media, and of course that big beautiful black bucking bovine. Yet, she unexpectedly made a special connection with another bull—Mind Freak.

"The more she was here, the more she kind of took to Mind Freak; she had that sparkle in her eyes," Kenny told Justin Felisko, who chronicled the relationship for PBR.com. "It is kind of crazy because Mind Freak took to her, and he is kind of the same way. He is real personable, and you can love on him. He took to her real quick. I think she fell in love with him here."

"The bond was so immediate it was crazy," Cristy said. "When she left, I didn't realize the impact she'd have on our family."

A few days later, Apper sent a message to Cristy, admitting "a bull crush" on Mind Freak.

The McElroys already had developed a special level of empathy for Apper. Kenny had survived a huge cancer scare in 2012, successfully battling the pernicious disease after nine inches of his colon and twenty-five surrounding lymph nodes were removed. He's been cancer-free since then. The family talked about their new friend amid a tough physical and emotional battle, and they hatched an idea. "She was struggling with treatment, and we wanted to do something to help her fight," Cristy said.

The couple remembered Apper saying that when she had the means to do so, she hoped to own a bucking bull. At the same time, they remembered how the bulls inspired Kenny during his battle, helping him stay positive and productive during the most difficult days.

Mary would attain that wish. K-Bar-C Bucking Bulls renamed the bull she had taken a shine to as Apper's Mind Freak. Mary would even get down in the bucking chutes for an up-close view of the bull competing.

"I have gone through the same thing she is going through, and I know how hard it is," Kenny told Felisko. "With my family and friends—these bulls helped me the most. I know if Mary had something like this, she can stay positive and have something to look forward to."

Kenny's deep respect for the military—his father served in Vietnam and his grandfather in WWII—also influenced the decision.

Apper had joined the U.S. Navy in 2006 and at the time of her medical retirement in 2017 was a Damage Control Petty Officer First Class. She had been deployed five times, four of which came aboard the *USS Chafee* (DDG-90) and once on the ground in Afghanistan. She had received numerous awards for her service, including the National Defense Service Medal, Army Commendation Medal, Afghanistan Campaign Medal, Navy Commendation Medal (four times), NATO ISAF Medal, and Expert Marksmanship Medals for both the pistol and rifle.

Mary gave her service flag to Tony Nevarez (Sonni Nevarez)

    Mary Apper's compassion and sense of service would intersect with the sport she loved and the fellow fans she grew close to. In the 2019 season, she crossed paths with another PBR superfan, Tony Nevarez, who is a popular fixture at PBR events along with his mom, Sonni. The two have attended nearly fifty PBR events. Tony, who has cerebral palsy, always brought his prized possession, an American flag covered with the signatures of dozens of PBR riders.

At home with the riders (Bull Stock Media)

In May 2019, mother and son were on the way from their home in San Diego to the Ty Murray Invitational in Albuquerque, one of their favorite events because it's named for the rider known as "King of the Cowboys" and held in a small, loud arena known as "The Pit" where the University of New Mexico Lobos play. Tony loved the energy of the intimate venue, and his signed flag was draped over his wheelchair in the back of Sonni's Ford truck as she sped to Albuquerque. Somewhere along the way, the flag blew out the back window. By the time Tony and Sonni discovered the flag was missing, it was too late. It could have been two miles back. Or fifty. The story of the one-of-a-kind lost flag made the news in New Mexico, but it was never found.

Mary Apper heard about this. She was not one to be given bad news and let it sit. She made plans for her U.S. Navy retirement flag to be given to Tony on his thirtieth birthday during a special presentation in the Honda Center when PBR visited Anaheim later that season. Since then, Tony had been taking Mary's new flag to every PBR event, including World Finals in AT&T Stadium, keeping it on his lap.

Now becoming friends with Mary, Sonni still chuckles at the memory of the decorated military warrior turning shy and star struck at the PBR Heroes & Legends dinner in South Point Hotel & Casino in Las Vegas, holding a white leather riding glove, wondering how to get PBR World Champion Chris Shivers to sign it. "She was so nervous to ask him; she couldn't get up the courage," Sonni remembered. "Cody Nance was there, so we had Cody take her to Chris. She was absolutely tickled."

After Mary's passing, her mom sent Cody and his wife, Korie, two patches taken from her U.S. Navy uniform—her name and the "backward" American flag. It's standard practice for the military to sew a backward flag on the uniform, making the blue field the highest position of honor placed on the right side with the stars facing forward to illustrate a soldier's unending dedication to facing adversity head on. Just as Mary lived.

If the measure of a person's life is their impact on others in their allotted time here on earth, Mary has done very well.

"Mary Apper was sent to cross our paths, I believe, and remind all of us to never give up, don't lose hope, live for each second of time," wrote Karrie Martin Eiden, a PBR fan from Mesa, Arizona, in a heartfelt online tribute. "She taught us yesterday is not a do-over, tomorrow is not a guarantee, and today is to be celebrated. Mary's message was to love with a passion, to help others when needed, to support those you care about, to fight for what is right. These are all the reasons we love Mary, and we are thankful to have had the honor of having her cross our path."

Two days after her passing, PBR honored Mary during the CBS telecast of the season opening broadcast from Ocala, Florida, where Apper's Mind Freak reigned supreme in dumping Marco Eguchi in 2.75 seconds and then beating João Ricardo Vieira in 7.4 seconds in the championship round of the PBR Monster Energy Invitational. "I have never seen him buck so hard," Vieira said. "This week I think he was bucking for Mary. I met her before. I am sad she passed away."

Exactly a year prior (January 19, 2020), Vieira had taken Apper's Mind Freak for 90.25 points in Manchester, New Hampshire.

"Apper's Mind Freak bucked awesome today!!!!" Apper wrote on Facebook after that ride. "I love him so much and am so proud of him! Also, congrats to JRV on an outstanding ride!!"

Mary had one final opportunity to talk to her namesake bull when Kenny and Cristy McElroy Facetimed Apper around Christmastime, about three weeks before her passing. "Everyone says we did so much for Mary, but the truth is she did even more for us," Cristy said.

Apper's Legacy

Fans continued to see Apper's Mind Freak compete in 2021 as PBR's premier series first started a swing through outdoor rodeo arenas across the South to keep bucking during the pandemic before heading back indoors. In memory of their dear friend, to ensure Mary Apper will never be forgotten, Kenny and Cristy McElroy gave the son of Apper's Mind Freak a new name.

The bull is now known as Apper's Legacy.

Love & Try

26

"RUMBLE IN THE ROCKIES" HERO STANDS FOR AMERICA

(Travis Strong)

He gave both legs for his country. On a Saturday night around Halloween in 2018, that didn't keep him from standing for the national anthem.

When the PBR "Celebrate America" tour hit Broadmoor World Arena in Colorado Springs that October, U.S. Army Staff Sergeant Travis Strong, who had been injured severely in Iraq a decade prior, was honored for his extraordinary sacrifice and bravery and given the opportunity to share his story of valor, love, and try.

Travis grew up north of Los Angeles with a yen for speed and adventure. He played high school football as a strong safety and raced dirt bikes on the high desert flat lands. The stepson of a Vietnam veteran, he had always wanted to be part of the military. He proudly joined the U.S. Army in 1997.

Strong was stationed in Italy, honorably discharged in 2000. But the routine slack of civilian life was not for him. After the planes hit the World Trade Center and the Pentagon, and a fourth one was brought down in a field in Pennsylvania by passengers who fought back, Strong wanted to do the same. He re-enlisted with the Army's First Stryker Brigade, named after the ceramic-armored mobile combat vehicle designed to protect troops from all but the most potent explosives.

On November 27, 2006, two days after Thanksgiving, Strong's unit was on night patrol in their Stryker rolling down an empty street near Baghdad. Strong, the vehicle commander, was seated in the middle of the Stryker. Then, a crushing explosion; a powerful EFP (Explosively Formed Penetrator) bomb had detonated, engulfing the eight-wheeled vehicle. A quiet road turned into hell on earth.

"I remember the smoke, the smell, the fire, and everyone yelling," Strong said.

His right leg was gone. His left leg was mangled.

"I don't remember any blood or not seeing my leg or feeling any pain," he said. "I just knew I was hurt very badly. It was the worst experience anyone could feel; that dread of dying, and there was nothing I could do to stop it."

His lungs collapsed. The men were shouting for Strong to breathe. He was fading in and out of consciousness.

Strykers travel in groups. Operating procedure was to stay together. This time, a soldier from Colorado took off solo, smashing into cars and anything else in the way to get the dying sergeant to the field hospital at Camp Liberty.

"I was in limbo, fading in and out," he said. "They were asking me questions, but I don't remember my answers. I could feel my clothes being cut off."

He would flat-line four times. The medics frantically worked on him. He woke up in a Baghdad hospital drugged, dazed, and confused. His left leg was lost. The battalion commander and chaplain reassured him, "You're still with us, you're alive."

Strong drifted away. Next time, his eyes opened to a group of familiar men—his platoon lining the room. "It was really cool to see them but also a very somber moment," he said. "My driver, who had become a good friend, couldn't look at me. He sat on the edge of the bed, his head down. It was hard for all of us."

Strong was sent to a military hospital in Germany. He then shipped back to the U.S. to Walter Reed National Military Medical Center followed by Balboa Naval Hospital in San Diego, closer to family and friends. He gritted through painful complications from bone growth and skin grafts on his leg. Emotionally, too, the first year following the blast was very difficult.

"I went through every emotion: anger, sadness, depression, and despair," Strong said. "But I never gave up. I knew everything had changed, but this was also the start of a new life."

Strong would spend five years in a wheelchair, each day vowing not to give up on his recovery and keep moving forward. He met a beautiful girl, Cara, and promised he'd walk down the aisle to take her as his wife.

A wonderful organization called "Homes for the Troops" hooked him up with a house in Colden, Colorado. Scores of volunteers—carpenters, electricians, plumbers, and roofers—came together to build the elevator-equipped house in three days.

The faith-based Wild River Ranch, supported by the Green family of Hobby Lobby, became a respite for relaxation and fun. He learned how to snow ski, tackling the most difficult black diamond slopes. He now plays sled hockey, competes in obstacle course races and bike marathons, and jumps from planes. Next up is wheelchair rugby.

Travis and Cara attended bull riding events at Denver Coliseum and Cheyenne Frontier Days. They own two gentle bulls, Gus and Monty. The plan had been that one day the bulls would make for a few good dinners. Then the couple discovered that bulls love kisses. Now Gus and Monty are family, like big, beloved dogs.

"I've done crazy stuff but getting on top of a bull is genuinely crazy, and it's a lot of fun to watch," Strong said after coming down to the dirt to be part of a PBR's "Stand for America" initiative, in which the sport's riders voluntarily pledged to always stand for the national anthem in honor of those who have died in preserving our freedoms and all who serve today. "To be honored was quite humbling, when I was just doing my job."

"I believe these [NFL] guys have every right to protest; that's why I fought. But I feel they are doing it the wrong way," he said. "To anyone who has served—cops, veterans, first responders—the flag means so much.

It symbolizes all the blood shed throughout the years for our freedom. We are proud of the country and our flag, and that's why we put our lives on the line. On the same hand, a lot of Americans, and we see them every weekend at PBR, do support Old Glory and our troops, and that makes me feel good."

Strong will accept being called a hero if it helps get out his story. But go easy on the H word. "It was like a lottery that I didn't hit so good," he said. "A lot of my friends didn't make it. In my mind, they are the heroes."

Nonetheless, he feels honored when asked to tell his story—not to recount tales of courage and valor but to share vital life lessons about overcoming obstacles. "When something traumatic happens in life, you don't give up. You keep living. If my story and what I do inspires one person, maybe they can help make the world a better place."

When Travis Strong walked down the aisle using a cane to meet his bride, it's safe to say every single person in the chapel was pretty darn inspired.

27

A CYCLONE BOMB OF LOVE

(Mandi McCary)

Nobody has to be a bull riding fan to work at PBR. But it sure helps.

Nobody is required to love animals, either. Though try meeting someone in the organization—or at any number of stakeholders making the sport go—who isn't a genuine animal activist, in the sense of doing things to help animals versus playing a political agenda. A special bond with the creatures sharing our land, and those competing every weekend, is routinely demonstrated in ways big and small across the sport.

Witness the actions taken after the powerful late-winter Cyclone Bomb devastated the Northern plains and Midwest in winter 2019. Combine a hurricane and blizzard into one weather event, and these so-called "Cyclone Bombs" can wreak devastation of biblical proportions. In mid-March, ice chunks big as sports cars ripped through ranches and farmhouses. Grazing and crop fields became inland seas. Baby calves were swept into freezing floodwaters, washing up lifeless along the banks of swollen rivers.

Thousands of larger animals had simply vanished.

"Snow drifts were so high, people worried for their cattle since they couldn't even get out of their homes to check on them," said Mandi McCary, a member of the PBR Public Relations team, who has a ranch in South Dakota where she and her husband spend summers.

McCary woke up the day after the historic storm to see a disturbing video on social media: a bull trapped under twelve feet of snow being frantically dug out by an entire family.

Speaking with friends and neighbors, she found out hundreds of animals were missing. Considering the thousands of square miles affected by the storm, how many more were trapped in snow tombs?

And this being calving season, how many cows in trouble were pregnant or had just given birth?

It was time to act.

McCary, who manages advance and onsite PR for many bull riding events in the central and Western regions including PBR World Finals, had already been creating plans to promote the April premier series event in Sioux Falls, where PBR is always active in the community. She used her creativity, scary-efficient organizational skills, and nearly inhuman work ethic to put together a PBR-funded team that would find and save cows, bulls, horses, and buffalo in grave danger. And since ground travel was virtually impossible, she hatched a plan to take to the skies to find the missing animals.

McCary speed-dialed Native American tribal council members and area sheriffs to identify where the need was greatest. Local connections helped find a handful of volunteer pilots who'd serve as eyes above, relaying directions to ground crews below going in to save the located animals. PBR quickly signed off on supporting the plan, including funding the planes' fuel.

The morning after that harrowing Facebook video with the happy ending, the first "PBR plane" took to the air from the Dakota Flight Center in Mitchell, South Dakota, searching for thousands of missing animals. One of the first pilots out, Scott Dorwart, who founded the flight center, teamed up

One of hundreds of animals rescued (Mandi McCary)

with four cowboys on the ground and found a group of 120 cattle. "We were looking for any animal stranded, abandoned, or in trouble," Dorwart said. "We could see the cattle so much better from the air than they could from the ground."

In the first four days, the flights covered three thousand nautical miles. They were not without peril. "You put the flaps down and slow as safely as you can without falling out of the air," said Dorwart, who owns a high-performance Cessna 182 RG. "If you get too slow, you lose lift, stall, and can fall out of the air. There's not a lot of grace space when you're two hundred to five hundred feet off the ground, trying to avoid power lines and other aircraft."

Livestock weren't the only beneficiaries of the pilots' heroism. Dorwart flew a thirteen-year-old girl from South Dakota to Kansas to reunite with her father in Wichita.

Like Dorwart, pilot Todd Priebe, a former rancher who sold his cattle a few years ago, jumped on the opportunity to fly the missions, and he headed to the Badlands in his Bellanca Super Viking to search for animals. "I'm just trying to give back to everyone who needs help," said Priebe, already an avid bull riding fan who attends every night of the annual event in Sioux Falls with his wife, his daughter, and her fiancé.

As McCary arranged for a helicopter to fly over a remote area of the Pine Ridge Indian Reservation where buffalo—a main revenue source—were missing, word spread of her efforts. She was getting phone calls at all hours

Teaching the author the basics of event PR.

A Cyclone Bomb of Love

from people from all over South Dakota and Nebraska, praying, crying, and begging her to brainstorm ideas to help. "It was very grounding to see an entire community decimated and not knowing where to start," she said.

Some phone calls were difficult. One sheriff observed everyone was in pretty good shape except "one ol' boy who could use a little help."

Willard Ruzieka, a sixth-generation farmer in his '70s had lost everything. His family-owned farm was pummeled by ice, flooded, and demolished, save a lone stone building. "Willard told me, 'I'm not saying I'm homeless, but I have no home anymore.' He was already determined to build again," McCary said.

His twelve bulls were presumed dead. But there was a small chance a few might have found high ground on a farm that has been in his family since 1871. The farmer was left speechless when McCary reported she scheduled a plane to search for any surviving bulls. PBR rider Matt Triplett, who is a skilled rancher then living in Montana, volunteered to scout the mission. Triplett then helped develop a game plan to head in on horses and evacuate the hungry bulls.

The plane took off from Dakota Flight Center. The sights from several hundred feet were grim. "The icebergs were huge. We didn't see anything alive. I wouldn't be surprised if none of them made it," Triplett said following the mission, his voice trailing off. Other search efforts for the cattle continued.

Despite that setback, the PBR flights located more than 3,700 cattle, horses, and buffalo.

"The devastation is almost beyond words," McCary said. "A lot of cattle died and beyond that tragedy it means millions of dollars of income and people who need to put their lives back together. There are ranchers with their entire feed supply gone; they can't feed the animals who survived. There are farmers who won't be able to plant their crops. There will be a need for money and assistance for quite some time as the water recedes."

Until then, and afterwards, McCary was taking phone calls, praying, crying, and brainstorming. She was doing everything she could to help save animals. Everything, except sleeping.

Love & Try

28

FROM THE SANDS OF IRAQ TO THE STAGES OF PBR

(Bull Stock Media)

It was a sultry, late August night in 2017 at the United States Military Academy at West Point. More than 1,300 new cadets were filing onto "The Plain," the academy's main parade field. The new cadets, having passed a rigorous entry selection process, marched crisply in unison. After the formal ceremony, they joined their new companies.

Following the acceptance ritual, the new cadets relaxed (ever slightly) to visit with their families while waiting for a concert by the West Point Band. It was a gorgeous night at the historic Trophy Point Amphitheater overlooking the Hudson River.

Soon, an announcer's voice boomed, *"He's a former Black Hawk helicopter pilot and chief warrant officer in the United States Army! He is the new Patriotic Voice of the PBR! Ladies and gentlemen, please welcome Ryan Weaver!"

A lean, muscular figure in a cowboy hat bounded onto the stage, backed by a group of soldiers known as The Benny Havens Band, and launched into a set of high-energy, all-American country rock.

Ryan Weaver's rousing West Point set was a fitting warm up to the national stage he would step onto several months later in Las Vegas at the PBR World Finals. The rocking combat veteran officially debuted as the voice of "Celebrate America," the sport's initiative honoring American heroes, inspiring youth, and bringing together local communities. Starting at World Finals that November, Weaver began providing an all-American soundtrack for the only pro sport whose athletes signed a pledge to always stand for the national anthem.

His EP song, "Celebrate America," recorded for PBR, channeled its proceeds to benefit charities helping the families of fallen heroes. During the 2018 PBR season, Weaver also performed at stops along the sport's elite tour.

Weaver, the son of a Marine, knows the grief of losing a family member to war. Both his brother and brother-in-law were killed in helicopter crashes in the Middle East. Ryan, too, was a Black Hawk helicopter pilot. The Florida native began performing in 2000 in karaoke competitions in Alabama during flight school to make ends meet. After returning from Iraq to the U.S. in 2004, he cut his teeth on the local Alabama bar scene, advancing to larger venues and festivals. Weaver has opened for artists including Charlie Daniels and George Jones, played with Lynyrd Skynyrd, and performed at the Grand Ole Opry.

"Ryan Weaver has red, white, and blue coursing through his veins," PBR Commissioner Sean Gleason said. "He understands hard work and sacrifice, and his love for this country comes out in song in a way that every fan appreciates."

Gleason met Weaver in 2016 during a performance at the Colorado Freedom Fest, an all-day fundraiser supporting the American Soldier Network, a charity to help prevent veteran suicide. Nobody knew any of Weaver's original songs. Yet as he introduced the tunes, the crowd was hanging on every word. The rocking country music with a serious message had the PBR boss engaged. When Ryan told the story of losing two family members,

Gleason says he became a fan and wanted the impassioned veteran to join the league's community building.

"Ryan came on stage like a twister and didn't stop through the entire performance. It wasn't a big crowd, but you would have thought he was performing at a sold-out Madison Square Garden," Gleason said. "His personal service in the military was enough to earn the respect of everyone in the house. The fact that he lost two family members in Iraq and Afghanistan while Ryan was on active duty made him a performer you'd never forget."

The timing was perfect. Gleason had been searching for artists to create original music for the league to own and use. He stumbled across an authentic American warrior who was turning the concepts of service, sacrifice, loss, and love of country into patriotic foot-stomping rock 'n' roll.

Gleason was intent on finding a place for Weaver just as fans were getting behind Celebrate America. Bringing in a credible new voice for the patriotism-soaked initiative honoring heroes and their families was the logical next step.

"I didn't have to change who I am," Weaver said. "My mission, story, and songs align with how the sport is honoring heroes and trying to unite communities. I am so grateful for this unique opportunity and hope that fans hearing my story and songs will be further inspired to love their communities and each other."

He dedicated his performances to his departed brothers, including tributes to U.S. Army Chief Warrant Officer Aaron Weaver, who is now enshrined in the Infantry Hall of Fame along with his brother-in-law, Randy Billings, one of four family Army Aviators.

Growing up in Citrus Country in west central Florida, Weaver lived with eleven children under one roof. "There were enough 'steps' and 'halves' under our roof to field a football team," he said.

Ryan had one full-blood sibling, Aaron, his idol.

"My brother was an American superhero," he said. "He was an awesome leader. He was tough as nails. Everyone wanted to follow him, and nobody ever had a bad word to say about him."

Some of Ryan's finest moments in the military were when Aaron visited his unit in Baghdad. Ryan would be giddy with anticipation waiting for his brother's aircraft land. When Aaron arrived, Ryan would proudly parade him around to the other Rangers.

Everyone at the base knew Aaron for his role in Somalia. As a twenty-two-year-old sergeant, Aaron was enmeshed in the 1993 Battle of Mogadishu in Somalia—where eighteen U.S. Army soldiers lost their lives. The fight was chronicled in the 2001 movie *Black Hawk Down.*

In Mogadishu, he was one of two men who volunteered to lead a unit toward the downed helicopters, saving one serviceman's life. The Army Ranger's vehicle took a direct hit from a rocket-propelled grenade, but he walked away unscathed.

To Ryan, the guy was Superman. Aaron would survive Mogadishu. Then he'd battle and conquer testicular cancer.

Aaron was so tough and committed to his country that after the cancer surgeries and nearly dying from an intestinal infection from a botched suture, he convinced doctors to sign a waiver allowing him to serve in Iraq for one more tour. No way his buddies were going back to war without him.

Ryan would get to see his brother in Baghdad when Aaron flew in every other month for medical tests to screen his blood for cancer. The cancer was in remission, making for happy and upbeat meetings.

The brothers would also meet on sadder occasions.

On January 2, 2004, Capt. Kimberly Hampton, an Air Cavalry Company commander in the same squadron as Aaron in the 82nd Airborne Division, was shot down by hostile fire south of Fallujah. She was the first female Cavalry commander to die in combat. Ryan flew several military brass to Al Taqaddum Airbase, west of Baghdad, for Capt. Hampton's memorial service. The solemn day was brightened somewhat when seeing Aaron, who had tears streaming down his cheeks.

"You never saw that. But becoming a father softened my brother," Ryan said.

Aaron and Ryan Weaver in their last photo together before Aaron's helicopter was shot down (Ryan Weaver)

Ryan proudly showed Aaron his aircraft. The older brother had been piloting a state-of-the-art flying machine that was much more advanced with its sleek glass cockpit and a clean, bright, high-tech display. The throwback cockpit of the antiquated aircraft he was now touring was more an optometrist's dream with its dizzying array of navigational signals.

Aaron poked his head inside, gave a low whistle and marveled at the labyrinth display of buttons and switches. He commented how his kid brother had to be pretty smart and talented to fly this old bird.

Ryan was standing a little taller in the glow of the respectful props from his brother. These kinds of compliments didn't come often. When you got them, they meant that much more.

As the men got ready to say goodbye, Ryan's crew chief asked to take a photo of the Weavers. Ryan was a hugger, and Aaron a shaker. This time, when Ryan went to shake his brother's hand, Aaron came in for a big, warm bear hug. Somalia made Aaron hard, but something more powerful had softened that tough exterior.

"Being a dad changed him," Ryan said. "He was happy and complete."

The great American superhero strolled down the tarmac. He turned around and smiled at his kid brother.

Two days later U.S. Army Chief Warrant Officer Aaron Weaver was killed in action.

He'd been riding in the back of a med-vac helicopter on his way to his blood test when the chopper crashed. Eight other soldiers perished as well.

NYPD Det. Rich Miller and Ryan Weaver at MSG (Bull Stock Media)

From the Sands of Iraq to the Stages of PBR

CWO Aaron Weaver was thirty-two years old. He left behind a wife, a young daughter, and a son. He also left behind a brother intent on honoring him every day along with a family forever crushed by the day they lost their son, brother, nephew, and cousin.

The chances of an American family becoming a Gold Star family by losing a member to combat is slim. Lightning struck the Weavers twice. On December 17th, 2013, Ryan's brother-in-law, Chief Warrant Officer 2 Randy Billings, was killed in action in Afghanistan. The Black Hawk he was piloting was taken from the sky by a ground-exploded Improvised Explosive Device (IED) on a remote Afghanistan hillside, killing all but one on board.

Ryan had come to know Randy as his instructor at Warrant Officer Candidate School just before Randy met his sister, Ashley. "Ashley loved, and still loves Randy with all of her heart," Ryan said. "Most people search their entire lives and never find what they had."

While remembering these fallen heroes, Ryan has brought fans to their feet as he chases his country rock dream. His popular music videos include "Crank It" and "BURN," featuring Benghazi survivors Kris "Tanto" Paronto and John "Tig" Tiegen with clips from the movie *13 Hours: Secret Soldiers of Benghazi*. His song "Unfriendly Fire," featured on the album, *Songs that Save Our Lives* with the Benny Havens Band, was short-listed for Grammy Award consideration in the American Roots category.

After leaving the military in 2012, Weaver took on two jobs while attending Embry-Riddle Aeronautical University. While working as a bar back at the Wild Horse Saloon, he was also studying his brains out, nailing a 4.0 GPA in in Aeronautics with a minor in management at a place known as "the Harvard in the Sky."

"Hard work, dedication, and putting your heart into something you believe in is the basis of the American dream," Weaver said. "That is my message, and I've seen how the amazing fans of the PBR have related to it."

When PBR was creating a special video to highlight the season's final Celebrate America opening in Las Vegas, Weaver introduced the organization to Rich Miller, a decorated New York City detective who had planted an American flag at Ground Zero following the 9/11 terrorist attacks. Miller had never spoken publicly about retrieving the flag from a nearby high school and attaching it to the antenna that had stood atop the North Tower. The detective knew several firemen among the 343 who had perished on 9/11, and he didn't want to take anything away from their heroism and valor.

After sixteen years, Miller decided to give his first interview for a special video to be shown at World Finals. He said he believes in what the sport is doing to honor true American heroes and coming together as a country, as imperfect as it is, through respecting the ideals Old Glory represents.

Miller triumphantly carried the stars and bars out to the dirt at T-Mobile Arena during 2017 World Finals, and the packed house then sang a stirring a cappella version of "The Star-Spangled Banner."

The following season, as the sport went even deeper on red, white, and blue, Ryan Weaver's song "Never Forgotten" played during Celebrate America openings, with images of his brother and other heroes reminding all in attendance why everyone in the sport stands.

"Hitching my wagon to the PBR was a big deal in terms of exposure to millions of passionate sports fans," Weaver said. "I am grateful fans learned my story, and I hope I have inspired them in their love for their communities and each other."

PART V

AMERICAN DREAMS

Those of a certain age will remember school lessons on "The American Creed," in which everyone born equal in the eyes of God can go as far as they push in life through talent, hard work, and determination. Bull riders, from here or abroad, come from all socioeconomic conditions. Many grew up dirt poor. They chased their dreams and made it to the top through applying basic values—blood and guts, love and try.

Anyone who gets on a bull is judged and rewarded as an individual, based purely on their performance. "When you do something wrong, it's all on our shoulders," J.B. Mauney said. "If you don't ride, it's nobody's fault but your own."

Bull riders take responsibility for their performance. If they don't ride for eight seconds, they don't take a dime from the promoter. It makes their sport one of the pure remaining meritocracies, a throwback driven by values that may be quaint to some, outdated to others. But for fans and competitors, they are essential don't-tread-on-me principles. Many fans told me that what

29

SHOOTING COWBOYS, DISCOVERING AMERICA

(Author photo)

More than forty years ago, in a small town in France, little seven-year-old Chris Elise sat with his grandfather, watching dubbed TV Westerns, and falling in love with cowboys.

He began dreaming of coming to America.

Chris had always been fascinated by photography, a hobby of his father. In 1997, his father tragically passed at forty-six, and Elise took possession of his dad's Nikon FE camera and one 50mm lens. He shot portraits, including musician Ravi Coltrane—son of John Coltrane—and dabbled in wedding photography.

Years later, a girlfriend asked about his biggest dream. Chris finally heard his voice saying aloud what had always been deep inside: "*My dream is to live in America.*"

It was go time. He'd need to support himself. He loved that Nikon. And sports. Why not put the two together and make a run at a new career ... using the universal languages of pictures and sports to cross the ocean?

"French was my mother language, so if I drop the pen and pick up the camera, I don't have the language barrier," he explained in an accent thicker than the hollandaise sauce at Le Bernardin. "I had always loved sports, so it was an easy way for me to walk into the USA and not have that barrier."

Elise hooked up with a photo agency in California and began covering the NBA for the French basketball magazine *Reverse*. Several sports agencies took notice, and he became a French photo correspondent in the USA, covering pro hoops while going on assignment to cover sports in exotic places like the Sahara Desert, Cuba, and the Dominican Republic.

Elise is now a renowned sports photographer, and, in November 2020, he drove his Chevy pick-up from Los Angeles to Texas to shoot the PBR World Finals as his new favorite sport played in a giant football stadium usually hosting the Dallas Cowboys. When it was announced that the 2021 season would start with a southern swing through iconic small-town outdoor rodeo grounds, the first media member to ask for credentials was none other than Chris Elise.

"My first love was the cowboys, so yes, I have come full circle," he said with a good laugh.

Elise had initially become intrigued with bull riding after seeing a single picture—a soaring bull and sprawling bucked-off rider, captured from ground level. "I was really impressed by the picture. These men were riding bulls! I wanted to see this sport and shoot it," he said.

In 2017, he was in Las Vegas to participate in a documentary pilot for a French TV show and out for a drink. He looked up at the TV and saw a cowboy hanging on to a furiously bucking bull at the PBR World Finals. He took out his phone and bought a ticket for the next night.

"I didn't know a thing about it, but I go there and fall in love right away," he said in an accent that sounded like a tour guide at the base of the Eiffel Tower eager to win his group's affection. "The bulls were spectacular, the cowboys so brave. PBR knows how to put on a show. It was really fantastic."

Months later, in Denver to shoot the Nuggets, he contacted PBR for credentials for its event in Sioux Falls. Chris explained that he may be an NBA photographer, but he loved cowboys and wanted to be involved with bull riding and the Western culture. The organization, eager to introduce the sport to media covering other sports, immediately credentialed him.

"It was my first time in Sioux Falls, in South Dakota, my first time shooting bull riding, and I loved everything about it," he said. "I would come to experience how PBR takes care of the media like nobody else."

With his afro exploding to the heavens, French accent, tattoos, and fingers dangling with conspicuous heavy silver rings, Elise brings a coolness quotient ratcheting the hipness level of any night's media contingent.

Working press normally don't make it into the slate of zany hijinks that goes down between death-defying rides, but he drew the attention of PBR Official Entertainer Flint Rasmussen. The funny back and forth banter between rodeo clown and seemingly out-of-place French photographer by way of LA went up on the video board.

While the NBA remained Chris's bread and butter, his PBR immersion continued. The cast and crew barnstorming the country week to week were eager to learn more about the tall, affable photographer with the Waylon Jennings tattoo on his arm dressed in cool denims and vintage seventies-style button-down corduroy jackets.

An impromptu meeting at T Mobile Arena during the 2018 World Finals would show an intimate sports culture Elise has come to cherish.

"I'm leaving the arena and some guy shouts out, 'Hey!' It was [bull rider] Cody Nance. He'd seen me before and wanted to know who I was. We had a good chat—he wanted to know more about me, so he said he'd see me tomorrow."

Elise had been working in sports for sixteen years. This was a new experience with an athlete. "In LA, I'd shot the same team for six years, and a few players never have said hello once. This guy had just gotten on a bull at the

One of Elise's favorite bull riding shots (Chris Elise)

most important event in the sport, and he's genuinely interested in me. The values in this league aren't marketing BS; it's totally real."

The cowboy he enjoys shooting the most, the sport's biggest star, J.B. Mauney, also befriended Elise.

"J.B. is one of a kind," Elise said. "His attitude and approach personify the hero that is a cowboy. He never disappoints me. If I could be one cowboy, I would be J.B. Mauney."

The consummate professional who's routinely been around stars as big as Kobe Bryant and LeBron James has to contain his enthusiasm when in Mauney's presence. "I'm fifty years old, and I can say that I feel like a kid, and he is my John Wayne."

He was becoming more fascinated with the sport, but he didn't expect what would happen next as he covered the rides. Friendships began to blossom.

"I've never met real friends in other sports organizations like I have here. Everyone is outward and friendly. Being a fan is easy because PBR is true. The sense of a family is very rich and real. The cowboy values you see PBR pushing, they live by these values. The values and slogans you see the other leagues push, they don't live by it."

When living in Los Angeles with a famous, beautiful, and sassy novelist wife, Gigi Levangie (or as Chris says, "my American Dream hot wife"), he drove his beloved muscle cars—a 1968 Chevelle SS and a 1969 Dodge Super Bee—as well as his modern pickup to cover PBR in Montana, Nebraska, Nevada, Texas, Wyoming, and South Dakota. (The couple recently moved to Tennessee on a forty-acre ranch and Levangie has finalized a movie script about female bull riding pioneer Jonnie Jonckowski—chronicled here beginning on page 65—with Sienna Miller slated to play the barrier-shattering athlete.)

"Those flyover states, *that* is America," Elise said. "I tell people all the time that LA and New York are not America. Some people may think the worst about those other places but go there and you'll see honesty and sincerity in the small towns across this country. In the real America, people like you for who you are, for how you treat them. People in America are much easier to talk to than a place like France. I've never had a bad experience in all my years of traveling across America. Small towns and rural America are where I love to be."

Shooting Cowboys, Discovering America

When Elise gets to the next city and settles into his position next to the dirt, the lights go down and the "Be Cowboy" video comes up on the video screen, and the gladiator cowboys strut through fire during rider introductions, he gets chills. Every single time.

Elise's magazine and news agency work trained him to be ready for anything that might happen on the field of play. "I'm a good enough photographer at covering different sports to get some super-good photos and some that are just good. In bull riding, what happens in front of you is spectacular in any second. You could have a ride for only two seconds and still get a spectacular picture. When I get on the floor of the NBA, it's my happy place. I always enjoy that. PBR is the only other sport where I get the same feeling. Every time I shoot PBR, I get excited. I feel like I'm with my grandfather again as the Western movie starts."

Elise wanted to use his camera instead of a keyboard in America. He thought he'd do better with pictures than words. But even in a second language, he's downright poetic in describing the objects of his lens.

"PBR is this strange dance, this clash, this fight of a man and an animal. And that animal is a magnificent beast. There's a mythology to this bull. They're beautiful and dangerous. And then you have these cowboys, most of them skinny and tiny, not like football players or UFC fighters. You put them together, the cowboy and the bull, and the chemistry of their dance is completely unique."

Along with the Westerns airing on three TV channels available in France long before satellite TV and the internet, Elise learned about America by reading about baseball, and he likes to compare the two. "Bull riding is like baseball: two sports that are like a painting—the colors and shades, the confrontations on the field. In bull riding, you have the showdown of the beast and the man. Baseball has the pitcher staring down the batter, which is like how the cowboy looks at the villain in a showdown. It's a very interesting combination for a photographer."

As Elise shoots more events—he was the only photographer besides PBR's longtime official lensman and dean of bull riding photography Andy Watson working the Monster Energy Team Challenge closed-to-fans events at South Point Arena throughout June 2020 at the height of the pandemic—he is expanding his canvas.

A few more of Elise's favorite shots (Chris Elise)

"Every photographer has his eye and his aesthetic," he said. "You want a photo of a good ride—the hand is up, he's in control, everything is looking good. That doesn't always transfer to good photography."

Like that first photo that attracted him to bull riding, he is in search of the next picture revealing something entirely new. "Catching the bull looking through the slats of the chute can be a great moment. After the big picture of a great ride, the magic is to focus on something else. Maybe when the bull is running in the arena after jerking off the rider down on the dirt."

At every event, his curiosity grows. He's eager for more rides, new paintings, the next surprising discovery.

"I get more and more interested in the possibilities every time. It's eight seconds, but there's many interesting things going on in every single one of those seconds."

As a youngster in France, Chris Elise's first love was cowboys. He's grown up in America now, a newly minted U.S. Citizen, in his own boots, capturing cowboy magic.

And amid the wonder of heroes normalized, in the land he always dreamed about, he's still feeling like a little boy.

30

A TITAN OF TRY

(Bull Stock Media)

Tommy Lasorda was said to have been a Dodger from the bottom of his cleats to the top of his blue ball cap. The legendary baseball manager and personality who spent seventy-one seasons with the same organization may have had "Dodger blue" coursing through his veins, but his cleats carried more than just ballpark dirt.

Love & Try

Lasorda was a great friend and ambassador of the PBR. With Jeff Robinson, he co-owned a bucking bull named Deja Blu, who was one-half of one of the most notorious and buzzworthy stunts in the sport's history. While the bull had a solid record in allowing nineteen rides in eighty-eight attempts for an average ride score of 88.16, he'd attain national recognition when NFL star Chad "Ochocinco" Johnson attempted to ride him in Duluth in 2011.

Ochocinco lasted under *dos* seconds. He was fortunate not to be stomped.

"It's a tough, tough assignment," Lasorda said at the time. "We want the people to know how tough it is to ride on a bull for eight seconds."

The Pennsylvania native, who coached the Dodgers to two World Series titles and four National League pennants, would regularly attend events in Anaheim and Las Vegas to watch Deja Blu buck. And he never stopped marveling at the combination of guts and skills required to ride an elite bull like the one he owned. (Ochocinco, a world class athlete with six NFL Pro Bowls to his name who had spent thousands of hours in weight rooms and had exceptional coordination and body awareness, had trained for two weeks under the tutelage of Ty Murray. He lasted 1.5 seconds.) "I can teach a bull rider to play baseball," Lasorda once said. "I can't teach a baseball player to be a bull rider."

It was quite the scene seeing Lasorda sitting next to actress Bo Derek in the arena. And it brought great in-arena entertainment that could never make it on TV, like the time official entertainer Flint Rasmussen was doing a bit about a boneless chicken, flopping around on the dirt.

As Flint was on the ground imitating gooey poultry, arena announcer Bob Feist let the crowd know, "We have Bo Derek here tonight!"

Flint sprung to his feet. "Bo Derek! That'll put a bone in your chicken!" he exclaimed.

Tommy loved coming to bull ridings to be around the cowboys, too. Of course, he was welcomed. "Tommy appreciated how humble, down-to-earth, and genuine they were as professional athletes," said Randy Bernard, PBR's CEO from 1995 to 2010 and a friend of Lasorda for more than twenty years. "Despite his lack of experience on the back of a bull, it never stopped him from giving them some boisterous coaching and advice. He was more than a legend in sports, he was so caring and charismatic that he lit up every room he entered with positive energy."

A Titan of Try

One of those rooms was the riders' locker room. One year at World Finals, Bernard's motivational speaker had canceled the night before the event. Bernard called Tommy at 6 p.m., asking if he'd fly to Las Vegas to give the riders a pep talk the next night.

"In Tommy's inimitable way, he said he was at the Italian parade in Chicago and cussed me out for not giving him more notice," Bernard said.

Of course, Lasorda called Bernard back later that evening to accept.

He'd land about an hour before he was needed in the locker room. Security picked Lasorda up and brought him straight to Bernard inside the Thomas & Mack Center.

"Tommy walks up, takes my cowboy hat off, and puts it right on his head," Bernard said. "He says, 'I need this to talk to these guys today.' I had to send someone out to get him a cowboy hat so I could get mine back!"

With an awe-struck Justin McBride on one side of him and Chris Shivers on the other, Lasorda gave a rousing talk to jack up the riders before they hit the chutes. NBC ran a camera down to the locker room and featured Tommy's comments in the telecast. Lasorda was a big fan of McBride, and he'd often compare the two-time PBR world champion to one of the all-time great pitchers, southpaw Sandy Koufax.

"His go-to line was always: 'Justin is the Sandy Koufax of bull riding,'" recalled Keith Ryan Cartwright, then the senior writer and editorial director for PBR.COM.

Lasorda's words have stayed with McBride.

"Anytime you get a compliment from a legend of another sport comparing you to yet another legend, those things can mean more to you than any of the awards you get," McBride said. "There's nothing like the love and respect of giants."

Lasorda was one of the most charismatic and colorful figures in sports spanning back to the Dodgers' Brooklyn roots. He was full of piss and vinegar, and his passion, sense of humor, work ethic, and aversion for suffering fools was a good match for the rugged cowboys who suck it up in the face of adversity without mincing words. Most of all, Lasorda appreciated athletes whose try trumped their talent.

"Tommy would get up in the morning full of beans and maintain that as long as he was with anybody else," Vince Scully, longtime voice of the Dodgers, said in a statement issued shortly after Lasorda's passing in early

2021. "His heart was bigger than his talent, and there were no foul lines for his enthusiasm."

31
"EVERYTHING WE LOVE ABOUT AMERICA"

(Author photo)

At one point or another, for all sports fans, reality bites.

They follow the games and buy the latest merchandise, memorizing key stats and hanging onto their favorite athletes' every performance. Then one day, they meet their heroes. And all too often, the stars from the video highlights and Instagram posts there in the flesh are not who they're hyped up to be.

Cynthia Johnson and Evelyn Robinson have never had that problem with their sport—professional bull riding. The ebullient sisters from Brooklyn, now living in San Jose when not touring the PBR circuit, are veritable people magnets who quickly create friendships with just about anyone, including bull riders and the staffers and contractors forming the itinerant bull riding road show hopping city to city. The inseparable duo has traveled to nearly two dozen PBR events, and their heroes have yet to disappoint.

There they are chatting with two-time World Champion J.B. Mauney, the Dragonslayer himself, with little Jagger Briggs in tow, in Target outside of Billings, Montana.

There they are getting a bite at McDonald's in Bismarck, North Dakota, with veteran rider Lucas Divino, who was bringing a pungent fast-food haul back to his Brazilian countrymen.

There's nine-time stock contractor of the year Chad Berger, spotting the pair at breakfast in the Sheraton in Sioux Falls, South Dakota, serenading them with a sweet version of "Do You Know the Way to San Jose?"

There they are in the street in Del Rio, Texas, standing in the spitting rain, leaning into a car window to chat with PBR Official Entertainer Flint Rasmussen, who spotted the sisters on the way to arena, screeched to a halt, and jacked the rental in reverse to pull over and say hi.

There they are at the front desk in the Arlington Hilton, trying to join a special PBR Global Cup tour, after missing the scheduling email. It's too late. But overhearing this is PBR cofounder and Director of Livestock Cody Lambert, who drops everything and takes Cynthia and Evelyn to meet the riders from the five nations competing in "the Olympics of bull riding," along with the bulls in the special team event. The common perception of Lambert's public persona is that of a porcupine who got up on the wrong side of the log. Lambert is warm and friendly and funny, and, after the private tour, he brings his new friends behind the scenes of a TV interview with two-time world champion Justin McBride.

This is the new world discovered by two unlikely fans, who grew up in the Bedford-Stuyvesant section of in Brooklyn—a concrete-jungle neighborhood usually not associated with cowboys, although through television, two young girls could explore new frontiers.

"We grew up on cowboys and were glued to all the Westerns on TV: *Gunsmoke, Bonanza, Rawhide,* and *Wagon Train*; you name it, we watched them all," Evelyn said. "And we had family who raised tobacco in North Carolina and Virginia, so there's a connection to the energetic American spirit of cowboys that now comes to us. Like you see in the opening video showing a lot of diversity, cowboys come from everywhere. It's a clean sport, there's no politics. It's just come and have a good time. It's just everything we love about America."

"It's a family thing—you see children with their grandparents," Cynthia adds. "The sport honors the flag, prays, and recognizes the military—it's all the things we support, a true American sport and experience."

Their mother came from a Southern family of eight siblings and their dad had four brothers and sisters. They still have relatives in Virginia and North Carolina, including a ninety-four-year-old great aunt, with cousins up and down the east coast.

"Family is super important to us, and this is a family atmosphere," Evelyn said. "Everyone is kind and humble: the bull riders and bullfighters, the stock contractors, the big wigs all the way to Randy, who takes care of the dirt. The environment is awesome. Everyone looks out for each other. Every event is the next level. We go home and think, nothing is going to top that! And then PBR does it again! We wind up talking about it all week long."

Cynthia was first to go west with her tennis-instructor husband, in 1976, and Evelyn followed from Brooklyn six years later. The sisters attended rodeos, enjoying bareback events and barrel racing. And then eight years ago, while channel surfing, Evelyn came across Guilherme Marchi riding a bull to win an event. The percentages could have called that one: Marchi is the PBR all-time leader with 635 qualified rides. After seeing the square-jawed Brazilian smiling atop the shark cage with his latest event buckle, life would take a turn.

"I was hooked," Evelyn said. "I thought it was absolutely insane—that someone would try to ride an animal that powerful and unpredictable. I'd come to learn these bull riders are genuine athletes, but it's so different than sports where you can read the body language of your competitor. The bulls are unreadable; yet they're thinking, with their own strategies. They are so intriguing to me—powerful, fantastic athletes in their own right."

She started learning more about the bulls and developed her favorites: Little Yellow Jacket, Asteroid, Bushwacker, Bruiser, Chiseled, and Cochise.

"When you see these athletes up close—they're giant muscles with horns, but they're agile and they're smart. You can see them thinking as the riders are on them. These are not dumb animals you put a rope on. And they get great care, just living the life. Their owners give them massages and hydrotherapy. They worry about them like their children."

Ask the sisters about their favorite riders, and they'll say, "the guys who are humble and appreciate the fans." They'll talk about the Americans, and then segue into the Brazilians, and wind up with the First Nation riders, rattling off a list of down-to-earth good guys too long to print here.

They appreciate a sport harkening back to what used to be proudly taught in schools as "The American Creed"—where everyone is born equal and can go however far as talent, hard work, and determination will take you. Bull riders can be dirt poor and make it to the top through blood-and-guts try. They're rewarded as individuals, based on staying on their bulls and scoring well, making the sport a rare, remaining meritocracy.

Evelyn says she "recruited" her sister to watch on TV. Then the duo, separated by sixteen months, attended the PBR in Oakland in 2013. Later, in San Jose, they saw a confident, young Cooper Davis win.

"This was way too cool. After that we were off and running," Evelyn says. "TV is great, but we said, 'We *have* to go live.'"

They've been to events in Albuquerque, Bismarck, Billings, Nashville, New York City, Sacramento, and Sioux Falls, and they have gone multiple times to Las Vegas for World Finals and have also attended a special weekend pairing PBR with the Bill Pickett rodeo. When PBR ended the COVID-challenged 2020 season atop the *USS Lexington* docked in Corpus Christi, Texas, with an exhibition event raising money for military charities, they purchased premium seats, alongside only five hundred fans allowed onboard the iconic aircraft carrier.

When it was announced in 2021 that the sport would again end the season on top of the carrier the length of three New York City blocks, they booked a return trip. The second time on the boat dubbed "The Blue Ghost" by the Japanese (after they'd nearly sunk the ship four times, but she kept coming back stronger each time) was even more memorable. The twenty-four participating riders had donated the entire $100,000 purse to the family of Amadeu Campos Silva, a twenty-two-year-old bull rider who had been killed at a PBR expansion tour event the week prior in Fresno, California.

Up until the accident, it had been a promising weekend for the young rider who arrived in the U.S. with his parents, Flavio and Rosa, two years prior, living in Decatur, Texas, now an established enclave for Brazilian bull riders and their families. Campos rode his first bull in Fresno and made it to the championship round. On that ride, his spur got hung up in the flank strap on a bull called Classic Man. Slight of build, Campos was pulled underneath and stomped to death. The bull was bucking normally; he was simply caught in a freak accident. The tragedy sent shockwaves throughout the entire sport, particularly among the Brazilian contingent.

Amadeu was a shy and serene boy, polite and humble yet fun loving—truly a kid at heart. When the Brazilian cowboys got together for frequent cookouts, Amadeu, who barely shaved, would be found inside with the young kids playing video games. He still often slept in the same bed in a modest mobile home with his parents, who had come to the U.S. to help their son who couldn't read or write.

Described by Josh Peter of *USA Today* as "thin as a bull rope" at barely 150 pounds, Amadeu often fought injuries; he had only earned $42,000 in fifty events since coming to the US. He sent virtually every hard-earned dollar to his parents and his sister in Brazil, who he was helping support through law school. His dream was to buy his family a house on a dairy farm in Brazil, where they'd lived after young Amadeu, seven years old, offered to milk the farm owner's cows, giving his family somewhere to stay instead of being homeless. And now with his fellow riders donating the entire *USS Lexington* purse, PBR matching that (as well as fan donations up to $100,000 as well), and official partners like Ariat and Pendleton Whisky chipping in $50,000 each, the dream would be realized.

It is not lost on the sisters how many of the hungry Brazilian riders come from impoverished areas to the US, dreaming of helping their families, riding bulls as their ticket to the good life. They are fortunate and grateful to be drawing a nice salary in positions allowing for ample personal travel to attend events. "We do like that our attendance helps support the cowboys and stock contractors, and to be honest, we'd do all of them if we could," Evelyn said.

After COVID-19 had shut down all live sports in the second half of March 2020, and PBR was the first pro sport to return with closed-to-fan events, the sisters decided when fans would be allowed back in the arena, they'd be there. As soon as the mid-July Sioux Falls date with a new concept called "pod seating" went on sale, they booked their trip.

They would add to their list of new friends met at events: South Dakota Governor Kristi Noem. The rising firebrand GOP star had recently sent about half the nation into a tizzy by hosting President Trump at Mount Rushmore, then she opened doors enabling PBR to blaze the trail hosting fans in an indoor arena for the first time since the virus had arrived.

Noem grew up on a farm in South Dakota. She'd work all day long. At night her dad would take her to rodeos. Her plan was to go into the family business and raise quarter horses. When she was twenty-two, her father was killed in an accident on the family farm. He was forty-nine years old.

Suddenly, the family—asset rich and cash poor—was saddled with a crushing debt brought on by death taxes. Her father had just tragically passed; now her own government was soaking the family with nearly overwhelming taxes due.

Kristi's dad had never complained about things. He went out and fixed them. Enraged by the injustice paralyzing a family that had invested so much in land, machinery, and cattle, Kristi did what her dad would do. She became passionate about tax reform and fixing an unfair and often cruel system. She was elected to the South Dakota House of Representatives in 2007 and the U.S. House of Representatives in 2011. In 2018, she became the state's first female governor.

Her politics veered toward libertarianism. "The most important thing government can do is stay out of the way," she said. Noem's philosophy in dealing with COVID-19 centered on trusting the people in making their own individual decisions. When PBR had established proven protocols for holding events without spreading the virus, and it was time to bring fans back into an indoor arena, Sean Gleason knocked on Governor Noem's door. And now, here she was, in Sioux Falls, in July 2020, triumphantly riding her own horse, Ice Man, into the Denny Sanford PREMIER Center in Sioux Falls, in a grand gesture of blood-guts-and-country defiance to the basement naysayers as if she were a rough stock character plucked off the set of *Yellowstone*.

While Noem would become nationally recognized for her response to the virus (seriously, name one other South Dakota governor), helping her open state achieve the greatest economic growth percentage during the pandemic,

"Everything We Love About America"

As soon as fans were allowed back indoors, the sisters bought tickets (Evelyn Robinson)

the sisters found her another friendly and unassuming character on the PBR scene. "We have a few hundred country concerts under our belts," Cynthia explained about how they met Noem. "We know a lot of floor people. If you're in with the production guys and the dirt guy, you can meet just about anyone."

Great relationships make things happen. Fostering those connections, the sisters always opt in for the best seats in the house through Elite Seats. The tickets are more expensive, but well worth the investment. "The bulls are kicking up the dirt, and it comes up and hits you. I just love it," Evelyn says. "That kind of up-close-and-personal experience where you actually *feel* it just amplifies how awesome the sport is."

In fact, the sisters take a bit of dirt back from every arena they visit, put it in tubes, and label it. They've met great friends at events and started pairing up with a couple from Texas in a four-person "pod." Winding up at a Chad Berger barbecue, they became close with Elmer Blackbird, a Native who has sent them Lakota (Sioux) phrases to learn.

Among their memorable adventures, they are still recounting eight days marooned in Del Rio when attending their first PBR event of the 2021 season.

With virus infections peaking during the brief off-season following World Finals in November, the sport pivoted to small outdoor rodeo arenas to start up again on time in January. It was officially dubbed "PBR Unleash The Beast: American Roots Edition." Some insiders called it "The Tumbleweed Tour." Commissioner Gleason jokingly named it, "The Where the Hell Are We Going Tour," because setting an event schedule during the virus was the proverbial mind-numbing cluster. The sport would settle on going to three small cities in Florida—Ocala, Arcadia, and Okeechobee—then moved west to Texas, starting in Del Rio.

"Eight or nine months into the pandemic, the virus was even worse than when we first came back at the Lazy E so we started in Florida and Texas—two states where COVID-19 never existed," Gleason joked, referring to the wide-open, pro-business practices and policies adopted by Florida Governor Ron DeSantis and Texas Governor Greg Abbott.

The sisters put in for vacation time and arrangements to attend the mid-February start of the Texas leg of the Tumbleweed Tour in Del Rio. Gleason and his team planned well for the pandemic, but the sport couldn't sidestep Mother Nature. The sisters would be stranded in the Texas-Mexico border town after a historic winter storm had swept in, canceling the second half of the PBR event weekend. Power was out, and the water was no longer running, making it impossible for many fans and crew to safely leave town. Cynthia and Evelyn were eating gas station food and bringing pool water up to their room at the Ramada Hotel in garbage cans. Most would consider this inconvenient travel odyssey to be a traumatic episode to repress or a nightmarish debacle to complain about whenever a certain sport is mentioned. They turned the ordeal into a fun adventure, an opportunity to make new friends among the hotel staff and local neighborhood, and a reminder that good people do good things everywhere. Their consistently sunny attitude shows how to make the best of every day given to us, roll with the punches, and see silver linings in every dark cloud. It also shows how giving to others can reward them, too.

As part of Elite seats, ticket holders get special mementos. One is a plaque signed by two-time World Champion Jess Lockwood. As the sisters were accumulating Lockwood plaques, they came up with an idea, inspired by the

"Everything We Love About America"

"Cooper Tires Fan of the Night"—a promotion in which Flint Rasmussen presents a special belt buckle made by Montana Silversmiths at the end of each show to his favorite fan in attendance.

"Now we go out and pick our own fans of the night," Cynthia said. "We find a deserving young person and give them the signed Jess plaque. The little people are just so excited to get that."

In a sport that gives so much to them, Cynthia Johnson and Evelyn Robinson are becoming fixtures of their own, by giving back with their laughter and conversation, their curiosity and friendship, and now, special surprises a group of youngsters will never forget.

Love & Try

32

PBR ♥'S HUCKABEE

(Bull Stock Media)

It all started with the Beatles on Ed Sullivan.

On February 7, 1964, four mop-topped lads from across the ocean kicked into "All My Loving" on the country's most popular variety program. More than seventy million Americans—a huge chunk of the population—sat in rapt attention in front of black-and-white television consoles across the country. Crime in the big cities was said to come to a screeching halt. When the boys in matching suits launched into "She Loves You," the theater in New York City exploded. Legend has it, the cameramen couldn't hear the director's instructions over the hordes of shrieking girls. Considering the cultural revolution about to be unleashed, some claim it was the most important two minutes and sixteen seconds of music ever broadcast on American television.

Love & Try

It was a life-changing moment for wide-eyed, eight-year-old Mike Huckabee, who felt the very ground in his family's living room in Hope, Arkansas, shifting. Mike wanted a guitar. He'd ask for one again and again. But the family couldn't afford the instrument.

Finally, on Christmas when he was eleven, Mike was presented a ninety-nine dollar Penncrest house-brand guitar his parents bought on installment from the JC Penney catalog.

"I wore my fingers to the bone learning to play that guitar," Huckabee said, fifty-four years later, in the green room of Bridgestone Arena in Nashville, getting ready to hit center stage to perform with Ryan Weaver, the official patriotic voice of the PBR, prior to the Music City Knockout. Huckabee had just returned from a trip to Liverpool to visit the hometown of his favorite band, which had prompted him to share the story about the Beatles.

He would eventually switch to bass, Paul McCartney's instrument. But it wasn't solely because he appreciated Paul's musical inventiveness, bouncy bass lines, and knack for creating many classic melodies. It was more a matter of utility: Every band needs a bass player.

That kind of clear-eyed, practical thinking helped propel Huckabee to an extraordinary political career, rising to governor of Arkansas from 1996 to 2007, and a run for the White House in 2008 and 2016.

Then, with a popular TV show bearing his name, he would become better known to many as the proud father of one of the world's most recognized and controversial women, Sarah Huckabee Sanders, President Trump's White House press secretary. Sarah would also attend the Nashville PBR event to see her dad perform, and more importantly, with her three children in tow, to spend much-deserved family time at a fun event that opened with a splendid celebration of American heroes.

Serving as the mouthpiece for the most unconventional president in the history of the republic, each day facing a press corps that had transformed into sharp-fanged advocacy journalists hell bent on dethroning her boss, Sarah had been through a tough time. So much so that she needed secret service protection, a first for a press secretary.

Not that any bodyguards were on call at Bridgestone Arena. Fans embraced a hard-working mom with daunting professional responsibilities that allowed absolutely no margin for error. In fact, if there were one person in the capacity crowd with a job more difficult and punishing (in her case, emotionally) than the bull riders, it would be Sarah Huckabee Sanders.

"It's hard to put into words how grateful I am for the warm reception Sarah received," Governor Huckabee said. "When men like [bullfighter] Shorty Gorham and [arena announcer] Clint Atkins stopped me to say how much they respect and admire my daughter, it's the best thing in the world any dad can hear."

Huckabee would receive a special Montana Silversmiths buckle from Commissioner Sean Gleason, making him "Governor of PBRville." He then joined Weaver's band for the pre-show concert, laying a booming backbeat for the combat veteran's new song, "That's What America Means to Me"

Over the years, Huckabee had played gigs at big venues. But when the Bridgestone Arena lights were killed, and thousands of fans stood shining their smartphone lights—2018's version of the zippo lighter held aloft—it was a musical moment he said he'd always remember. The best part was his three grandkids were there, and they loved the bull riding even more than even their first major league baseball game.

"My five-year-old grandson said, 'Papa, I don't like it—I LOVE IT!'" Huckabee later told me as we watched bull rides with his daughter and grandkids from atop the bucking chutes. "This is an amazing display of some of the most highly trained and courageous athletes in the world wrapped into a full evening of wholesome, family friendly patriotism. It's a fast-paced, electrifying production where the energy starts at full throttle and never stops. It was easy to see why the arena was packed to the rafters—this is one of America's great and original experiences."

There were no politics involved in the performance; the music and message of "That's What America Means to Me" united all fans.

As bull riders, sponsor representatives, and stock contractors in the chutes got to meet and spend time with the governor and his daughter, hearing about their passion to serve their country to try to make it a better place while watching a family bond together at a good old-fashioned bull riding, a new picture of the two began to form, different from the popular narrative in the media. While the father and daughter may not wear cowboy hats or boots, they epitomize the cowboy values seen every day in the sport.

Love & Try

PART VI

TOMORROW'S STARS

Kids don't ride bulls or steers in school, in the street, or at the local park. That makes Western sports generational. Attending rodeos and bull ridings is a family tradition, and the sport is passed down through generations. Two-time world champion Jess Lockwood attended his first rodeo wrapped in a blanket when he was one-week old. Other current stars remember watching the film *8 Seconds* with their dads.

Some manage to find the sport on their own. But for every Ezekiel Mitchell who goes on YouTube to study bull riding moves, stringing up a barrel in his yard in dreaming of making it to PBR, thousands of kids are put on a sheep by their parents.

It doesn't matter how youngsters get introduced to the sport—if they catch the bull riding bug, they can't wait to get back on even when they're on the ground spitting dirt. Soaked in the influence of their parents or mentors, drawn to Western culture, and committed to pursuing their dream, they may just turn into shining disciples of love and try.

33
NAJIAH KNIGHT'S MOON SHOT

(Bull Stock Media)

Underneath a beige straw cowboy hat, Najiah Knight glides across the shiny concourse of Madison Square Garden light and easy in her Ariat boots, catching sporadic recognition before the New York Rangers hockey game in the big arena in the big city.

Love & Try

"*Is that the bull riding girl from Vogue?*"

"*Hey, I saw you on Kelly Clarkson!*"

These enthusiastic overtures were still surprising the newly minted teenager in January 2020, even as they'd become more frequent in her life. Najiah responds to each interruption with a gentle tilt of the hat and polite, buttery "thank you, ma'am" or "yes, sir." She's only thirteen, yet is wise enough to realize the quest she's on has already made her an ambassador and salesperson for the sport she loves.

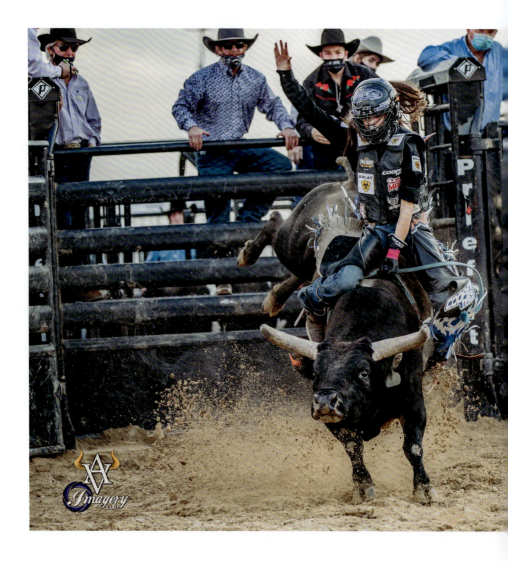

Recognition of the budding bull riding star among strangers outside the rodeo world continues as the night goes on. Najiah participates in a panel discussion with female sports pioneers (such a grown-up thing to do!) right before the Rangers host the Toronto Maple Leafs. And then during a break in the action, she is featured on the big screen above the Garden ice. The video shows riding highlights—some rides and a few big wrecks. Each time Najiah is thrown and dragged, she feels the intensifying buzz of a crowd pulled into the video, the "oohs" and "ahs" growing louder with each outrageous wreck. Hockey is a rough and tumble sport, and the home crowd is impressed. Skeptical New Yorkers aren't typically fast converts to the unfamiliar, but they sure seem to appreciate this fearless little cowgirl. When the reel ends and a healthy roar fills the whole place, what can Najiah do but stand there in the world's most famous arena with the world's biggest smile?

A nice lady from Madison Square Garden who has been escorting Najiah presents her with a beautiful blue Rangers jersey, and she wears it proudly, settling into the riveting action below. You can hear the skates carving into the ice as players sprint for the puck, which crackles their sticks with each crisp pass. Occasionally a loud "ping" rings out when a shot careens off the goal post. She loves the way every player hustles. Nobody is standing still. Everyone is working so hard to take possession of the puck then keep it, sometimes slamming the opposing player into the glass, which rocks back and forth. Her first professional hockey game is nothing less than great. She'd been in MSG once

(Philip Kitts)

already, and it is fast becoming one of her favorite places. Even the popcorn seems to taste better here.

Best of all, the Rangers come out on top. She didn't know much about the beloved local hockey team a few hours ago, but now, wearing the bright blue jersey with their name in red capital letters running diagonal down her chest, they sure are her favorite hockey team.

Following a big win over an original-six NHL team, the home crowd is buzzing. The electricity of the arena has seeped into the crowded corridors. Giddy fans are whistling a song, then screaming "Potvin Sucks" (which she's later told is a chant older than her parents, aimed at a loathed former player for the crosstown rivals, the New York Islanders, who aren't even in action that night). Led by a few of the more animated guys, the fans are breaking out into booming "Let's Go Rangers!" chants. Yet even in their post-victory delirium, some fans are doing double takes as Najiah files out towards Seventh Avenue with her mom, Missi, and dad, Andrew. Hockey fans being hockey fans, they'd been won over by the video highlight reel on the giant four-sided scoreboard hanging above the ice that had showed this skinny little girl being *rocked* by real bucking bulls, slammed into the dirt, nearly stomped, but always getting up, smiling, waving, onto the next ride. Fans exiting the arena are calling her name and shouting in beer-enhanced encouragement. In front of our eyes, a star is being born.

The theme is consistent: *NAY-jah! We love you! Keep it up! Go girl! Ride those bulls!*

Who wouldn't be rooting for an adorable thirteen-year-old still in braces and tipping the scales at eighty pounds and trying, amid grave personal danger, to accomplish a massive goal she plainly declares when asked?

"I want to be the first girl to make it in the PBR," Najiah says, sometimes with a hint of mischief, but more often with a plain "this is no big deal, why are you asking" tone people use when stating they're going to the grocery store.

It's a gigantic aspiration, and since hearty men have been killed riding bulls, Najiah's goal can make even some who sit on the women's empowerment panels a tad uncomfortable. Najiah is nonplussed. It is not that big a deal. Back home in Arlington, Oregon, a small town of 593, away from the video tributes, panel discussions, and jumbotron celebrations, life as the third of five kids in a tight family is still very simple. Help take care of the family's cows, pigs, chickens, dogs, and cats. Go to school. Hit basketball practice. Do your homework. Make goofy videos with your brothers. Lift some weights. Get on the bucking barrel that dad set up. Go to church on Sunday. Then pack your gear for the airport taking you to the next bull riding. Absent the confrontations with bulls, and questions from Kelly Clarkson, it's just a normal kid's life. By putting in the work, in a half dozen years when she's no longer a kid, the plan is to compete for the same gold buckle as her heroes J.B. Mauney, Chase Outlaw, and Jess Lockwood.

Make no mistake: to be the first girl in the PBR is Neil Armstrong-level audacity, a declaration as preposterous as the moon shot when first announced by President Kennedy.

It's never been done before. It's dangerous. It's expensive. The reasons this is not possible are too numerous to even list. Why try?

"Don't let anyone tell you what you can or cannot do," Najiah responds. "Be strong. Be proud. Work hard."

That is the "Najiah Way" starting to emerge. Be true to yourself. Put your trust in God. Block out negativity. Surround yourself with positive people who want you to succeed. Work hard. Don't be afraid to fail. Learn from the inevitable setbacks. Above all, have fun.

The more Najiah is interviewed, the seemingly unattainable starts to change into an affirmation. Because who, really, is the arbiter of what is possible or not? Who has the right to bang the gauntlet on the practical and appropriate and possible path for any of us?

The naysayers never hesitate to assert their point of view. Society has come around to agree that women should have equal opportunity and equal pay for the same work as men. There's no job a man has that a woman shouldn't hold. Yet Najiah has heard that girls have no place on top of a bucking bull.

"I don't do it for them," she says. "I do it for myself."

Missi has also privately fielded objections to her daughter's plan from those claiming a monopoly on the maternal rules for what's proper and right—and safe—for a young girl. "She's a wild child, and my job as a mom is to support her dream," Missi says.

Mom plays the role of business manager, working with sponsors Ariat, Cooper Tires, and Chad Berger Bucking Bulls, scheduling Najiah's appearances riding the seven hundred-pound beasts in Chris Shivers Mini Bull

Riders (MBR) tour and working with me to sort the interview requests and phone calls from newspaper reporters, filmmakers, and reality show producers. Missi also chronicles this accelerating rush to fame on social media. Her daughter is far from celebrity obsessed, but without seeking them out, has a knack for winding up next to the biggest names at the show. There's Najiah with Sylvester Stallone. Najiah with Scott Eastwood. Najiah with Chase Outlaw. Her mom does the social posting. (At a dozen events with Najiah, I've not once observed her head buried in a phone. She is always present.)

Missi, the wife of an occasional bull rider and now mother of a Western sports pioneer, understands and has witnessed the punishment this sport metes out without prejudice. The permanent licks are evident in the scar tattooed on Najiah's porcelain face following a stomping in Louisiana. (Her helmet was mangled, but it saved her life.)

Missi knows the score—helmets only go so far. So, she studied to become a certified EMT once it became clear Najiah's PBR dream was no fleeting obsession. If her girl ever gets in trouble, Missi is not about to put her life in the hands of strangers. Not when she now has the knowledge and permission to help.

Najiah says she's thankful every day for the people allowing her to pursue her dream: Missi, and her dad, Andrew, who woke up at 2:30 a.m. to drive two hours to the Portland airport to make it to New York for the women in sports celebration. "I wouldn't want to do any other thing," Andrew says. "I'd rather pack my kid down the road and let her prove herself. Let her build herself up. Let her show people there's another world out there, and she's gonna be in it."

The first time the Knights had flown to New York, the Miniature Bull Riders were being paired with the big boys of bull riding in the media capital of the world. Najiah rode, and she won her round on PBR Championship Sunday—the proudest moment of her career. With her mom and dad, she celebrated with authentic New York pizza. The Knights would take their daughter to a half dozen MBR events that season.

Andrew, a heavy equipment operator who also rides bulls in open rodeos out West, has the same calm, unflappable demeanor of his cucumber-cool daughter. Najiah initially caught the bull riding bug while standing in the chutes watching her dad get settled on a huge bovine. When he busted from the chutes, she could barely contain her excited glee. She told him she'd made a decision. That's what she wanted to do, too. Andrew built a bucking barrel for Najiah in the shop at their home in Arlington, Oregon, and he bucks it for her just about every day.

"Cowboy, cowgirl ... when you're in the sport, you're all the same," Andrew said. "Everybody's riding the same bulls. They're all cowboys out

(Christy Burleson)

there, so I don't treat her any different than I'd treat a boy. We just keep going and pushing down the road like she's any other kid."

The road next led to MBR's event in Lockney, Texas, in late February at the arena built by Cirilio Leal, a cheerful and kind man who, with his wife and daughter, along with support from PBR legend Chris Shivers, formed the youth bull riding organization that has helped produce riders such as

2018 PBR Rookie of the Year Keyshawn Whitehorse and young gun Cannon Cravens.

When Najiah came to compete at the Garden, I set her up with two great storytellers who appreciate quiet grace in the face of wide skepticism and a stacked deck. Kirsten Fleming of the *New York Post* and Cory Seymour of *Vogue* wrote about Najiah, and her story exploded.

Of course, the Western sports and rodeo press gets excited about bull riding, and they are eager to hear of any potential new riders to write about. The rest of the media? Meh. But Najiah has been different. In my seven-year tenure with PBR, beyond those endemic Western outlets, there's never been a stir for one of our athletes quite like the one created by this poised, pint-sized pioneer. Our small press team is creative and relentless; each day is a Groundhog Day exercise in scratching and clawing for coverage. Nobody in the general media wakes up thinking about cowboys and bulls. We're usually selling them something they don't believe they want or need. PBR doesn't own MBR, but it's still good for the sport to create a buzz about kids riding mini bulls, trying to make it to the top. With Najiah, we no longer had to concoct clever pitches and pray for a return call from reporters and assignment editors outside the rodeo outlets. Now it's *People*, *Today*, HBO, and *Access Hollywood* contacting us. Within the Endeavor network, she's signed with IMG Models for brand representation. Nike has featured her in a social media content series. Endeavor Content is planning a movie based on her life story.

The blinding klieg lights would overwhelm most kids. How could anyone not feel overwhelmed by the pressure when aw-shucks cowboys don't make a practice of promoting themselves ... especially when they're yet to win a World Championship. How could anyone's head not swell in being relentlessly reminded of one's wondrous life?

Najiah hasn't changed. If anything, she's becoming calmer and more courteous. She absorbs the adulation with uncanny graciousness and aplomb, smiling and having fun, tipping her hat to a growing group of adoring fans. She'll do the photo shoots and sit for the podcasts, but most of all she just wants to get her chores and schoolwork done so she can get on bulls.

In our world, abundant with keyboard warriors locked and loaded for the next triggering, it must be unnerving for any teenager reaching celebrity status to give sage words of wisdom on demand. How do you defend your choices, when just beginning to live your life? When asked how she has the gall to believe she is the one who could change a sport forever, because so many say it's not possible, Najiah offers a simple cowboy answer: "It doesn't matter what anyone else thinks," she says. "Just do what you love and always do your best."

Can anyone seriously be rooting against Najiah Knight making it all the way to the moon?

Love & Try

34

GIVING BACK EVEN WITH SIGHTS SET ON PBR

(Christy Burleson)

The top sports mentors are usually seasoned veterans sharing hard-earned advice with budding young athletes seeking a dream.

Bull riding has a mentor of a different sort already making a mark in the sport he loves.

Oh, and he's twelve years old, tipping the scales at eighty-three pounds.

Soft-spoken and stubbornly determined Canyon Trevino of Boaz, Alabama, first got on the back of a sheep when he was six years old. He wanted to be "like Mike." PBR Champ Mike Lee, that is, not Jordan of basketball fame.

Visions of championship buckles dancing in his head, Canyon moved up to calves and began riding six hundred-pound bulls on the competitive Mini Bull Riding circuit, held in arenas around the country alongside PBR elite events.

While touring with the PBR, Canyon helped by speaking at special youth seminars to introduce the sport to deserving young people from all walks of life. He shared his story and answered questions to teach cowboy values to youngsters from an array of local inner-city organizations who were seeing a bull riding event for the first time.

In 2016, Canyon published *Life's Arena*, a book chronicling his bull riding experiences. He wanted to inspire kids to go after their dreams—no matter how seemingly difficult or outlandish.

Canyon's mother, Kelly, has no clue for explaining the origins of this burning passion for bull riding. No one in the family comes from a rodeo or riding background.

Even young Canyon can't pinpoint what fired his jones to mount moving animals. "It might have been seeing PBR on TV, but I don't really remember," he said. "Just feels like I've always been hooked on the sport."

The elephant in the room is the human destruction inevitably wrought by a raging bull. Kelly and Santos Trevino fully support their son's quest to make it in the world's most dangerous organized sport. "I want him to realize there is a great, big world full of opportunities to offer," Kelly said in an email suitable for forwarding to the Mother of the Year Awards.

She has to dig deep to muster every ounce of support, counter to every protective maternal instinct, to keep him in this punishing game.

Both parents have made innumerable sacrifices to buoy Canyon's dream. When we had first connected, Kelly had recently driven 428 miles so her son could be an extra in a bull riding scene in the film, *Cowboy and Indiana*.

By the time Canyon was twelve years old, Santos had taken him to ride in Texas at least twenty times, often with Canyon's riding buddy, Ryder Carpenetti, who is a year younger. Father and son have made multiple trips to Las Vegas, Tennessee, Georgia, Louisiana, and New Mexico.

"They ended last season with a two-week, three thousand-mile road trip to ride in Texas, Colorado, Wyoming, and then hit an event in Oklahoma on their way home," Kelly said. "Then it was time to start PBR and NFR all over again."

Giving Back Even with Sights Set on PBR

The previous week was Mississippi, where Canyon won a Junior NFR qualifier.

Like the pros he idolizes—first 2004 PBR World Champion Mike Lee and two-time PBR World Champion Jess Lockwood—Canyon has endured his share of pain: eighteen stitches at Texas State Finals, a broken leg at the Youth Bull Riding World Finals, a busted arm, a dislocated collar bone and knee, deep bruises all over his body, and his bell seriously rung more than once. Yet he still rides in the hopes of moving up to full-sized, 1,800-pound bulls just like the stars of the PBR.

Like the big boys on tour, Canyon has an endorsement deal with American Hat Company, which has former world champions J.B. Mauney and Guilherme Marchi in its fold.

"It's hard to explain; I just know 'it' when I see it, and Canyon has it," said Keith Mundee, the president of American Hat Company. "Whether he rides a bull or not, he's an influencer. If there's someone who's new or uncomfortable, he has an ability to pick that out and go make that kid feel comfortable. He's got a great heart."

Along with empathy, the precocious kid has guts and moxie, equally important as core strength and balance in his sport. He sees opportunities and unabashedly goes for them.

Canyon contacted PBR to request a media credential for the 2017 World Finals in Las Vegas. He wanted to interview bull riders, media insiders, and those close to the sport for advice that he could pass along to other mini bull riders. He received access alongside the professional media. He interviewed top PBR riders, sat in the press box with credentialed press, and asked questions at each night's post-event press conference on the plaza outside T-Mobile Arena. Lockwood, then nineteen, won three World Finals rounds in a row—a first in the sport's twenty-four years. Canyon's questions for the young star were among the most insightful.

When he was in Albuquerque in March competing in a mini bull competition before the Ty Murray Invitational, Canyon appeared on the new Western sports digital network, RidePass, alongside Craig Hummer and Matt West. He handled the appearance as if he were a regular.

Before reaching his teen years, he had already established deep roots and a number of close friendships in the sport. He's been baptized (twice) by PBR bullfighter Frank Newsom at the Lane Frost Christian Bull Riding

School in Texas. "It was always hot there, so at the end of the last day of school, we would swim in the pond at Lane's parents' house," Canyon said. "Just in case I needed it again, I did it both times I was there!"

In a typical year, Canyon competed in more than two dozen one-day mini bull riding events and then in Las Vegas alongside the PBR World Finals while attempting to qualify again for the Junior NFR.

Canyon's new mentoring role is a classic case of receiving by giving. At each PBR event, he takes away something special.

"One of the first things I noticed when I started riding bulls was the kindness from the cowboys to people and animals," he said. "I started asking about this, and I kept getting the same answer: 'It's just the cowboy way.'"

(Canyon Trevino)

Giving Back Even with Sights Set on PBR

He's witnessed what that means firsthand, including at the 2019 season-opener when paired up with bull rider Neil Holmes at an event to expose inner-city kids to bull riding and Western values. The sport had rolled into New York City amid a once-in-a-generation cyclone bomb. The wind was howling with temperatures in the single digits. Following that day's youth outreach seminar, Canyon and Neil were walking to the arena in the deep freeze. Neil suddenly stopped. He needed to duck into a store.

"I was glad to get to warm up, so we went in to look around," Canyon said.

The bull rider thumbed through a few sweatshirts, spotted one sporting his hometown Houston Rockets logo and exclaimed, "This is the one!"

Leaving the store, Holmes started walking with purpose in the opposite direction of the arena. He stopped in front of a woman sitting on the freezing cold sidewalk.

"She was on the ground trying to stay warm with some flimsy cardboard and a small blanket," Canyon said. "Neil whispered something to her, gave her the bag, turned around, and started walking towards the Garden."

Canyon watched the woman peer into the bag. Her eyes welled into a fat pool of tears and nearly froze on her face as Neil's cowboy hat disappeared into the holiday-season sidewalk bustle.

The young rider ran up Seventh Avenue to catch up.

"I wanted to tell Neil that what he did was really nice. He just smiled and said, 'I'd like to think if someone I loved was ever in that position someone would do the same for them.' I guess that was just the cowboy way. Even on a very cold night in New York City."

Canyon Trevino wants to ride bulls at the top of PBR. But more than that, he wants to carry that torch and show the world the cowboy way. So far, he's doing a pretty good job of it.

Love & Try

EPILOGUE

(Author photo)

It's been seven years since I pulled on a pair of cowboy boots to check out a job promoting bull riders. I'm still living in the crowded concrete jungle, and, as much as I feel welcomed after leaving New York City to arrive at different arenas, I can't fully shake the fish-out-of-water feeling. Remember, I ride a subway, not a horse. And that's okay. It grants a license to continue to learn new things about life from some of the last remaining cowboys. I can stay wide-eyed and curious, a middle-aged man in schoolboy awe, scribbling memorable cowboy quotes on scraps of paper, and snapping photos of the bull riding scene like an excited tourist peering across the rim of the Grand Canyon.

Putting together this book, I flipped through hundreds of photographs. My favorite one doesn't show a cowboy valiantly soaring through the air to conquer a mighty bull to win an event or a rampaging bull with the upper hand, launching the rider like a midlife-crisis billionaire's rocket. The photo that really stands out was taken off the dirt, a few battered iPhones ago. It's not exactly coffee-book quality. The finish is grainy, the colors washed. But I treasure the shot for what it shows: a tired yet very content Cooper Davis holding his son Mack, sleeping peacefully in his father's arms. The then-reigning world champion was frozen in that position through an entire two-hour dinner at a South Shore restaurant after the bull riding inside Nassau Coliseum on Long Island, where I grew up.

Following the *PBR Buck Off the Island* in September 2017, a company of rambunctious bull riders packed into a sushi joint, trading stories and jibes as they tried to order steak with ketchup. Even amid the hearty guffawing that breaks out whenever Chase Outlaw holds court, still pumped from a night when he and his bull riding brothers put it all on the line in pushing for the year-end gold buckle, Mack didn't stir.

Cooper loves the way Mack smells and knows his boy sleeps best in his arms, his wife Kaitlyn later told me. The whole time, the bull rider sat still, cradling his boy in a glow of serene contentment. It's been some time since I could hold my own Gaby, now a twenty-something musical artist, tattooed with hair the color of an ever-changing rainbow snow yet seeming to be more fragile than ever. Wistful thoughts were filling my head about my only child, and how I spent my time, and too often squandered it.

Cooper does this all the time, Kait said. Won't let go of the boy once he falls asleep.

This is a world champion athlete, the top bull rider on the planet that weekend. But more than that, the picture shows a loving dad, just being a dad. Present to account for. Making the most of time. Because what is time but a constant stream of moments that wash away, like ocean waves crashing against the shore, and this moment like all others gifted to us was at once powerful and fleeting—here, and gone, and never coming back. After a night of try, Cooper Davis was spending precious time to love the one who matters most, someday the cycle to repeat.

ACKNOWLEDGMENTS

When joining PBR, the first bull rider I would work with was J.B. Mauney. That's like meeting your first painter, who happens to be Rembrandt. Two months earlier, in November 2015, J.B. had won his second world championship. He was in New York to appear on the Stephen Colbert show to teach the late-night host how to ride a mechanical bull. Getting ready for dress rehearsal, Colbert was acting like a Lord who would have had his portrait painted by Rembrandt. He delayed and delayed, and J.B. was stuck with me in the CBS green room for four hours. As the minutes ticked by, J.B. slowly began regaling me with daring and hilarious bull riding tales. By the end of the second hour, I knew there was a book to be written about his sport. If it were J.B.'s dream to ride bulls, it was my dream to have him contribute to whatever book would come of my PBR experiences. Thank you, J.B., for your Foreword and always living on your terms.

Love & Try wouldn't be in your hands or glowing on your screen without the support of PBR's John Sohigian, who I will enthusiastically join in raising a few cold ones at the PBR Bar.

Connections are everything in life. Fanchon Stinger made a great one in her introduction to Bill Horn of Cedar Gate Publishing, who embraced the idea of "love and try" and lined up the crack team who created this book product, led by Holden Hill and Randy Allsbury.

Sean Gleason and the Red Dawn gang—Josh Baker, Chad Blankenship, Chris Gallina, Rodd Granger, Robby Greene, and Kosha Irby—who led our sport's fight through COVID-19, as well as Endeavor's Christian Muirhead, Maura McGreevy and Ginger Chan, recognized the potential of the project and have my gratitude for their support.

A group of talented reporters laid important groundwork for several stories between these covers, including decorated writer Matt Crossman vividly capturing Dr. Tandy Freeman, J. B. Mauney, and bull-riding atop the USS Lexington; Marty Klinkenberg's riveting profile of Chase Outlaw; and bull riding savant Justin Felisko, thoroughly reporting virtually every aspect of the sport on and off the dirt including Mary Apper's story.

Love & Try

Some great podcasts—Flint Rasmussen's "According to Flint," Matt Merritt's "Roadcast," "Matt West Now," and Ted Stovin's "Cowboy Sh*t"—helped immensely with historical background, and Flint saved me from using the term "yee-hah" until this final page.

In phone calls often lasting longer than a podcast, cowboy raconteur and acclaimed author "Professor" Keith Ryan Cartwright has been generous in sharing his encyclopedic knowledge of Western sports and its culture.

While preparing her PBR documentary for Fusion, investigative journalist extraordinaire Mariana van Zeller allowed me to eavesdrop on conversations with Dr. Freeman, Jerome and Tiffany Davis, and J.B. Mauney. While Marianna's follow-on feature film documentary bringing J.B.'s life story to the silver screen was not funded, this book in part picks up her intention to shine a light on a man she called "the most charismatic and fascinating athlete I've ever met." Then again, maybe someone reading this book will see the light.

I want to thank longtime PBR photographer Andy Watson of Bull Stock Media whose photos appear throughout, supported by the work of Andre Silva. Additionally, the eminently talented Christy Burleson graciously provided several other phenomenal shots and Leah Hennel gifted the lead-off photo of J.B. Mauney.

Ken Danieli, an old Pepsi colleague from the Cola Wars, provided invaluable structural advice and precise copyediting assistance.

Several others outside the Western lifestyle have my deepest gratitude: My mom (Carol Giangola, so her name is in lights) for your proofreading skills, instillation of a lifelong appreciation of reading and writing, and constant encouragement; my daughter Gaby for always inspiring me; and my true love Malvina Schulz, who continues to prove that anything can be accomplished through love and try.

Thank you, all the loyal (and opinionated!) PBR fans who continue to cheer on the cowboys and bulls; the bull stock contractors "loving on" (a new term I learned) their marvelous animal athletes; our friends at CBS and Pluto TV bringing the sport virtually everywhere; the dedicated brand partners who put their dollars and promotional energies into the sport; each and every indefatigable colleague at PBR who does so much so often with so little; and most of all, every uncommonly optimistic cowboy and cowgirl across the span of time who has gotten on a bull with nothing more than a rope in their hand and a heart full of love and try.